The Black Prince and his age

The Black Prince and his age

JOHN HARVEY

B. T. Batsford Ltd
London

By the same author:

Henry Yevele
Gothic England
The Plantagenets
Dublin
Tudor Architecture
The Gothic World
English Mediaeval Architects
A Portrait of English Cathedrals
The Cathedrals of Spain
Catherine Swynford's Chantry

The Master Builders
The Mediaeval Architect
Conservation of Buildings
Early Gardening Catalogues
Man the Builder
Cathedrals of England and Wales
Early Nurserymen
Sources for the History of Houses
Mediaeval Craftsmen
York

Bibliographies:
English Cathedrals – A Reader's Guide
Conservation of Old Buildings
Early Horticultural Catalogues – A Checklist

Revised Muirhead's Blue Guides:
Northern Spain   Southern Spain

Edited with translation:
William Worcestre: Itineraries (1478–1480)

First published 1976
Copyright © John Harvey 1976

Filmset by Servis Filmsetting Ltd, Manchester
Printed by Biddles Ltd, Guildford, Surrey
for the publishers B.T. Batsford Ltd
4 Fitzhardinge Street, London W1H 0AH

ISBN 0 7134 3148 2

Contents

		page
ACKNOWLEDGMENTS		6
LIST OF ILLUSTRATIONS		7
PREFACE		11
INTRODUCTION		20
CHAPTER I	England in 1330	34
II	Heir to England	47
III	The Years of Youth	59
IV	A Share of Glory	71
V	The Days of Fame	84
VI	Castles in Spain	98
VII	Downhill	111
VIII	The Young King	122
IX	Brittle Glory	135
CATASTROPHE		147
APPENDIX: The Will of Edward the Black Prince, 1376		160
BIBLIOGRAPHY AND ABBREVIATIONS		168
NOTES TO THE TEXT		172
INDEX		178

Acknowledgments

The author and publishers here express their indebtedness to the following persons and institutions for permission to reproduce the illustrations mentioned: the British Library for Plates 8 and 9; the British Museum for Plate 17; the Dean and Chapter of Canterbury Cathedral for Plates 1, 5, 6, 16: also W. B. Moore, F.R.P.S. for 1, the National Monuments Record for 5 and 6, and the National Portrait Gallery for 16; the National Gallery for Plate 7; the Dean and Chapter of Westminster for Plates 2 and 15: also the National Monuments Record for 2 and the Warburg Institute for 15; the Warden and Fellows of Winchester College for Plate 14; the Dean and Chapter of York Minster and the National Monuments Record for Plates 3, 4, 10, 11, 12 and 13.

List of Illustrations

Map: Lands of the Black Prince *page* 9

Between pages 80 and 81

1   Edward of Woodstock, the Black Prince, from his effigy
2   The Black Prince, from his father's tomb
3   Edward III, in the Lady Chapel, York Minster
4   The Black Prince, York Minster
5   Joan, 'The Fair Maid of Kent', Canterbury Cathedral
6   Effigy of the Black Prince, Canterbury Cathedral
7   The Wilton Diptych
8   Joan of Kent, from Cotton MS. Nero D. vii, f. 7v, *c.* 1380
9   John of Gaunt, from Cotton MS. Nero D. vi
10 Henry, duke of Lancaster, K.G., York Minster
11 William, lord Latimer, K.G., York Minster
12 Thomas de Beauchamp, earl of Warwick, K.G., York Minster
13 William de Montague, earl of Salisbury, K.G., York Minster
14 William of Wykeham, bishop of Winchester, from a carving at Winchester College
15 Richard II, from his effigy
16 Henry IV, from his effigy
17 Richard II's quadrant, British Museum

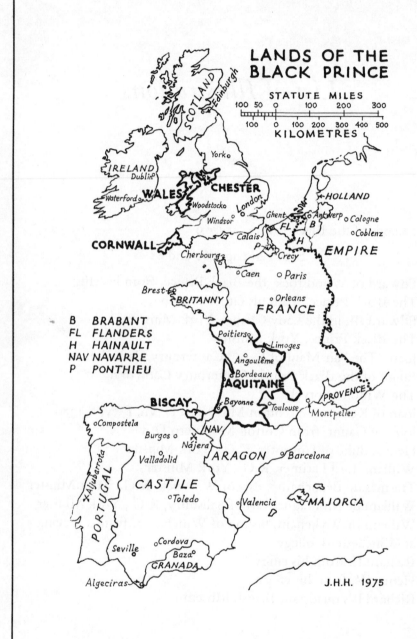

LANDS OF THE BLACK PRINCE

STATUTE MILES

KILOMETRES

B   BRABANT
FL   FLANDERS
H   HAINAULT
NAV NAVARRE
P   PONTHIEU

SCOTLAND
Edinburgh
IRELAND
Dublin
York
Waterford
WALES
Woodstock
CHESTER
London
HOLLAND
Ghent
Antwerp
Cologne
FL   B
Coblenz
CORNWALL
Calais
H
EMPIRE
Cherbourg
P
Crecy
Caen
Paris
Brest
BRITANNY
Orleans
FRANCE
Poitiers
Limoges
Angoulême
Bordeaux
AQUITAINE
PROVENCE
BISCAY
Bayonne
Toulouse
Montpelier
Compostela
NAV
Burgos
Nájera
ARAGON
Barcelona
Valladolid
CASTILE
PORTUGAL
Aljubarrota
Toledo
Valencia
MAJORCA
Cordova
Seville
Baza
GRANADA
Algeciras

J.H.H. 1975

In Memory of
Edward of Woodstock,
Prince of Wales and Aquitaine,
THE BLACK PRINCE,
for the Sexcentenary of his Death
8 June 1376

Preface

It is now well over a quarter-century since, in writing of kingship as exemplified by the Plantagenet line, I remarked: 'we are living in an age of swift transition towards what may be a new Dark Age of utter chaos, or which, more hopefully, we may diagnose as a new epoch of creative energy'. So far it seems that my gloomier prognostication is the more likely of fulfilment, though the worst has not yet happened in terms of the fears of 1947. None the less, wars and threats of wars, civil strife and galloping inflation have led to increasing misery throughout the world. In terms of number, there are now far more people than ever before, but are our problems in themselves worse, or different in kind from those which have beset earlier periods? It may well be that many of our difficulties remain the same in essence, in spite of superficial changes from age to age.

If the fundamentals of human experience are constant, we may be justified in seeking in the past for helpful parallels. Some comfort may be drawn from the discovery of suffering not less than our own, even from horrors such as the Black Death which, in modern times, Europe has not had to experience. Our present financial difficulties are not without their counterpart at several periods of English history, notably in the inflation of the fourteenth century largely caused by the great pestilence. It is possible to see in distant view, as if through a telescope, the impact of debt on a national scale in the latter part of the reign of Edward III and throughout that of his grandson Richard II. Those two reigns put together lasted from 1327 to 1399, a little more than one scriptural span of threescore years and ten. England's plight, and her survival, in that age are not without lessons for our own time.

Occasionally the resemblances between our former and our present state are even startling. The Hundred Years War, like the two World Wars, brought rationing of food and clothes, and the provision that all church bells should be rung in the event of invasion. Perhaps a contrast is more revealing: that between the swiftly declining value of modern paper currency and the standard of English money instituted in 1344. In 1914 an American student of the London School of Economics, Schuyler B. Terry, wrote in his book *The Financing of the Hundred Years War* that 'an indication of the increasing prosperity of the English is the beginning of gold coinage in 1344. . . . Too great emphasis cannot be laid upon the value to the English of an unfluctuating coinage. It is one of the chief causes of their success.' In the past sixty years we seem to have proved the converse: that a fluctuating currency spells failure. Without a standard of value as stringent as those of length or weight or capacity, civilizations slide into bankruptcy.

This is to consider only material values, and it is the logical outcome of our system of education that such material and quantitative standards are applied. There is a tendency to measure progress in terms of increase in population, gross national product, output. We laugh at statistics, yet rows of figures dominate the news. Even beauty is described by numerals as though it were they rather than the female figures that called for admiration. What is more serious is that unintelligible groups of numbers are steadily invading the realm of human personality. Registration numbers of all sorts have proliferated within our own time, and numerical languages are coined for feeding into computers. At times it seems as though the machines are already in control, in spite of their observed inefficiency. Whether or no these developments are welcomed, their tendency is towards a level uniformity and diminution of individual characteristics.

It is in this respect that, notwithstanding the points of close resemblance between the two Englands, of six hundred years ago and of today, the comparison breaks down. The surviving works of art and craftsmanship of every kind show marked individuality and a wide range of inequality between the persons who made them. The spectrum of humanity and of human endeavour displayed more startling contrasts. This can be experienced in any of those older towns and cities which have not yet been redeveloped as more or less identical units. Each place has its own character so well marked as to amount to something approaching personality. This is true too of the greater buildings, the castles and cathedrals, and of the several thousand parish churches. The artefacts of the Middle Ages, like the products of nature, differ from one another in quality.

It is easy to see why mediaeval and modern times are so distinct in this respect. The vast bulk of our products is made for a more or less uniform range of taste; what appeals only to a few is discarded as unprofitable. As the years pass there is a diminution in the number of competing sorts of product of any one kind, so that progress is towards a dead level. In the Middle Ages, on the contrary, most of those who could afford to buy things of lasting utility had high standards of taste which demanded fine quality and that capacity to please the eye which constitutes beauty. Similar attributes spread over into goods of consumption: even what was very soon to disappear, such as the food on the table, tended to be made into attractive shapes and colour-schemes as a work of art and not merely one of adequate skill.

Herein lies the great attraction for the moderns in the study of the mediaeval: the difference of approach which distinguishes every part of life. The men and women of the Middle Ages, in common with those of many eastern nations even now, were surrounded by objects of hand craftsmanship appealing to all the senses and deliberately designed to have this appeal. The best objects were made for those with the highest quality of taste, and it was for the most part this group of persons, an élite, that was also primarily concerned in government. Primarily, but not exclusively, for in England there was already by the thirteenth century if not earlier a career open to talent among the clergy – who provided the civil service and almost the whole administration – and also among the arts and crafts of aesthetic production. The peak of this society was the Court, and at the pinnacle the person of the sovereign. For several centuries it was the individual qualities of the ruler that called the tune, not only in the maintenance of law and order and of prosperity, but in the pursuit of beauty as well.

The Middle Ages as a whole are typified by this principle of the individual ruler, leading his people in peace as in war, and calling forth if not actually dictating the triumphs of art. Within the overall period of several centuries there were some generations in which effectiveness in cultural activity reached a peak, just as in other civilizations. Exactly as we discern such high-water marks, reflected in surviving art or in recorded achievements, in Twelfth Dynasty Egypt, Periclean Greece, T'ang China, so we may discover comparable manifestations near home. The same attractive pull, exerted by a Court, is found at the end of the Dark Age in the Ottonian Empire, and in the Ottoman Turkey contemporary with the Tudors. While in England we had to wait for our greatest literary outpourings for the Reformation and the secular theatre, the chief masterpieces of national architecture were built in Gothic style during the reigns from Henry II to Henry VIII. That same epoch included the personal achievement of Chaucer and a mass of other poetry in the vernacular, a large output of prose, mainly in Latin, and a growing body of exquisite music. In the first half of the fifteenth century the English composer John Dunstable set the pace for Europe.

Between the twelfth century and the sixteenth we have to seek for the particular age which best exemplified the highest quality of life in this country. The task of precision is not easy, for much of our art, literature and music spread over several centuries can take a worthy place in a hierarchy based upon world-wide standards. It is not chauvinism to claim excellence for many products of mediaeval England. In power of line, forceful execution and sensitivity of detail the cathedrals of Wells and Lincoln, the octagon at Ely and chapter-house at York, the rebuilt Westminster Hall, Wykeham's colleges at Oxford and Winchester, Henry VI's at Cambridge, Henry VII's Chapel at Westminster, need fear no comparisons. Little remains of painting on a large scale, but the riches of English illumination and such surviving panels as the Westminster Retable and the Wilton Diptych represent a supreme peak of European achievement.

We have concerned ourselves with England as the place, what then was the time? From the onset of a national Gothic architecture at Wells around 1180 until the dying away of church building in the 1530's, where did our art reach its zenith in terms of human generations? Art cannot be considered alone: the quality of living as a whole, and social and economic factors too, have to be included in the assessment. Soon the possible period is narrowed by one factor or another. Before the time of Edward I, England was as yet hardly English; the language was exiled from the Court; building, painting and carving were largely based on French models. On the other hand there is no denying a falling off after 1400, not only in art but in everyday affairs: law and order were displaced by piracy and civil discord; relative prosperity gave place to severe depression lasting over two or three generations. The span of time closes about the fourteenth century or, at most, the reigns of the first three Edwards and of Richard II.

The qualities of Edward I were epic; his reign unfolds on an exalted and well-nigh superhuman plane. Law and policy, the reduction of Wales and campaigns in Scotland, left little chance for the display of social graces. The country was becoming, but had not yet become a leader of the western world. Its greatest architecture was in progress but little of it was complete, the highest flights undreamed. The English language as a literary instrument barely existed, and indeed appears as the medium for real poetry almost for the first time in the verses written on the death of the old king: 'The goodness might I never tell, that with King Edward was.' Edward I was probably the greatest of all our sovereigns in sheer achievement and had a flair for justice seldom equalled. His personal character was noble yet intriguing, endowed with humour, filial, conjugal and paternal affection. But he did not live to see the flowering of any of the seed he set.

Few would contend for Edward II, though his rejection almost endows him with a power of converse attraction. A murdered victim, he was in some sense a martyr, and was long regarded as a saint. His historical importance lies, negatively, in the fact that his deposition was unlawful and was to become a symbol of the tension between the theory of divine kingship and the material considerations that dragged it into the arena of power politics. We must move on in our search for time and place together. By all the marks of greatness, it is the successive reigns of the third Edward and of his grandson Richard that embrace our target. What then of the gold within: the loved one who for a few short years came together with place and time in a single unity? It is Edward of Woodstock, eldest son of Edward III and father of Richard II, who fills the bill.

Known to us as the Black Prince, Edward was in his own time successively earl of Chester, duke of Cornwall, prince of Wales and later of Aquitaine. To his contemporaries he was Prince Edward or simply the Prince, and there is no certainty as to the origin of his famous cognomen, not found in English until the sixteenth century. There is, however, some rather shadowy evidence that he was described in French as clad at the battle of Crecy *'en armure noire en fer bruni'* – in black armour of burnished steel. Whatever its source, the name has stuck for over four hundred years and must be accepted as a necessary anachronism. The fame of the man has stood for six centuries; his name remains one that moves the hearts of Englishmen. The secret of such enduring reputation lies in his personal character and demonstrates in him an unusual rare quality impressive to his contemporaries and to posterity. As no other figure in our history he symbolizes the finer side of the Middle Ages: chivalry, desperate courage, true love, and a debonair liberality so greatly admired in his day as *largesse*. A national hero among a troop of heroes, his figure dominates those of the chosen knights who were his mentors and his brothers in arms.

So much is certain: it is less easy to discover precisely why he captured the imagination in a way that his father – in spite of his popularity – never did. We know too little of the strictly personal temperament of mediaeval personalities, even kings and princes, to be sure of the exact impression they made. One factor was certainly the generosity of Edward III towards his son: the father never showed envy of his boy's prowess and deliberately gave him the lion's share of the glory of Crecy. By mediaeval standards the Prince was certainly one of the great commanders and his military career was glorious. Besides the share he had, at the age of 16, in the victory of Crecy, he won outright against heavy odds at Poitiers and at Nájera. Arbiter of western Europe for a few years from his princely court at Bordeaux, his lack of political success was more than compensated in the eyes of the world by his prowess as a warrior. In a martial age he towered over the scene, nearer to Alexander or Caesar than to Marlborough or Wellington. Yet this almost exclusively military fame, derived from the chronicles, does him an injustice. The Black Prince deserves to be celebrated also for his magnificent taste in art and in the niceties of life, as a triumphant human being, not least in the long years of patient suffering as painful illness dragged him down to death. He represented the most admired standard of excellence as a soldier, a man, and above all as a deeply religious and sincere Christian. He struck the keynote of an age.

What was that age of the Black Prince? It cannot be limited to his life of barely 46 years from 1330 to 1376, but extends to cover the rest of the century to the point he would have attained at threescore years and ten, in 1400. Dying a year before his father, he never ruled, but much of the mantle of his glory and his popularity descended upon his young son Richard who, on 22 June 1377, came to the throne. By the tragic turn of events, it was the son who died on 14 February 1400, four months short of 70 years from his father's birth. Many of the contemporaries of the Black Prince did survive until about that time and gave to the age those monuments and works of imaginative art that have come down to us from a vastly greater output. For practical purposes the age was that lifetime that began at the time of prince Edward's birth and his father's overthrow of Mortimer in 1330, and closed with the fourteenth century. The same year 1400 saw not only the death of the deposed king Richard, supreme exponent of mediaeval monarchy, but also those of the first great English poet Geoffrey Chaucer and of our finest architect, Henry Yeveley.

As has been said, we know little of the intimate personal details of mediaeval men and women: the sources, such as letters between friends, hardly exist, even for kings, queens and princes. Biographies, such as they are, can only be careers at best, enriched with scattered anecdotes that have come down to us by chance. Even for the Black Prince, so outstandingly famous, we have little beyond the detailed accounts of his military engagements given by Froissart, and a sprinkle of facts from other chroniclers. Much has indeed been written on aspects of his life as a soldier and a ruler by serious historians, and apart from the mediaeval sources there have been several highly competent lives, starting with the one by Arthur Collins (1740), the London bookseller who also wrote the *Peerage* and *Baronetage*. The most serious and extended study, in two volumes, was written by George Payne Rainsford James (1799–1860), historical novelist and historiographer royal to William IV. This was first published in 1836 and, substantially revised, in 1839, and holds the field still as a work of scholarship. Apart from several other biographies of the Prince issued within the last hundred years there is the good factual life by R. P. Dunn-Pattison, *The Black Prince* (1910), and several historians have produced scholarly works on aspects of the Prince's career.

There is, then, no room for yet another life of the Black Prince in the normally accepted sense. What is here attempted is to set his life and character against the cultural background of his time in a way not previously possible. It is only in comparatively recent years that the progress of studies in social history has opened up new vistas in the artistic and scientific life of England in the later Middle Ages. Where previously was a wide desert of anonymity there is now a field full of folk; hundreds of names and dates are known, linked to advances in literature, art or technology. The details, as in the case of the highest ranks, are jejune, yet the sum total is not negligible. It is not too much to claim that the Middle Ages as a whole, and perhaps more especially the fourteenth century, now appear to have been a highly sophisticated epoch, very far removed from the simplistic view of gorgeous savagery that has held sway for so long. Real progress was being made in medicine, in botany, and in chemistry both pharmaceutical and commercial. Not only were improved techniques making it feasible to construct larger and more neatly articulated buildings, but their design was becoming better integrated and proportioned. The shops of London and the other larger cities were stocked with luxury goods, builders' merchants could hire out scaffolding or pile-drivers, and gardeners supplied turf by the thousand ready for laying.

All this was made possible in the first instance by enlightened patronage, and at the apex of the pyramid of patrons were King Edward III and his sons, notably the Black Prince; and later King Richard II. The quality of what was produced was improved in response to the value-judgments made by royal and noble purchasers in competition with one another. This sphere of values lay in aesthetics; but value was also assessed in the field of ethics. It is in this respect particularly that the world of the Black Prince differed so sharply from that of today. Made concrete in Edward of Woodstock and in his friends and companions, it did not reject the material or the profit-motive; but these were subordinated to higher personal concepts of behaviour, not paramount. There was indeed a bitter struggle in progress between the highest ideals of honour and loyalty and the trickier methods of power politics with which we are now so familiar. The contrast is seen at its clearest in the behaviour of the Prince and of his enemy Charles V of France. The great French soldier Du Guesclin, captive at Bordeaux, taunted the Prince that he did not dare to set a ransom, knowing that the code of his chivalrous captor would impel him to name some high price which the king of France would be glad to pay. The Black Prince named 100,000 francs, and honourably released Du Guesclin even though this was rightly judged by his Council to be a fatal move. On the other hand, King Charles at the same period captured the Prince's Gascon supporter the Captal de Buch and refused ever to release him unless he swore never again to take up arms on the English side. The Captal declined, and died in prison. Public opinion universally applauded the Black Prince's quixotic behaviour and condemned the French king's lack of sportsmanship.

The essential theme of this book is this other, contrasting set of values, based upon an instinctively felt code of honour. Throughout the recorded history of mankind there has existed this faithful allegiance to what is felt to be right; the avoidance, even to death, of any act felt to be wrong or unworthy. Page after page of Froissart relates incidents of honour and of its inseparable accompaniment, loyalty. Loyalty, an essentially personal quality, was owed first to God as the supreme monarch requiring the loving obedience of all mankind; next to an earthly sovereign; and in third place to those to whom one is rightfully bound by ties of blood, marriage, pledged word or sentiment. While he lived the Black Prince was the highest exponent of this chivalry, based on honour, on loyalty, and on steadfast courage.

★   ★   ★

As a general rule quotations from texts in mediaeval English and from Berners' translation of Froissart have been modernized in spelling but not otherwise. I must confess my own former error by pointing out that the name of the famous architect is now spelt Yeveley (not 'Yevele') to avoid both phonetic and topographical error. Accents are preserved on foreign place-names and personal names which have not been anglicized; but omitted where the word has become part of English history, as with Crecy and Bretigny. It is now accepted that Queen Philippa's famous servant was really named Mauny, not 'Manny', but the error is too deep-seated to correct now, and as Sir Walter Manny he must remain famous.

I am grateful to Colonel J. G. O. Whitehead, M.C., R.E., for the original suggestion for this book as well as for his discussion of Henry Yeveley as a military engineer (now in part published in *The Royal Engineers Journal* for 1974); and to Mr Claude Blair, F.S.A., for his kind help in regard to the origins of gunpowder and of firearms. The background of the book owes much to the late George F. Powell, with whom over many years I was able to discuss details of mediaeval culture and the problems of European dynasties. I am also thankful for generous encouragement given long ago by the late Professor A. M. Hocart. In the course of my research I have been greatly helped by too many librarians and archivists to name, but it is a pleasure to mention the courtesy and patient information received at the British Museum, the Public Record Office, the London Library, and the libraries of the Society of Antiquaries and the Society of Genealogists.

The illustrations consist mainly of portraits, and it must be emphasized that deliberate portraiture, intended to catch a likeness, was already mature in England by the fourteenth century. Even as far back as the twelfth, the ideal of individual imitation of features by artists was recognized, and far too much has been made of the alleged inaccessibility of sitters. The king and his courtiers were habitually on the move so that regional as well as court artists would have opportunities to study features and expression. Furthermore, there seems to be no doubt as to the mediaeval origins of the practice, firmly entrenched by the sixteenth century, of distributing 'type' portraits of the sovereign, and possibly of other members of the royal family, to be copied locally.

True portraiture was particularly well handled by sculptors and we get characteristic impressions of the leaders of the age. Notable among the surviving portraits are those of the Black Prince himself (Plates 1, 2, 4) and his wife (Plate 5), as well as the great statesman William of Wykeham (Plate 14). This last, carved as an external label-stop of the east window of Winchester College Chapel, opposite to a noteworthy head of Richard II (reproduced in *Archaeologia,* XCVIII, 1961, plate XIb.), is here illustrated from a plaster cast made in 1907 before weathering had proceeded so far as it has now. The original must date from about 1393 when Wykeham was 69, and may be provisionally attributed to William Wynford, the king's master mason who was also architect of the College.

Of outstanding importance for the portraiture of the Court is the series of busts in the Lady Chapel of York Minster, to which attention has been drawn by Mr. T. W. French, F.S.A., in his paper on 'The Dating of the Lady Chapel in York Minster' (*Antiquaries Journal,* LII part ii, 1972, 309–19). Mr French suggests a date of 1368, and in any case before 1373, for these heads, and these are absolute limits: probably the date is not later than 1369 in view of the inclusion of the old earl of Warwick who died in that year. From the series, six portraits are here illustrated (Plates 3, 4, 10–13), demonstrating the marked individuality achieved.

For help in connection with portraiture I am grateful to Mr Douglas Sellick and to Mr Robin Gibson. The book as a whole has benefited from the assistance of my publishers and particularly from the care taken over its production by Celia Hollis. My wife has spent much time in discussion of the period and its personalities, and has read the whole of the proofs.

John H. Harvey
December 1975

Introduction

The Black Prince: theme of three notes on a distant trumpet, echoing and re-echoing yet not diminished. Reputation may wax and wane, but almost always the successive waves grow less and less, and in the end disappear. To only a very few of the human race has been granted the magic gift of a name endowed with perpetual motion and a kind of earthly immortality. Among these choice names is that commonly given, nobody quite knows when or why, to Edward of Woodstock, eldest son of King Edward III of England. Unlike the Black Boy, King Charles II, the prince was of fair complexion and golden hair; it was not the man himself that was black but almost certainly the burnished suit of plate armour that he wore in battle. His image rides high on a great charger, in full panoply of war, leading his men to victory sword in hand at Crecy, at Poitiers, and at Nájera in Spain. Cast in bronze we see him exactly thus in Thomas Brock's equestrian statue in the City Square of Leeds. Mediaeval romance invades the stronghold of modern industrialism.

At Leeds, which has little claim to any special relationship with the prince, his figure is the spirited creation of a gifted Victorian sculptor; but at Canterbury, where the man himself lies buried, are his helm and crest, his gauntlets, his shield and the scabbard of his sword, beside the life-size effigy of bronze made at the time of his death, showing him as he lived, fully armed in plate of war with his sheathed sword by his side. This splendid figure on the tomb, surrounded by enamelled shields bearing the prince's arms and his mysterious badge of ostrich feathers, is the culminating point of a visit to the interior of Canterbury Cathedral, as surely as the pinnacles of Bell Harry dominate outside. Fifty or sixty years ago, before war damage and rebuilding, the streets of Canterbury were not unlike those the prince had known, through which his coffin was borne and by which his friend Geoffrey Chaucer's pilgrims reached the shrine. The shrine of the controversial archbishop Becket had long since gone, but boys and girls on holiday were forced, a weary penance, to follow the harrowing story of his murder related with all too vivid pantomime by a black-robed and clucking verger. After the gory horrors of 1170 and the climb to the Trinity Chapel came the joyous relief of re-entry to a saner world. There, in the coloured light thrown by the windows lay the hero of England, encompassed by his strange alien mottoes: the familiar *ich diene* and the puzzling *houmout*.

I serve: surely he had served if anyone ever did, his parents, his countrymen, his God. Brought up in royal pomp but seeking no affected reverence, he won men by his courtesy to all, his kindness, his generosity, his simple ways. The pattern of knighthood, embodiment of chivalry, symbol of the officer, he had been among the first to identify himself not only with his companion knights and squires but with the whole body of his troops. Famous in his life as ever since as a soldier, victorious in three of the most desperate battles of history, he yet sought God's forgiveness for having won. His service too could be literal: captor of a king, the prince served his prisoner at table with bended knee, yielding the palm of the day's valour to his enemy.

High courage, *houmout*: from his childhood trained to the joust and tourney, bravery of the ordinary sort became second nature. Given the chance to win his spurs in the bloodiest moments of Crecy, barely saved in the nick of time beneath his great standard of Wales, the prince was a man at the age of sixteen. For more than twenty years on he was to take risks gladly, never counting the cost in personal exertion and hardihood, equally ready to embark upon the stormy seas of Biscay or the Channel, to lead his army through the snow-clad passes of the Pyrenees in mid-winter, to endure the torrid heat of summer in Spain. In this he went too far, and the remorseless law of cause and effect killed him after nine years of wretchedness and agonizing pain. Throughout he never complained; men who were sometimes unsure if he still breathed, wondered in this strait also at his high courage. On the very last day of his life he composed his will and ordained his tomb; directed the inscription of the French poem on Death which must have been his contemplation for long years. In that he could visualize his inevitable future state, from which his spirit might be redeemed by the grace of God and through the prayers of passers by; at the end, high courage.

Forced to leave him at Canterbury we may follow in reverse some part of his life's pilgrimage, seeing still the remains of buildings that he knew. Nothing is left of his last earthly home, the little palace within the great palace at Westminster; but there remain the Norman walls of his father's Hall, and the undercroft of the chapel of St Stephen as he knew it when it was first built. Close by, though transformed in many ways, is the abbey church in which he often worshipped. Across the Thames, at Kennington, there is nothing but fragments of his own palace, surrounded with its gardens and vine-clad arbours. At Berkhamsted, 30 miles away, the broken walls and turf-covered courts of his favourite country house are glimpsed from the express train as it rushes through the Chilterns where the prince hawked and hunted in moments of peace. At Windsor, scene of many of his feats of arms, much of his father's castle survives, though his birthplace has been obliterated to glorify a later warrior. We must go back still further to understand the Black Prince and the age in which he lived.

★   ★   ★

England in the fourteenth century was a small country and relatively a poor one. When the century opened the king, Edward I, was straining every nerve to overcome the resistance of the Scottish followers of Robert Bruce to the concept of a united island, comprising England, Scotland and Wales. The great Edward who, a quarter-century earlier, had been the most famous warrior of Europe on his return from Crusade, and universally acclaimed for his impartiality and strict sense of justice, was to fail in this last and most fundamental of his endeavours. England's greatest natural advantage, her island position, had been half cancelled by the existence of two hostile and rival states within the same boundaries. Wales had been overcome as a disruptive force within Britain, but three centuries were to go by before the dynastic union of Scotland with England under a single sovereign. All the rest of the mediaeval period in England was overshadowed by the threat of enemy raids over the Border. France, the 'natural enemy' under the aggressive policy of the kings of the House of Capet, was always able to count upon an eager ally ready to attack England in the rear. Whatever our view of English expansionism, it must be recognized as the response to a continual threat of simultaneous invasion from north and south at once.

The royal policy of the kings of England was in part the direct outcome of these geographical and strategic circumstances. It was also conditioned largely by their inheritance of the family tradition of their own House which, though anachronistically, we term Plantagenet. The state of affairs found in the fourteenth century derived directly from the succession of events ever since the Norman Conquest of 1066. The key lay in a series of royal marriages. Firstly, in 1100, the Conqueror's younger son Henry I had married Edith Matilda, heiress of the Saxon line; in this way his father's victory was legitimatized and possible rivalry thwarted. In second place came the marriage of Maud, the daughter of Henry I and Edith, to Geoffrey Plantagenet, count of Anjou. Their son Henry was able, after the civil wars of Stephen's reign, to come to the throne peacefully in 1154. Henry II, in his turn, had married the divorced wife of Louis VII of France, Eleanor of Aquitaine. In this way the heirs of

Plantagenet came into possession, not only of the northern domains of England and Normandy, but of a great empire in the south between the Loire and the Pyrenees and stretching from the Bay of Biscay to the Rhone.

For a time it seemed as though it was the king of England who would hold France in his grip, rather than the other way round. The crusading zeal of Richard Coeur-de-Lion overtaxed his empire, as did the enormous ransom paid to rescue him from the duke of Austria. The next reign, that of his inept brother John, soon saw the loss of Normandy and all the northern section of the French holdings of the Plantagenets. A century later all that was left of that empire to the king of England was a strip of coastal land centred on Bordeaux, less than 200 miles long from the Charente to the Bidassoa, and some sixty miles wide. This remnant of Aquitaine, governed from England, brought valuable southern trade and supplies of excellent wine, and was strategically important for its common frontiers with the Spanish kingdoms of Navarre and Castile. England thus obtained a counterbalance, albeit an insecure one, to the Franco-Scottish pincers: English friendship with Spain was rational, and the marriage of Edward I to Eleanor of Castile in 1254 led to close links with the Peninsula. Eleanor was the sister of the wise king Alfonso X of Castile whose promotion of astronomy and the physical sciences was of prime importance for the future of civilization.

In the Spanish marriage of Edward I there lay hidden the Iberian involvement of his great-grandson the Black Prince. It might be thought that one-eighth of Spanish blood would count for little, and so it might have done in other circumstances. It was the fact that prince Edward was by 1366 the actual ruler of a greater Aquitaine bordering upon Spain that emphasized the remote ties of kinship that bound him to Don Pedro of Castile, his fourth cousin. We may suspect that a good deal more than consanguinity was involved: for the whole life of the Black Prince followed a pattern that is far more familiar in Spanish than in English history. Heroic deeds, attachment to honour above all but God, and deep religious devotion – all keynotes of the prince's life – are typically Spanish characteristics. Some accidental genetic predominance may account for it, but we are here concerned only with the effects.

Through Queen Eleanor England had acquired a small but important toehold in France, often overlooked: the county of Ponthieu with its capital Abbeville. Only about 25 miles square, it was nevertheless of considerable value as a bridgehead and lost its importance only after the taking of Calais in 1347. Apparently an analogy to the British possession of Gibraltar or the Spanish occupation of Ceuta and Melilla in Morocco, the enclave of Ponthieu leads to a necessary consideration of the completely different view of nationality taken in the Middle Ages. Though there had been, more especially in England, such a concept as that of nationhood as far back as the time of the Venerable Bede in the early eighth century, it was personal allegiance more than any other factor that made up the mediaeval national structure of Europe. Men were subjects of the king of England or the king of France. It was the king in his own person who was 'England' or 'France' – Louis XIV's famous phrase was no boast but the reaffirmation of a well known truism. '*L'état c'est moi!*' might have been said, and with philosophical truth, by almost any mediaeval king in Europe.

Language might be used as a shibboleth against a foreign military caste, as it was in the Sicilian rising against the French in 1282, when all unable to pronounce *ceci* (chickpeas) were massacred; but this was unusual. In England the dominant language for three centuries after the Conquest had been French, and until 1350 it was actually the language of instruction in schools, apart from grammar schools which insisted on Latin. Multilingual states, though now relatively unusual, still exist, but generally with an increasing rivalry and bitterness between the tongues, as in Belgium. Throughout the Middle Ages the allegiances in most countries were multiple and Spain, for instance, included until the late fifteenth century the four Christian kingdoms of Aragon, Navarre, Castile and Portugal, as well as the Muslim principality of Granada. In the kingdom of Aragon the Spanish and Catalan languages co-existed and do to the present day. King Alfonso X of Castile, a poet as well as a lawgiver and scientist, wrote verse in Portuguese as well as in Castilian Spanish.

Whereas England in the fourteenth century was at last becoming an English-speaking country of a single allegiance, it must be remembered that English was also the chief speech of Scotland. On the other hand France was divided, without respect to political allegiance, into the two languages, northern and southern, of French and Provençal. It was highly desirable for members of the ruling class, whether they were partisans of the king of France at Paris, the king of England, or of the German emperor in the region east of Saône and Rhone, to be masters of both tongues, as Richard Coeur-de-Lion had been. It was, all the same, northern French based on the use of Paris – but in England seldom a very faithful copy – that served over the greater part of western Christendom as the medium of diplomacy and business. Kings, nobles and knights from most of the places involved could all communicate through French, perhaps helped out with Latin.

This state of affairs was to come to an end soon after the time of the Black Prince. His life was, in more senses than one, the swansong of an international civilization, in principle Christian of the Roman rite yet owing a deep loyalty to the code of chivalry, which in some departments of life transcended religion as it did national frontiers. Doubtless the code had imperfections, but its great value lay in its ideal quality as an absolute arbiter of conduct rigidly excluding the consideration of material factors. It brought into the everyday life of the highest social classes something spiritually akin to the mysticism of the Muslim dervish. It is indeed probable that chivalry as practised in Europe from the twelfth to the fourteenth century owed a good deal to contacts with Islam, in Spain, in Sicily, and in Palestine in the days of the Crusader Kingdom. In spite of routine denigration of the Prophet and a great deal of nonsense about the supposedly 'idolatrous' practices of his followers, Christian knights were able to appreciate the courtesy and high ideals of their infidel opponents, as Richard Coeur-de-Lion did the generosity of Saladin.

Even if the last of the truly great knights of the age of chivalry, the Black Prince perhaps represents better than any other the best type of the chivalrous man. That side of his character most difficult for moderns to understand, his extravagant generosity without counting the cost, won him friends everywhere. This was not, as we might now cynically suppose, for obvious material reasons. Quite early in his career he was brought up against the economic difficulties that stand in the way of such generosity, and he was unable to offer much in the way of well paid careers. Yet he was as loyally followed as Napoleon, far more beloved and with better reason. The difference between mediaeval and modern man could hardly be more sharply brought out than in the contrast between Napoleon's cold-blooded kidnapping and judicial murder of the duc d'Enghien, and the Black Prince's magnanimous treatment of his prisoners, King John of France – who had ordered his troops to give no quarter to the English – and Du Guesclin, the most dangerous of all his opponents. The prince fought to win, but not at any cost: the one sacrifice that could not be made was that of honourable behaviour. It is probably not too much to claim that what passes for the British spirit of fair play and the sporting chance owes more than a little to the superb example set by Edward of Woodstock.

Here we should anticipate by taking from the end of his military career the incident of the sack of Limoges, often held up as an instance of mediaeval barbarity. At all periods war is barbarous, and there may be little to choose between its exponents, eastern or western, or of ancient times or today. But there is at least a distinction between unrestrained violence, 'no holds barred', and war fought according to some set of accepted rules, no matter what those rules may be. The accepted rules of mediaeval warfare were indeed harsh, particularly in the lack of any understood obligation to spare the lives of prisoners. It was not a breach of 'fair play' to kill the captured *at once* upon the field of battle. The difficulties of guarding and feeding captives on the migratory campaigns of the Hundred Years War were very great. The surprising thing is that nevertheless there were extremely few cases of deliberate slaughter of the vanquished. It was the Black Prince himself who, after the victory of Nájera, persuaded Don Pedro 'the Cruel' to spare the lives of all his enemies (traitors captured in arms against their lawful king), except for the abominable Gómez Carrillo.

The case of Limoges is different in at least two ways: firstly, it has hitherto been discussed on the basis of uncritical acceptance of the 'first edition' of Froissart's chronicle. Froissart, writing far from the scene, stated categorically that 'more than three thousand men, women and children were slain and beheaded that day', but in the second recension of the work the number was deleted. Alfred Leroux in 1906 was able to show conclusively that no surviving local chronicle of the period supported Froissart's original statement, but that it was an exaggeration of the chronicle of St Martial's abbey at Limoges, which states that over three *hundred* persons were put to death 'because of their rebellion against my lord Edward, duke of Aquitaine'. This is the crux of the matter: the three hundred or so who were killed at the taking of the town were legitimate victims, since they were in deliberate rebellion and had rejected their chance to surrender. This, the second and vital point, is what differentiates Limoges in 1370 from most cases of capture of an enemy town. Limoges was the prince's own city, gone over to the enemy under its traitor bishop. Incidentally, though the prince threatened to have the bishop beheaded, his life was in fact spared.

Gratuitous aspersions have also been cast at the prince on the supposed ground that he was hated by his own tenants for extortion. Rents had, of course, to be collected, and landlords as a class cannot be considered popular, but there is little evidence that the prince's extravagance and generosity were particularly resented. On the contrary, all sources of the time concur in telling of his immense popularity in contrast to dislike and suspicion of his brother John of Gaunt. It should at once be added that the reasons for objection to Gaunt were political rather than personal and that he, like his brother, tended towards leniency and generous treatment of subordinates and the tenants on his estates. In 1351 the prince ordered a thorough investigation of complaints from the manor of Bensington (or Benson) in Oxfordshire, both as to high rents and the arbitrary behaviour of the steward of his court in the Honor of Wallingford. Gaunt likewise allowed personal appeals from the villeins on his estates and remitted rents or lowered taxation of the duchy of Lancaster. Both the brothers permitted the sons of bondsmen on their manors to attend school and to take holy orders, thus opening to them the clerical career normally reserved to freemen born.

The royal family in the fourteenth century seem to have been decidedly advanced in their attitude towards serfdom. Villein tenants in England were never slaves, but they were subject to humiliating restrictions and could neither marry nor move without the leave of their lord. The brighter aspect of their lot was that, in most manors, they had perpetual security of tenure at very low customary rents, at any rate by the opening of the fourteenth century, when the commutation of heavy labour services into money rents was making great strides. Occasional riots and revolts are no more to be taken as proof of victimization or unfair treatment than are strikes accompanied by violent picketing in our own time. It has to be accepted that abuses of power always occur and are a constant of history, but they do not necessarily constitute an indictment of a whole society or, more to the point, of its individual leaders.

In comparison with most other countries of Europe, England's social attitudes were conspicuously favourable to the poorer classes of society. The lead in this was taken by the Crown, and whereas certain of the nobility were eager to exploit their peasantry and to keep them in perpetual subjection, such behaviour was checked by the king. The intervention of Edward I in 1306 to save the poor commoners of the forests from losing their rights to the lords of disafforested lands was a conspicuous example of active paternalism at the cost of incurring opposition from the baronage. Edward III in 1340, in demanding a tax of a fifteenth to prosecute his claim to France, completely exempted 'the poor and those who live of their labour'. It was the great lords who so bitterly opposed Richard II, the Appellants as they were called, who in 1388 passed an act in savage repression of begging and vagrancy. In 1391 a bill was introduced into the Commons to prohibit the education of villeins, but was vetoed by the personal action of Richard, who also in the same year insisted (in his Statute of Mortmain) that when a church was appropriated to a monastery, a proportion of the profits should be distributed to the poor of the parish.

Considerate treatment undoubtedly had a great deal to do with the successful military collaboration between knights and men-at-arms in the campaigns of Edward III and his sons. The English soldier was typically a volunteer – admittedly often in the hope of plunder – but was regarded as a match for any two pressed men of the continental armies. The popularity of the prince as a great leader survived the years of his illness, defeats and inaction to be transformed into universal and apparently sincere mourning at his death. Five years later, at the famous confrontation between Richard II as a boy of 14 and the rebellious commons at Smithfield, the spontaneous enthusiasm of the rebels when the young king put himself at their head must have been founded upon memories of the noble prince his father.

Whatever may have been the ultimate reasons, there is no doubt that England had abandoned at a very early date the hard-and-fast class divisions of feudal society. The gradations from the higher nobility, largely intermarried with the royal family, down through the gentry to the yeomanry, often the descendants of younger sons of gentle families, came to no abrupt cleavage. Many craftsmen were of yeoman stock, some few at least were of armorial families, and the regulations of many guilds, and notably those of the free masons, called for a code of behaviour that was honourable rather than merely honest, and quite as strict as the etiquette of the medical and other learned professions. By 1300 English society had reached a condition of elasticity that was not to be attained by most continental nations even in 1900. For better or worse, we knew nothing of the concept of *ebenburtigkeit* until, about 1800, the start of the Industrial Revolution had brought the new snobbery of mere wealth in its train.

England was not only exceptional in its social and political freedom – relative rather than absolute though that might be. English thought of the period was far less shackled than that of the French philosophers. Back in the thirteenth century the closed circuit of scholasticism had been challenged by Roger Bacon, and during the first half of the fourteenth the fight for free investigation was carried on by another English thinker, William of Ockham. In theoretical science, where the dead hand of Aristotle had to be cast aside, and in technical advances by experimental trial-and-error, England was already leading the western world. This can be seen most clearly in the visual arts and especially in architecture, where English masons were the first to break away from the norms of classical French Gothic and, in a wide range of personal styles showing creative imagination, to fire the whole of the West to develop what in central Europe became *Sondergotik* and, ultimately, Flamboyant in France. The passing of artistic domination from French to English masters was significantly first marked at Strassburg Cathedral in 1275, when the building lodge claimed and obtained autonomous jurisdiction 'after the English fashion'. This was a year after Edward I's triumphant return across the continent from his Crusade and when English influence was at a peak.

After the recession of Edward II and the minority of Edward III, English influence once more flowed outwards following the assumption of power by Edward in the autumn of 1330, within a few months of the birth of his son the Black Prince. The psychological fillip given to Edward III by his fatherhood is evident, and to that extent the baby Edward of Woodstock played a vital part in events from the day of his birth. It has to be remembered that the king was only 18 when his son was born – indeed, not much over $17\frac{1}{2}$ – and had some forty years of active and on the whole glorious life before him until senility set in after the death of Queen Philippa in the plague of 1369. The effective start of his reign not only coincided with the infancy of his eldest son, but with the opening of a wholly new and specifically national phase in art. This new age had its counterparts on the continent, particularly in the musical 'Ars Nova' of the Parisian Philippe de Vitri and the new poetry and learning of Italy exemplified by Petrarch.

The rise of nationalism from within the theoretically unitary Roman Christendom of the West seems at first sight a strange phenomenon. Within the limits of a 'world' of considerable extent there was a single religion employing a single language, Latin, by means of which all men of good education could communicate. The religious hierarchy had at its head the Pope, who claimed and in fact exercised many of the prerogatives of the Roman Emperors and of more ancient chief priests of pagan times. Thinking men looked back upon what they knew of the Roman Empire with some nostalgia for its quasi-universal extent, for its power, its wonderful organization, and its lasting dominion over intellectual life. It might have been expected, after the terrible experience of the barbarian invasions of the Dark Ages, that a genuine unity would arise, based upon the recovery of civilized values and recognition of a common heritage. No doubt some of the blame for the failure of Europe to achieve anything resembling this ideal must be borne by the individual rulers of emergent states. Personal ambition in many cases overcame constructive activities. As long as the Christian princes had to contend with the Muslims of Sicily and the Peninsula, or the heathens of the North, there was a high degree of co-operative alliance. Once the enemies from without had been halted, however, there began that syndrome of intermittent civil war from which Europe has suffered ever since.

How may men honour and cherish the neighbours of their own tribe or nation without scorn or hatred of others? How can courage, endurance and mutual assistance be displayed as well in peace as in war? How are men of fundamental goodwill to be brought together for common purposes rather than divided from one another by the principles or programmes of party? A genuine love of one's own country, coupled with affectionate admiration for its great personalities of past and present, is in no way ignoble. Yet, *corruptio optimi pessima*, Johnson's dictum that patriotism is the last refuge of a scoundrel is all too often verified in real life. The Middle Ages, before the period of decline after 1400, knew little of patriotism in this pejorative sense. There is an uneasy consciousness that its sinister figure was lurking in the wings when Saxon Englishmen rebelled against William the Conqueror; when Scots banded to support Bruce against Baliol; when the Portuguese refused to accept the accession of a Castilian sovereign. In some way the foundations of a persistent fallacy were being laid: that a frontier could be determined on the ground between men who *by law* owed allegiance to one state rather than another and who by the accident of birth had no freedom of choice. That special characteristic of the English freeman at the time of Domesday that 'he could take what lord he pleased' became a dead letter. Still worse, a quasi-religious mysticism could be adduced to wrap up the political motivation of French nationalism under Joan of Arc. That indeed may be said to have marked the end of the Middle Ages and the beginning of modern times.

The particular relevance of the fourteenth century to the tragedy of the twentieth is that it provides the most recent example in our country of a different kind of allegiance: to a person rather than to an abstraction. The highest side of this is brought out in the anecdote of the Black Prince's companion Sir Hugh Calveley, related by Mr John Barnie in his recent book *War in Medieval Society*. After the Peace of Bretigny in 1360 contingents of soldiers of fortune from many nations fought in Spain on behalf of Enrique the Bastard in his attempt to wrest the throne of Castile from Don Pedro. Among them was Calveley, who served under his former enemy Bertrand du Guesclin. A plot to assassinate Du Guesclin was hatched among the English troops and revealed to Calveley, who refused to be a party and at once told Du Guesclin, 'for he did not wish to be culpable for, nor consenting to, the death of so noble and valiant a knight'. The murder of an opponent, however much feared, was an unworthy act. On the other hand, when Calveley soon afterwards heard that his king's decision was in favour of Pedro and against Enrique, he took leave of Du Guesclin because 'he could not and should not be against his lord the prince'. We can see here the two sides of the principle of strict honour, operating in the same man.

War fought under the leadership of men actuated by such exalted principles must necessarily be less destructive, not only of life and property, but of transcendent human values, than war of the modern type where the aim is victory at *all* costs. Chivalry will always provide a better safeguard than the Official Secrets Act and atomic weapons. Yet chivalry, like patriotism, is not enough. And it is precisely in the age of the Black Prince that this was grasped, at least in part, by the prince's son Richard. We shall see that Richard, in the catastrophe of the later years of his reign, was attempting to apply the principles of the loftiest chivalry – taught him by his father – to the attainment of a lasting peace rather than military victory or continuing war. The prince and his son were the obverse and reverse of the same medal: the father as nobly successful in war as any commander of history; King Richard, seeking peace and failing, no less nobly. The stars in their courses fought against them: Edward of Woodstock died after nine years of illness at 46; Richard in humiliation and imprisonment at 33.

Whether or no we are to believe in the influence of the stars and planets on human affairs, or (as orthodox Muslims accept) regard them as cosmic indicators comparable to the hands of a clock, there is certainly a mysterious parallelism in certain dates and ages. The Black Prince, who had turned 46 at his death, was the same age as Napoleon when he was finally defeated at Waterloo; almost the same age as Babur, conqueror of India. Richard II, dying at 33, was as old as Jesus in universal tradition, as Alexander the Great, Julian, and his successor Richard III, the last Plantagenet, in historical fact. Threescore years and ten may be a normal limit to the average human life (even though that norm may not yet have been generally reached), but much shorter lives seem to be the rule for many sovereigns and statesmen, not necessarily through death in battle. Others survive approximately to the scriptural limit: Timur 69, Elizabeth I 70, Socrates 71, Confucius and Charlemagne 72, Lao-tzu 73; while a few greatly exceed it: Louis XIV 77, Kublai Khan 78, Victoria 81, George III, Justinian and Solon 82. It is as though there were peaks of greatest risk upon a master graph or model of life.

These ages of great men and women are, of course, scattered through history. But we have already seen that there is a different aspect of this apparently mathematical process, shown in the remarkable coincidence of deaths in 1400, the end not merely of a century in the Christian era, but of an age typifying a way of life. With slightly less exactitude queen Victoria just lived into 1901, surviving by a year Ruskin (almost 81) and by a few weeks Oscar Wilde. Here we cannot follow out these mysteries, but they serve to sharpen our awareness of the multiple strands of events in time as in space. Although we are here concerned with a particular period, a life-span of 70 years between 1330 and 1400, this cannot entirely be cut off from all reference to the historical continuum existing before and after, or from the happenings in many places remote from England as well as in her immediate surroundings.

So far as England is concerned, the period was made by the thoughts and actions of three generations of the same family: Edward III, the Black Prince, and Richard II. The scene had been set mainly by the far-reaching activities of Edward I in the course of his reign of 35 years. On the other hand, the twenty years which elapsed under Edward II were a time of English decline and defeat, relieved only by the proliferation of architecture and other works of art. It was this period of decline, coinciding with the boyhood of Edward III, that must have acted as a goad to his mind and as a springboard for his later activity. In the wide world outside England a great deal was happening, tending to change the fundamental concepts of western society. An age of technology was dawning, and from the far Orient at that. Inventions already ancient in China at length reached Europe, and Britain: bellows for producing a forced draught worked by water-power; the casting of iron; machinery for working silk. A time-lag of several hundred or even more than a thousand years had elapsed, but around 1300 the knowledge worked its way through to the West. The extraordinary career of Marco Polo at the court of Kublai Khan and his return to Venice in 1295 provide at least part of the explanation. The founding of a Christian archbishopric in Peking in 1307 opened another chapter that was destined to close in 1368 when the Ming dynasty recovered China from the Mongols and once more sealed the frontiers.

It was not only from the eastern end of the immense Mongol empire that new things were reaching us. The great shake-up administered to the whole

world by the outswarming of the Mongols in the middle of the thirteenth
century was pushing out refugees, many of them skilled craftsmen, who left
Turkestan, Persia and the Near East to seek safety in the western Muslim states
along the coast of North Africa, and in southern Spain. In Asia Minor the
Seljuk kingdom of Rum came to an end with the death of Mes'ud III in 1308,
making way for another and more famous Turkish dynasty, that of Osman.
From a group of obscure villages Osman and his son Orhan expanded their
inheritance into a major state, taking Brusa on 6 April 1326, crossing the
Dardanelles into Europe in 1353, moving their capital to Adrianople (Edirne)
in 1361; thence to Constantinople on 29 May 1453, to become the last dynasty
of the Eastern Empire until 10 November 1922. From the succession of Osman
in 1281 until our own times the Ottoman ruling family provided not merely
a link with the Middle Ages, but through their conquest of Constantinople
with the cultural traditions of classical antiquity.

While the East produced great empires, Europe was splintered into relatively
small principalities. The largest realm was that of the (western) Empire, comprising most of Germany and northern Italy, but the Emperor's control over
it was generally slight. The poet Dante was attempting, in Latin prose and in
the years around 1310, to work out a theory of universal Roman monarchy on
behalf of the Emperor, owing spiritual allegiance to the Pope; but his book
remained a theory. The real battle of practical politics was that between France
and England for dominance, but behind the scenes an even deeper struggle for
power was that between the new mercantilism of great cities and the attempt
of the feudal nobles to control them. This was the precipitating cause of the
Hundred Years War: Jakob van Artevelde led Ghent and the other cities of
Flanders against their Count, a member of the French royal family, seeking
help from England. Edward III, with his own inheritance of claims to the
throne of France, had an equal interest in allying himself to the Flemish
merchants. The English king soon afterwards made a close alliance with the
Emperor, Louis IV the Bavarian, who appointed him Vicar-General of the
imperial provinces on the left bank of the Rhine, with power to raise troops
for foreign war for seven years from 1338.

The journey of Edward III to the Low Countries and Germany led to
unusually close relations of his court with the continent. His sons Lionel and
John were born at Antwerp and Ghent ('Gaunt') respectively, in 1338 and
1340. Queen Philippa remained in the closest touch with her mother, countess
of Hainault, an imperial fee divided from French Flanders by the river Scheldt.
Philippa throughout her life was loyally served by Sir Walter de Manny and
other Hainaulters attached to her at the time of her marriage. We owe to her
compatriot Jean Froissart of Valenciennes the best account that has come down
to us of the events of the fourteenth century touching England, France and

Spain. The complicated story of the smaller principalities of the Low Countries, their rivalries and alliances across the frontier between the Empire and France, lay very near to the England of Edward III, his queen Philippa, and their children. Hainault passed by marriage later in the century to the ducal house of Bavaria, and it was to Albert, duke of Bavaria and count of Holland, Zealand and Hainault that Richard II was, in 1397, to confide his most intimate thoughts on the political problems which beset him.

The western world into which the Black Prince was soon to be born was, then, a place of great and prosperous cities backed by agriculture on fertile lands. A frightful famine had, it is true, struck the continent in 1314, but did little to obstruct the march of the burghers to riches. New machinery and other inventions, whether from the remote East or developed on the spot, were offering the chance of still more profit and a rise in the living standard for craftsmen and labourers. The arts were flourishing and royal and noble patrons were ready to spend enormous sums on houses, paintings, carvings, tapestries and clothing, and – most costly – upon jewellery and plate of gold and silver. The little that has come down to us from that age is enough to show the almost incredibly high standards of taste reached in the fourteenth century. It is rare to find any piece that shows signs of vulgarity: line, form and colour were harmonious and exquisitely compounded. By the humdrum light of our own times this is seen as a fairy land of amazing beauty. Even those, the great majority, who could not possess such works were able to see them, and to enjoy the great feasts and public entertainments put on to celebrate victories, royal marriages and meetings, and, every year, the festival of the birth of God at Christmas. Behind the colourful scenes hidden forces were moving: chivalry, religion, greed, rivalry, patriotism, mystical sensibility. At the highest level it was an age of kingly governance of peoples for good; of eager listeners to poetry, French, Italian, Spanish, Portuguese, German, English; and above all a time in which artists and craftsmen laid up a richer harvest of creative imagination than has, for quality and perhaps quantity as well, ever been seen in Europe.

CHAPTER I

England in 1330

The inequality of nature is nowhere better displayed than in historical geography. Significant forces have at times sprung from an extremely small base to control great areas, and at one and the same time there may be a virtual equipoise between one state of vast size and another relatively so small in extent as to appear geographically irrelevant. On the surface of the globe the whole island of Britain seems unimportant; England alone almost negligible. Yet the far larger islands of Madagascar and New Guinea, respectively more than four times and more than six times as large as England, have hitherto had virtually no impact upon history. Most of the major civilized powers have controlled great land masses: China, India, Persia, Rome, the Mongols, the Ottoman Turks in the past; China still, Russia, and the United States of America at present. A minority has always existed, contradicting the general rule: cultures with an importance vastly out of proportion to their minuscule base: Minoan Crete, ancient Athens, Portugal, Holland and England.

This phenomenon of disproportionate importance is due to two main factors: exceptional capacity on the part of the rulers, and what may be called a high quality/quantity quota in the population. England had already enjoyed this combination at a relatively low level under King Alfred in the ninth century and again under Henry I early in the twelfth. Under the Plantagenets, after 1154, it became clear that in spite of its small size and relative isolation, England was a substantial power. Her standing depended almost entirely upon the personal capacity of the reigning monarch: high under Henry II and Edward I, low under John and Edward II; under Henry III, in the course of his long and chequered reign, politically mediocre but artistically in the first flight. The trend was throughout in an upward direction in spite of setbacks. By the second quarter of the fourteenth century England had reached a level of aesthetic culture and technological civilization equal to that of France, but little below that of Italy, and in the West only notably bettered in the south of

Spain. In Germany and the Low Countries technology and commercial development were more advanced, but artistic inspiration was still in second place, north of the Alps, to both France and England.

Step by step, from the Conquest onwards, England had acquired specific advantages over her continental neighbours. The fact that William of Normandy had won the country by force of arms put him in a position of complete authority hardly rivalled elsewhere. He deliberately strengthened the hand of the Crown in two ways: by carrying out a survey (Domesday Book) of the taxable value of every estate; and by insisting, through the Oath at Salisbury, that every feudal tenant owed allegiance directly to the sovereign and not to an immediate overlord. Under his younger son Henry I, married to the heiress of the Saxon line in 1100, integration between victors and vanquished made strides, and Englishmen of Saxon origin once more reached high positions. Henry, though perhaps not himself as learned as his nickname Beauclerk might suggest, was a notable patron of learning, and it is in his reign that England first took a leading place in science, scholarship, and the arts and crafts. Advances in building construction and the use of machinery marked the practical field, while scholarship was conspicuously exemplified by Adelard of Bath, the translator of Euclid, and the converted Jewish doctor from Aragon, Petrus Alphonsi, who became the king's physician. The royal minstrel Rahere (died 1144) founded St Bartholomew's Hospital in 1123 and so made possible the continuous tradition of medical experiment and teaching in this country.

The size and reputation of London, among northern cities, was of importance for the country as a whole even before the Conquest. A century later it was one of the major capitals of north-western Europe, though not to be compared with such centres as Cairo, Constantinople or Cordova. It is likely that intensity of organization, under skilful masters, more than made up for lack of numbers. By the middle of the twelfth century there were many guilds of weavers in England, and the trades came as time went on to play an ever more important role. The building trades, used to the construction of very large monasteries and castles, led the way in the deployment of capital on a large scale as well as in highly sophisticated technical skills and the logistics involved in getting the necessary work-force to the site. Military engineers constructed the giant catapults which formed the artillery of the period before gunpowder, as well as crossbows and other examples of ingenuity put to a destructive use. In all this and in much else England had already been equipped for more than a hundred years before the Black Prince's time.

The refinements of civilized life, superadded to its necessities, were largely introduced by Henry III, and very probably to satisfy the elegant requirements of his queen, Eleanor of Provence. Her upbringing amid Mediterranean

culture doubtless made her insist upon the improved sanitation, fitted bathrooms, and window glass which suddenly made their appearance. Walls and
ceilings were finely painted, or hung with cloth or panelled in wood. Table-
cloths of linen were supplied for the king's use at Christmas and other feasts,
and it is necessary to insist that by 1250 there was no longer any question of
English kings and their courts existing in magnificent barbarism. The surroundings of life, as led by royalty and by the upper classes, displayed as much
elegance as at any period of European history, even though they might fall far
short of the refinements of China, Japan or Persia. Parks set with trees and
pools, houses surrounded by gardens and orchards, had descended to a new-
rich bourgeoisie by 1250, in less than 150 years from the introduction of such
delights by Henry I at Woodstock in 1110.

The thirteenth century saw too a great development in the keeping of
records. England, perhaps fortunate by mere chance in the survival of Domesday Book and of numbers of financial accounts – the Pipe Rolls – going back
even as far as 1130, abounds in documents of all kinds after 1200. From the
middle of the century even private documents, yearly accounts and records of
the courts of manors, have come down to us and continue in a wider and wider
stream of written matter down to the present day. Whereas much that went
on, in many departments of life, is virtually a closed book before 1100, and
even up to 1200, information becomes abundant by the reign of Edward I.
The names of individual artists and craftsmen and even intimate details of their
lives can be discovered. The title deeds to the property of ordinary men and
women, not only those kept by great landowners; their wills, often registered
as part of their title; and even a few business and private letters can be found.

Though it is generally impossible within the Middle Ages to unravel the
delicate interplay of personalities, revealed only when there is a substantial
survival of correspondence and memoranda, we do get thumbnail sketches of
character from the chroniclers, and some individuals begin to emerge from
the generally faceless obscurity. Even where this is not possible, such records
as registers of craftsmen who took up the 'freedom' of cities begin to provide
rather more than merely statistical information. By 1300 it becomes possible
to distinguish particular families, not just of the nobility and gentry, but of
burgesses and artist-craftsmen, and to obtain some idea of their local standing,
their wealth or poverty, and their municipal or parochial influence. The
attribution of works of art to known authors is the rule rather than the exception, and throughout the fourteenth century we can get a reasonably clear
idea of the personal responsibility for a high proportion of the really significant
developments.

Who then were the personalities who set the tone of English life in the
period around the birth of Edward of Woodstock in 1330? Bearing in mind

the relatively low expectation of life in mediaeval times, it is evident that the generation concerned was mostly born between 1270 and 1310, roughly the reign of Edward I. Every age depends upon its predecessor, and we can see this happening if we think of the post-war generation born after 1918, surrounded by the activities and taste of late-Victorians mostly born between 1860 and 1900; or the French born after Waterloo and conditioned by an environment largely consisting of those whose memories extended back to the *ancien régime* before the Revolution. Where the Black Prince had luck in the highest degree exceptional, was in being the first-born of a very young father. Edward III, the leader of English society from his son's first year, was himself the youngest of all in England who counted. The era into which the prince came was that inaugurated by his father's birth as recently as 13 November 1312. For once the gap between the generations hardly mattered, and the Black Prince was able – as very few heirs to thrones – to grow up under and remain on the best of terms with a father whom he sincerely admired and loved.

Throughout the prince's boyhood his father was engaged in one campaign after another. The king took Berwick in 1333 and routed the Scots in the first pitched battle in which he took command, at Halidon Hill on 19 July. By 1336 he was in effective control of most of the Lowlands and English garrisons held the fortresses of Roxburgh, Edinburgh, Stirling and Perth. It was perhaps a pity for the long term peace of Britain that he was distracted from Scotland by the results of his claim to France. By 1337 it was clear that war was inevitable, and Edward III first used the title of king of France, though it was not until the beginning of 1340 that he quartered the French arms and regularly used the year of his French 'reign' as well as his English one on documents. Meanwhile he had sailed on his first expedition against France in July 1338, and during the 18 months of his absence it was his son who nominally represented him as keeper of the realm and summoned parliaments in his father's name.

In these early years the young prince spent much of his time with his mother, one of the best hearted and deservedly beloved of all the consorts of England. The marriage of Edward and Philippa was, like most royal matches, an arranged one, and arranged well in advance. When she was not yet nine, in 1323, the bishop of Exeter was sent over to Hainault to report upon her to Edward II. In the absence of photographs, the envoy brought back a detailed verbal report: 'The lady whom we saw has not uncomely hair, betwixt blue-black and brown. Her head is clean-shaped; her forehead high and broad, and standing somewhat forward. Her face narrows between the eyes, and the lower part of her face is still more narrow and slender than the forehead. Her eyes are blackish-brown and deep. Her nose is fairly smooth and even, save that it is somewhat broad at the tip and flattened, yet it is no snub-nose. Her nostrils are also broad, her mouth fairly wide. Her lips somewhat full, and especially the lower lip. Her teeth which have fallen and grown again are white enough, but the rest are not so white. The lower teeth project a little beyond the upper; yet this is but little seen. Her ears and chin are comely enough. Her neck, shoulders, and all her body and lower limbs are reasonably well shapen; all her limbs are well set and unmaimed; and nought is amiss so far as a man may see. Moreover she is brown of skin all over, and much like her father; and in all things she is pleasant enough, as it seems to us. And the damsel will be of age of nine years on St John's day next to come, as her mother saith. She is neither too tall nor too short for such an age; she is of fair carriage, and well taught in all that becometh her rank, and highly esteemed and well beloved of her father and mother and of all her meinie, in so far as we could inquire and learn the truth.'

Three years after this queen Isabella and her son, later Edward III, visited the count and countess of Hainault, and the marriage was definitely arranged. Philippa was married by proxy at Valenciennes in October 1327, soon afterwards travelled to England, and on 24 January 1328 married Edward III in York Minster, where their second son, William of Hatfield, was buried as an infant eight years later. All that we know of queen Philippa proves that she was kind and generous-hearted, and she may have been inclined to spoil her children. The king gave special orders that Edward was to stay with his mother and follow the Court, but a great deal of the boy's childhood was spent at Woodstock. Later he was to profit from tuition at the hands of the learned Dr Walter Burley. Burley, a Yorkshireman and an Oxford graduate, took a doctorate in theology at Paris in 1324 and was the greatest commentator of his time on the works of Aristotle, still regarded as the fountain head of all science. It is disputed whether Sir Simon Burley, son of Sir John, was a relative of Walter, but Sir Simon was in due course to stand tutor to the prince's own son Richard, and ultimately to lose his life for his loyalty to his royal pupil. Traditionally at least the Black Prince was one of the early students at The Queen's Hall (now College) in Oxford, founded by Philippa's chaplain Robert de Eglesfield in 1341 with the queen as co-founder.

Walter Burley, besides being a leading scholar, was a diplomat of standing, and the prince's capacity for tact and charm doubtless owed much to thorough training as well as to his innate qualities. He was from his early years in touch with some of the best minds of his time who centred about his father's court. Though the personalities of most of the leading statesmen and advisers of Edward III remain shadowy, we know a good deal about one of them, Richard de Bury, bishop of Durham from 1333 to 1345. He had long been in the service of Edward III and may have been his principal tutor about 1323–26; he was certainly one of the king's closest friends and worked to build up a court party on his master's behalf. It was largely due to Bury that the young king was able to escape from the tutelage of his mother Isabella, and get rid of her paramour Mortimer, in 1330. Bury reaped his reward in the highest offices of government: treasurer in 1333–34 and then chancellor – in effect prime minister – for the next year, and thereafter employed on the most vital diplomatic concerns until ill health struck him down in 1343. Bury, as he himself tells us in his entertaining *Philobiblon*, was 'reported to burn with such desire for books . . . that it was more easy for any man to gain our favour by means of books than of money'. He is careful to point out that, in accepting gifts of tatty and worm-eaten old volumes, he strove to forward the affairs of the donors so long as 'justice suffered no disparagement'.

Bury was a close friend of Burley, and we can still sense their immense enthusiasm for learning, and the penetration of all the riddles which the world and life might afford. Petrarch, who met Bury in Avignon in 1333, described him as 'a man of ardent genius and by no means ignorant of letters, from his youth up beyond belief curious concerning hidden matters'. It is refreshing to read Bury's unbounded enthusiasm, not limited by the common round of the Latin learning of his day, but concerned to study Greek and Hebrew, and aware of the need for knowledge of Arabic to study its 'numerous astronomical treatises'. This interest reflected the concern for languages of the Council of Vienne in 1312, when Raymond Lully persuaded Pope Clement V to decree that professorships of Greek, Hebrew, Arabic and Chaldee (Aramaic) should be set up at Rome, Paris, Oxford, Bologna and Salamanca. This great project had originally been urged upon Pope Clement IV (1265–68) by Roger Bacon. The diocesan bishops failed to carry out the papal decree, but even at the end of his life Bury was hoping for its fulfilment. An ill man, nearing his deathbed, he could at any rate by 1344 congratulate Britain on receiving the visitation of 'admirable Minerva', goddess of learning.

Spiced with sly remarks at the expense of the French, Bury's comments are surprisingly modern in tone. He remarked that 'the Palladium of Paris has been carried off in these sad times of ours'; 'that noble university, whose rays once shed light into every corner of the world, has grown lukewarm, nay, is all but frozen.' The French scholars 'wrap up their doctrines in unskilled discourse' while 'our English subtleties, which they denounce in public, are the subject of their furtive vigils.' Bury realized that culture in course of time moved from place to place: Minerva had 'already visited the Indians, the Babylonians, the Egyptians and Greeks, the Arabs and the Romans'. Having passed by Paris she had now come to dwell with us in 'Britain, the most noble of islands, nay, rather a microcosm in itself'. Finally the chapter concludes with a neat dig at the enemy across the Channel: 'it is conceived by most men, that as philosophy is now lukewarm in France, so her soldiery are unmanned and languishing'.

Even when we make allowance for some literary exaggeration, Bury's picture of monastic decline is striking in that he wrote two hundred years before the Dissolution. He found little enthusiasm for books among the monks of the early fourteenth century. 'Flocks and fleeces, crops and granaries, leeks and potherbs, drink and goblets, are nowadays the reading and study of the monks.' Yet he was a serious scholar and a fair-minded man, and adds that there remained a few elect ones in whom lingered some slight vestige of the fathers who had gone before. The canons regular of St Augustine he considered quite as bad, only thinking of getting through their prayers quickly to go hunting or hawking, spending on their dogs what might have been given to the poor, or playing games of dice and draughts. For Richard Aungerville de Bury, both as bishop and as statesman, books were the one correct answer.

Beneath the exalted level of prime ministers and royal tutors we have to seek for the main body of distinguished Englishmen of the time, for it was into a world shaped by their endeavours that the young prince Edward came when he emerged from his mother's care at the end of boyhood. Most serious writing, whether literary or scientific, was still in Latin, but it is from the opening of the fourteenth century that there begins to be a trickle of English verse and prose. In spite of the long period in which English had become a downtrodden language of country folk, it quite suddenly about the reign of Edward I (who spoke English in public, as well as Latin and French) took on a definite shape. It became instead of an uncouth dialect a true language, on a par with the other new vernaculars of Europe though younger. Apart from short lyric poems, some of great force and charm, the first outstanding works were religious, such as the *Handlyng Synne* of Robert Mannyng of Bourne in Lincolnshire, finished in 1303. Mannyng then turned his attention to re-writing English history and produced his *Rhyming Chronicle* in over 25,000 lines, covering the whole story from the arrival of Brutus the Trojan to the death of Edward I in 1307.

Mannyng's work was not finished until 1338, but it was still in time to have had a hand in shaping the young prince's attitude towards the dynastic history of Britain, and the belief that our civilization, like that of Rome, stemmed directly from royal refugees of Trojan stock. It was such ideas, whether historically well founded or not, that gave spiritual backbone to the leadership of the country for several hundred years. The concept of Britain, in Bury's words, as 'the most noble of islands, a microcosm in itself' underlay the forging of English nationalism and, in the long run, the creation of the British Empire. For we must remember that the idea was by no means new in the fourteenth century: without counting the patriotism of the Venerable Bede long before the Norman Conquest, there had been the amazing development of Geoffrey of Monmouth's *History of the Kings of Britain*, written in Latin and finished by 1136. The poetic prophecy of the goddess Diana, appearing to Brutus in a dream during his flight through the Mediterranean, had gained acceptance and provided a chart and, as it were, a blueprint for ultimate success.

> Brutus, beneath the setting sun beyond the realm of Gaul
> In ocean lies an isle where giants once did dwell.
> Now it is desert, fitted for thy race.
> Seek it: for ever will it be thy seat;
> In it another Troy shall rise for all thy sons.
> Of thy descent shall kings be born; to them
> Subject shall be the globe of all the earth.

Geoffrey's *History* was certainly brought to the notice of English sovereigns, for one of the original manuscripts was dedicated to the new king Stephen, who had just succeeded Henry I. The taste for the 'British History' and the romance of King Arthur had been inculcated by his work, and formed basic reading matter, in Latin or French, for generations. By a happy accident we know that Edward I carried about with him on Crusade a volume of British Arthurian romances, which Rusticiano of Pisa was able to borrow, to found upon it a version of his own. The *History* was indeed, as R.W.Chambers wrote, 'one of the most influential books ever written in this country'. The seed fell upon fertile soil, and the harvest began to be reaped in the time of the Black Prince's youth. Hitherto all the versions accessible to the reading, or listening, public had been either in Latin or in French. The main source used by Mannyng was the French rhyming chronicle of Peter de Langtoft, likewise brought down to the death of Edward I in 1307. For the first time the whole story was available for everyone who had learned to read his own language in the church porch, or who – though themselves illiterate – listened to the public readings or recitations which formed one of the few intellectual recreations of the Middle Ages.

Nor was the new tradition set by Mannyng's English version confined to mere history of past events or the legendary treatment of the dynasty through Arthur and Belinus back to Brutus the Trojan. Popular verse in English, celebrating the prowess of Edward III in the immediate present, poured from the pen of Laurence Minot during the twenty years from 1333 to 1352. This was popular in the special sense that it stressed an identity of interest between the Crown and the ordinary common man of the English countryside. During the king's absence on the campaign of Crecy in 1346 Philip VI of Valois, the French king, sent to David II of Scotland asking him to invade England from the north. The Scots complied and crossing the Border sacked and destroyed towns and monasteries, but on 17 October were heavily defeated at Neville's Cross by a home-guard army raised by William Zouche the archbishop of York, and consisting largely of priests and clerks, shepherds and countrymen. The king of Scots was captured and the victory had a decisive effect. Minot's version, though it needs re-spelling, is intelligible enough if we bear in mind the old use of 'let' for prevent or hinder: –

> Sir Philip the Valois, sooth for to say,
> Sent unto Sir David and fair gan him pray
> To ride through England, their foemen to flay,
> And said, none is at home to let him the way.
> None lets him the way to wend where he will,
> But with shepherd staves found he his fill.

and so on through many verses.

As we shall see, the Black Prince when in command before the battle of Poitiers ten years later made two separate addresses to his troops, one to his companions of the knightly class, and a second to the archers. The private soldier of no social rank or status was, almost for the first time in history, urged to remember that he and his officers shared the same lot, and stood or fell together. Once again we find that the innovation was not wholly new, for it had been foreshadowed by Edward I during the war in Wales: when cut off by floods with a small body of men the king went share and share alike with them, not only in the little food available, but with his single cask of wine. Such behaviour is commonly miscalled 'democratic', but has nothing to do with rule by the people. It had, however, a decisive effect on English history and was one of the biggest ingredients in long-term success. One of the factors, at least, in the conspicuous failure of the French armies in pitched battles was the contempt of the lords and knights for the rank and file.

Behind these changing attitudes, tending towards a national consciousness specifically English, and an identification of the people as a whole with the aims and actions of the sovereign, there lay the solid successes of the long reign of Edward I. England had been left in 1307 in a strong economic position, with the wool trade as its greatest asset and an adequate population, on the whole robust and probably better fed than the European average. Prosperity had reached the point where the small farmer could find cash to pay a money rent every year instead of performing menial labour services on the land of his manorial lord. The lords of manors, both the lay squirearchy and the monks of most orders, were finding that it was more advantageous to lease out their land for money rents, so that they did relatively little farming themselves. For the time being money was available, rents came in, and the landowners could pay their way rather than eat the actual produce of their estates, visited in turn. The high cost of transport, of victuals as of everything else, could now be met, and there was still a surplus which could be spent on works of charity and upon personal luxuries.

It is this surplus expenditure, or a proportion of it, that produced the amazing output of architecture and the arts, backed by superlative craftsmanship, that is now the chief tangible survivor from the age. From the royal family downwards to the parochial level through lords and prelates, country gentlemen and burgesses of the towns, there was a growing determination to live in more beautiful as well as better equipped surroundings. The taste for finer clothes made of richer stuffs went so far down the social scale as to have to be restrained by sumptuary laws. Though we can follow the changing fashions through paintings and sculpture, extremely little of the clothing itself has come down to us. There is little furniture and not very much in the way of domestic fittings and utensils, though recent archaeological excavation gradually reveals more and more of the surprising richness and complexity of daily life. The striking thing is the high quality of aesthetic taste coupled with the notable efficiency of craftsmanship shown in most artefacts. This is also displayed in the highest degree by the buildings.

Architecture, the Mistress Art, set the fashions in design and decoration, followed by the related and subordinate arts of painting, sculpture, joinery, embroidery and tapestry. Metalwork too, under the aegis of the great goldsmiths, used architectural detail in many ways. The creative designers, whose imagination led the way in all this immense output, were mostly the masters of the stonemasons in collaboration with leading carpenters responsible for timber construction. The linguistic movement away from French towards English as a national language was exactly paralleled by developments in architectural style. Ever since the middle of the twelfth century, when the new Gothic art had been imported from France, it was usually French influence that had been paramount. The latest fashions in and around Paris tended to be copied within a few years, but towards the end of the thirteenth century there was a close association with the regional style of Champagne. This had a directly political basis in the marriage of the widowed countess Blanche in 1275 to Edmund of Lancaster, younger brother of Edward I. Lancaster was in actual charge of the great province, with its cities Rheims and Troyes, for over ten years. The artistic connection is perhaps best exemplified by the resemblance between the design of the eastern parts of Troyes Cathedral and the nave of York Minster begun in 1291. Even before the dynastic marriage of 1275 the master of the works of the important and artistically revolutionary church of St Urbain at Troyes had been John 'Anglicus', the Englishman, for several years before he went on pilgrimage to Jerusalem in 1267.

England had already diversified its approach to Gothic in three main regional styles of the thirteenth century, in the South-East, the North, and the West, though the style of the South-East was dominated by the personal approach of the masters directly employed by the Crown, and so comes to be called the Court Style. In the last quarter of the old century this was directed by Master Michael who came into Edward I's service at Westminster from the priory of Christ Church at Canterbury. Master Michael, working at Canterbury in 1275 and still alive and in charge at the palace of Westminster in 1321, was succeeded by Thomas of Canterbury and Walter of Canterbury, almost certainly his sons. Thomas was in charge of the king's most important building works until 1335. The development of the southern Gothic style passed into the hands of Thomas of Witney, who trained on the works of St Stephen's Chapel under Master Michael in 1292–94 and later had charge of work at Winchester and Exeter cathedrals, probably also at Wells and several other great churches. In the North a very different movement of style took place, towards a richly flowing line, producing what has been termed the Curvilinear Style. This was initially the creation of a master concerned both with Carlisle cathedral and York Minster, and with other works in the diocese of York. He seems, upon a basis of very strong probability, to have been the architect who worked for William Melton, archbishop of York, Ivo de Raghton, whose name came from the village of Raughton not far from Carlisle. This style is of considerable significance in that it appealed to the taste of continental masters and, after the middle of the fourteenth century, appeared abroad in forms which led to the foreign Flamboyant.

Perhaps because its flowing lines were fundamentally out of keeping with English linearity, the fully developed Curvilinear did not become a phase of the Court Style, and development went in a quite different direction. A tendency towards stiffness and the introduction of more straight lines into decorative design began about 1330 and steadily grew along with the Black Prince, its exact contemporary. This tendency became stylized and codified into what was described by Thomas Rickman as the Perpendicular Style. So far as any architectural style can be said to have been invented, Perpendicular was the creation of William Ramsey, member of a distinguished family of Norfolk masons. Their original surname was Curteys, as descendants of one Alfelin 'the courteous' (*facetus*) who had held property in Upwell under the abbot of Ramsey before 1150. William Ramsey worked on St Stephen's Chapel, Westminster, under Thomas of Canterbury in 1325 and in 1332 was engaged by the dean and chapter of St Paul's to design their new chapter house and cloister. It is the fragments from these buildings, destroyed after the Great Fire of 1666 and now preserved in Wren's St Paul's, that first show the specific character of the new style. Ramsey succeeded Thomas of Canterbury as the king's master mason in 1336 and carried out work at Norwich and Lichfield as well as at Westminster and Windsor Castle. He died in the Black Death in 1349.

Ramsey's colleague, the carpenter William Hurley, was another of the craftsmen who gained experience on the king's works at St Stephen's Chapel. Besides official work, at the Tower of London, Tonbridge Castle and Caerphilly Castle, Hurley was in charge of timberwork at the chapel of the Guildhall in London, and visited Ely to take charge of the amazing wooden vault and lantern over the new octagon at the centre of the cathedral. This is a work of quite exceptional genius, both in construction and in aesthetic quality, and is completely unparalleled elsewhere. It may be that it was inspired by the success of the wooden 'dome' which spans the chapter house at York without the aid of a central pillar, but the span is some ten feet greater and the inclusion of a lantern enormously increased the difficulty of the technical problems to be overcome. Hurley was also responsible for the original timber roof over St Stephen's Chapel. The success of these roofs, and especially the cantilevered construction of that at Ely, paved the way for the outstanding invention of the hammer-beam truss, one of England's chief contributions to building method.

Ramsey and Hurley were the greatest architects of the second quarter of the century, but they were leaders of an army of designers at work all over the country. Many are known by name and it becomes possible for the first time in our art history to attribute to individual personalities, who are also historical figures, most of the important movements in our art. We shall meet a number of these artists as time passes. They included not only architects in stone and timber, but sculptors and painters. In 1332 Master Richard of Reading carved statues for the front of St Stephen's Chapel, and was probably the Richard of Farleigh known to have been working for Reading Abbey by 1334, when he also had work in hand at Bath Abbey and was engaged as mason by Salisbury cathedral. Distinguished painters included a succession of masters from St Albans, perhaps three generations of the same family, culminating in Master Hugh. He designed the great scheme of wall paintings in St Stephen's Chapel, of which drawings and some fragments survive. Hugh of St Albans very probably visited the south of France and Italy, and when he made his will in 1361 he possessed a valuable painting of Lombardy in seven panels. He died in 1368 and had probably been born between 1310 and 1320, as he first appears as a groom of the king's chamber in 1348, painting the king's ships, flags and 300 pennons with the arms of St George. The cult of St George as national patron, thus artistically exemplified, formed part and parcel of the new outlook in English society. It is not to be supposed that Hugh painted everything with his own hand: at St Stephen's, where he and his chief assistant were paid 1s. a day each but did not work there every day, we know of at least 16 subordinate painters by name, paid at lesser rates. Among them was Hugh's successor, Gilbert Prince.

Besides the wall and panel painters there were many illuminators who enriched the splendid manuscript books made for wealthy patrons. Although some illuminators were connected with great monasteries, among which both Peterborough and Norwich were particularly important in the early part of the fourteenth century, most of them were lay craftsmen rather than monks. Glass-painters too were very numerous and had shops in London and in the greater cities, where they can be identified in the rolls of freemen as well as occasionally in accounts for work and in title deeds. The large number of craftsmen in all these artistic fields is astonishing, and though little has come down to us of their output, what has survived is of superb quality. In gold-smith's work, for instance, the King's Lynn Cup, silver-gilt and with exquisite enamelling, is almost unique in showing what could be done by about 1340. English embroideries of the first half of the century are, on the contrary, quite numerous, and present a glowing picture of the coloured enrichment of the Church and the Court. We can still see in the Cluny Museum at Paris the remains of an English horse-trapper, embroidered with the leopards of Edward III: here is just a single glimpse of the glorious visual world which surrounded Edward of Woodstock from the moment of his birth.

CHAPTER II

Heir to England

When Prince Edward was born at Woodstock, on 16 June 1330 at 10 o'clock in the morning, the king his father was 17½ and his mother, Queen Philippa, a week short of her sixteenth birthday. She was a child-mother and it is natural to suppose that she treated her first-born as an animated doll. The supremely cheerful and debonair temperament of the Black Prince in later life confirms this; we know too that Philippa insisted on breast-feeding him herself. Both parents certainly regarded him as good fortune and a harbinger of better things: the freeing of the king from the irksome control of his mother 'the She-Wolf' and the setting up of his personal government within months of the boy's birth. The messenger who brought the good news to Edward III, Thomas Prior, was rewarded with 40 marks (£26 13s. 4d.) a year; the prince's nurse, Joan of Oxford, got £10 a year, and Matilda Plumpton, whose duty it was to rock the infant's cradle, 10 marks (£6 13s. 4d.). Peter de Eketon, another messenger who took the news to Henry, the old earl of Lancaster, was granted by the earl a rent of 10 marks for life. The heir to the throne of England got off to a good start and, it would have seemed, under the happiest of auspices.

A birthplace may of itself have little influence upon the subject, but a child-hood home can be of considerable importance. Prince Edward was not only born at Woodstock, but spent a good part of his early years there. The estate survives as the great park of Blenheim Palace, but of the mediaeval royal manor-house nothing is left, and the landscaping of the eighteenth century has destroyed much of the contours. The old house stood on the top of the low hill to the north-west of Blenheim, at the far end of the bridge across the lake. Less than a quarter-mile to the west of the house was the separate walled garden-pleasance of Everswell, known as Rosamund or Rosamund's Bower. This had been started in 1165, perhaps in historical fact for Henry II's mistress Rosamund. The enclosure consisted largely of an orchard, planted with a hundred pear trees for Henry III in 1264, and had a series of pools fed by the natural spring of Everswell. By the pools the queen's garden was laid out, imitating the type of oriental garden now best known to us from that of the Generalife at Granada, but also found by the Normans in Sicily.

Woodstock had been a royal residence even before the Conquest, but its special character was due to Henry I, who in 1110 had the park surrounded by a stone wall and turned into a menagerie or open-air zoo, far-off predecessor of Whipsnade. As far as we know, this was the earliest 'paradise' in England based on the ancient Persian and Mesopotamian model which had been brought by the Arabs to north Africa and into Spain. There was at least one distinguished precedent in Normandy at Coutances, where Bishop Geoffrey de Montbray after visiting his relatives in southern Italy soon after 1050, built a palace and laid out a park before the conquest of England in 1066. Acorns and the seeds of other forest trees were sown and pools were formed, and a vineyard planted. Deliberate landscaping of this kind is implied by what little is known of Henry I's activities at Woodstock. It became the model for all the country estates of royalty and the greater nobles. At Kenilworth Castle, for instance, the private apartments looked on to the lake and park through large windows 'comodyouslye to se the deer courssyd and to se the fysche takyn' as an old survey put it. Similarly in 1352 a balcony was built outside the chamber of the Princess Isabel to give her a view of the park at Woodstock.

Among the many royal homes the others where Prince Edward spent most time were King's Langley in Hertfordshire and his own palace at Westminster, inside the great royal palace on the side towards the Abbey. Of Westminster, apart from the surviving great hall, much is known, but Langley like Woodstock has disappeared and left hardly a trace. King's Langley was another royal residence particularly noted for its garden, and one must imagine the fair-haired boy spending a good deal of his days in the open air, rolling over and over on the turfed plots, racing up and down the alleys of the arbour and fishing in the pools, or attempting to fish. Although in his mother's charge, the prince had a great establishment of his own paid for with 500 marks a year out of the earldom of Chester; and before he was three he was created earl of Chester and endowed with all its profits and with the castles of Chester, Beeston, Flint and Rhuddlan. When Edward was seven he was also made duke of Cornwall, with all the special rights of the Stannaries, and the tax on all the tin mined and smelted. A month before reaching 13 came investiture as prince of Wales, the appanage assigned to Edward of Caernarvon by his father Edward I in 1301 and reserved for the eldest son and heir of the reigning king ever since.

Queen Philippa was deeply religious and had a special devotion to the Holy Trinity. This she inculcated in her son at an early age, and it was beneath a magnificent painting of the Trinity that he came in the end, by his own particular wish, to lie buried at Canterbury. The boy's religious education probably lay largely in the hands of Dominican friars. Edward II in 1308 had established them beside the royal manor at King's Langley, and we know that the prince's son, Richard II, chose Dominican confessors. The royal family during the whole century kept strictly to the paths of ecclesiastical orthodoxy, and there is every reason to regard their devotion as sincere and remarkably unbigoted. Under the tutelage of such men of learning as Walter Burley and Richard de Bury, education must in any case have been strongly tinged with religion and reading would involve constant study of the breviary and psalter, if not of the Bible as a whole. Along with the Latin language there was no doubt some teaching of points of philosophy and theology and at least a working general knowledge of the subjects required by a ruler: principles of law and the theory of kingship. The deposition and murder of the prince's grandfather Edward II cannot have been hidden from him as he grew older, and here too our knowledge of the attitude taken by Richard II indicates that the importance of the principles involved was handed down from father to son.

The theory of kingship was taken very seriously in the Middle Ages, not only by kings themselves. It was recognized by all thinking men that the governance of worldly affairs was placed by God in the hands of princes. The doctrine of Render unto Caesar, and the implications of the Psalms, accepted as the personal composition of King David, provided a firm framework into which all other aspects of political life had to fit. The fundamental questions, as in all periods, concerned the difficult cases of kings of personally bad character, and the clash of right with right when it came to deciding matters of succession. Both of these crucial issues came under discussion, and caused much of the wars, civil and foreign, of the century. Looking back we can see the case of Edward II leading on to that of Richard II, to the much later tensions between the Crown and over-mighty subjects in the times of Charles I and his two sons, and even the abdication of Edward VIII in our own day.

England has no written Constitution, and never has had anything of the kind, unless we count Magna Carta. What passes for constitutional, or has so passed at any given date, has been merely what was ground from the mills of God at the end of the day, and in the long run either might or cunning has been proved 'right' in the sense of acceptable without a renewal of civil disturbance. Unlike this civil constitutional process of the development of governing forces in internal politics, which has gone on and is still continuing, the great external problem of the Middle Ages was solved once and for all, though it took a war of well over a hundred years to settle it. The life and working career of the Black Prince has to be seen mainly in the light of this external struggle, one between the king of England his father, and the *de facto*

king of France. The issue was to decide whether or no England and France
were to remain bitterly opposed rival powers, or were to be united under a
common sovereign.

Problems of this kind were formerly common, when the basis of government was almost universally the general acknowledgment of a particular person as sovereign by legitimate inheritance. It can be said at once that, in the
earlier Middle Ages, there was no strict rule of inheritance, or of legitimacy in
this sense. Thrones did not necessarily pass to eldest sons, nor even to legitimate
children born in wedlock – witness the succession of William the Bastard to
Normandy and, in the fourteenth century, of John I to Portugal. Actual
failure of issue, or failure in the male line, was likely to lead to national crisis.
This had happened in Scotland in 1286–90 after the successive deaths of
Alexander III and his granddaughter Margaret, the Maid of Norway. There
were 13 claimants to the Scottish throne, though only two had claims generally
regarded as serious. Edward I, admitted by all the competitors to be overlord
of Scotland (in exactly the same way that the kings of France were overlords
of Normandy and Aquitaine), after a year's search of historical records and the
best legal advice, adjudged the crown to John Baliol rather than to Robert
Bruce. The essential point at issue was that, both claimants being legitimately
descended from the admitted root of claims, David of Huntingdon, Baliol
represented David's eldest daughter but was David's great-grandson; Bruce
was descended from the second daughter, but was grandson of David and so
closer in blood by one degree.

According to the laws of succession as they later became accepted throughout Europe, there was no question that Baliol had the better claim. Yet it was
the grandson of Robert Bruce who, after long wars and many vicissitudes,
established the claim of his line mainly by force. Might triumphed over what
was held by the lawyers to be right, and this triumph of might took more than
half a century to establish after the coronation of Robert I (Bruce the grandson)
in 1306. A closely similar series of events took place in regard to the French
succession, and it was the resulting dispute that caused the Hundred Years War.
The Royal House of France, descended from Hugh Capet, had reigned in
undisputed line since 987, but the last of the direct male descendants died in
1328. Edward III of England, son of Isabella the sister of this last king Charles
IV, was his nearest male relative, and claimed the right of regency since the
late king's widow was pregnant. The French baronage, determined not to
admit the claims – even to regency – of a king of England, trumped up a completely unhistorical law of the Salian Franks, that 'no woman, nor by consequence, her son, could succeed to the throne of France'. They chose as regent
Philip of Valois, grandson in male descent of King Philip III (1270–1285), and
so first cousin of the late king. A daughter was born to the widowed queen,

and Philip VI succeeded to the crown of France in virtue of the alleged 'Salic Law'.

In spite of the fact that this imaginary tribal law was ever afterwards observed in regard to the throne of France, it is doubtful whether any serious observer at the time regarded it as other than a political subterfuge. In 1329 Edward III agreed to do homage in words for that part of Aquitaine which he held of the king of France, but he refused to perform the ceremony of placing his hands between Philip's, which was held to acknowledge him as liege lord. This, in the eyes of the chivalric world, constituted a bond which no knightly man might break. It seems clear that Edward, who at the time had no intention of waging war on Philip, had genuine doubts as to Philip's claim to the French throne. Like his grandfather Edward I, who had hoped to settle the problem of Scotland by a royal marriage between his son Edward and Margaret the Maid of Norway, Edward III hoped that diplomacy might provide a satisfactory long-term solution. By 1331–2 he was sending envoys, including the bishop of Winchester, John Stratford, his chancellor, and the great lawyer John de Shordich, to arrange a summit meeting with Philip to discuss a marriage between the prince, not yet two years old, and the French king's daughter Joan.

These attempts failed, as they were perhaps bound to fail. The kings of France had matured over many generations a policy of aggrandisement which was to continue with greater or less success for another four centuries, until France had reached to the Rhine and the Pyrenees, and a prince of the blood of France sat on the throne of Spain. We do not know whether there was ever anything in the nature of a deliberate programme, even a written directive passed on from one king to his heir, but the events of history actually suggest that such might have been the case. There was nothing haphazard about the steps taken to ensure the steady outward expansion of the realm of Parisian influence. This is in such striking contrast to the ebb and flow of English and later British aims as to indicate a profound difference of approach. On the whole the kings of England were most English in this: they adopted a tentative and empirical approach, at times even opportunist, but seldom calculating or stealthy.

Edward's opportunity did not come for several years, while his son was growing through boyhood towards youth. Some things seemed to be playing into his hands. There was, for example, the strange scandal of Robert of Artois, count of Beaumont, brother-in-law to King Philip. Robert's grandfather, Robert II count of Artois, had been killed at the battle of Courtrai in 1302, four years after the death of his only son Philip. The county was adjudged to his daughter Mahaut, but Robert produced forged deeds to the parlement of Paris, the supreme French tribunal, claiming Artois as his by right. The affair that ensued was as notorious in its way as that of the Diamond Necklace four hundred years later. We need not attempt to unravel all the intricacies of the plot, which included forgery and the counterfeiting of seals by a woman called the Damsel of Dijon and a clerk, the clerk's counter-accusation that the abbot of Versailles had forged the seals, and the sudden deaths of Mahaut the countess, and of her daughter Jeanne, widow of the late king Philip V, predecessor of Charles IV. Rumours of murder became current, and King Philip solved the problem by cutting the Gordian knot: Robert of Artois was outlawed from France. He was made welcome in England, and spent his time for the next few years in trying to urge Edward III on to claim France and so give Robert vengeance upon the king who had exiled him.

Ever since the time of Henry II, well over a century before, the paradox that an immense tract of territory, geographically part of Gaul – or, as we should now say, of France – belonged to the kings of England, necessarily led to continuous difficulties. The highest court of appeal for lawsuits in Aquitaine lay not in London, but in Paris, yet a frontier across which hostilities might well be in progress had to be crossed on the way from Bordeaux. Depending on all sorts of local and personal interests, the Gascon nobles and gentry were inclined either to the French or the English side. Whenever a new king succeeded, homage had to be rendered for the territories held or claimed, and the kings of England had had to develop a skilful technique in wording their homage to cover, not what they held *de facto* at that moment, but 'what they ought to hold' as feofs of the king of France's realm.

To those brought up in an atmosphere of Victorian and post-Victorian moral strictures, this may be criticized as prevarication, but the whole background has to be taken into account. In England (though not in Scotland), and in northern France (but not in the South), the whole system of mediaeval law was based on custom, not upon written Roman Law or later specific statutes covering the whole field of human behaviour. Even much of Spain was ruled by customary law-codes of an analogous kind. In such systems the custom had to be precisely obeyed, and this included the exact methods and forms of pleading. A single infraction of the minutest technicality invalidated a suit. It was essential for every pleader, whether a trained counsel working on behalf of his client, or a king making his own case before a feudal superior – the relative position of the kings of England to those of France – to observe with the utmost strictness every detail of his position. Nothing might be admitted, even by implication; nothing allowed to go by default.

It has to be admitted that, from a merely practical and realistic point of view, the political and geographical situation was one likely to yield a maximum of difficulty and of grounds for conflict. It is remarkable, considering all the factors, that the kings of England should have been able to maintain control continuously for three centuries of some part of the richest provinces of France, across a dangerous sea-passage of more than 700 miles (London to Bordeaux). The facts speak loudly and tell us several things about the situation. Firstly, they show that the resistance of the provinces of France to the centralizing policy of the French kings was very strong: the distant rule of a king far away in his island was to be preferred to direct rule and taxation from Paris. Secondly, English rule must have been reasonable, fairly efficient, and not humiliating to local sentiment. Thirdly, the personal characters of the kings of England of the Plantagenet line, in their chivalry, romantic adventurousness, and flamboyance, must have appealed far more to the volatile Gascons than the cool statecraft that typified the Capetian and Valois sovereigns.

While merely popular sentiment counted for little in the Middle Ages, there was a strong body of educated public opinion throughout the chivalric classes, including royalty and not merely the nobility but all substantial landowners. There were two threats to which this body of opinion was sensitive and likely to react forcibly. One was really outrageous behaviour, offending against the code of chivalry, on the part of one of the members of the 'chivalric body' as a whole. King John was never legally convicted (in spite of a legend to the contrary) of the murder of his nephew Arthur; but this was so widely believed at the time by those whose opinion counted as to be the decisive factor against him. The forfeiture of Normandy and all the northern provinces which had formed part of the English dominion in France was effective largely because in 1204 there was a real backing of outrage behind the king of France. The second type of threat was the converse of the first. Whereas outraged opinion might be in favour of confiscation by higher authority of the lands of one felt to be grossly unworthy, nothing short of this could justify any sustained attack upon property-holders as such. We shall see that at the end of the century the straw that broke the camel's back was the seizure by Richard II of the whole of the estates of the Duchy of Lancaster after the death of his uncle John of Gaunt. The heir was in exile, perhaps rightly condemned; he might have had to wait for years before being able to enjoy his inheritance; this would have been accepted by all and perforce by Henry of Lancaster himself. Total sequestration of his rights was another matter: every owner of great estates felt himself attacked and, however loyal to the Crown, obliged to stand up for Henry's ostensibly limited claim, to his own inheritance.

This counterpoise of forces, internally within England, France, or any other major kingdom composed largely of great feofs; and externally as between the opposing claims of the two sovereigns over provinces of France, accounts for the relative peacefulness of relations hitherto. The position was uneasy for both parties, but it had on the whole been better to endure it than to seek to end it by a trial of strength. War as an instrument of policy was normal in the

Middle Ages, but its aim was generally strictly limited. One party rarely sought the complete annihilation of the other and the subjugation of the vanquished was unusual. The fact that what was to become the Hundred Years War took on the aspect of a struggle to the death, in which one side or the other would be at the mercy of the victor, was due to fresh factors. One of these we have already noticed: the new national patriotism involving Englishmen generally in the aims of their king. Another was economic: England, which about 1300 had reached a peak of prosperity in the wool trade and in the general export balance, was losing ground. The advances in material civilization, as at many other periods, were tempting people of all ranks to live beyond their means. Finally, and probably the really decisive point in terms of individual psychology, Edward III came sincerely to believe that he had the best claim to be king of France, and that it was his duty as well as his right to prosecute his claim to success.

To grasp this is perhaps not easy in the entirely different atmosphere of the twentieth century. To level against Edward III the accusation that sheer greed and ambition made him seek an excuse for aggression is to simplify unduly, and is besides unfair to a noble and courageous man. Kings, as human beings, were taught by their confessors of their religious duty to their subjects: it was God who had entrusted these subjects to them. To neglect their governance might even be to imperil their own immortal souls. In reading, for instance, the exceptionally revealing last will of Richard II, we cannot doubt the passionately held belief behind his words: 'we have already for some time since our tender age submitted our neck by the mercy of the supreme King to the burden of the government of the English'. The royal burden was a very heavy one, hard to bear and not to be laid down. God in His wisdom might see fit to add to that load.

What we may well ask is the reason why Edward's claim was not put forward seriously at an earlier date. Charles IV of France had died on 1 February 1328, one year after Edward III's accession as a boy of fourteen years. Edward's claim to the regency of France was really made by his mother Isabella, who held the reins of power. Philip of Valois, at the time strongly supported by Robert of Artois, had no difficulty in becoming regent and, only a few months later, in succeeding to the vacant throne. The legal and historical fact, that the throne was not vacant, had been skilfully obscured by the red herring of the fictitious Salic Law. At the English end of the tussle, nothing could happen until after Edward had freed himself from his mother's grip late in October 1330. By that time a great many other matters urgently demanded his attention. First of all he had to establish himself as master in his own house, and it was during this period that he performed, with reservations, homage for his French territories. He made a serious attempt to engage his young son Edward to a French princess, and negotiated with Philip with a view to their joint leadership of a Crusade, urged upon them by Pope John XXII.

Trouble again broke out in Scotland in 1332. Robert I (Bruce) had died in 1329, and was succeeded by David II, a boy aged only five. His minority offered an opportunity to all those Scottish lords who had been dissatisfied with the victory of the Bruce faction. They joined Edward Baliol, son of the John who had been king in 1292–96, and with the help of English archers easily won the battle of Dupplin Moor on 12 August 1332. Edward Baliol was crowned king of Scots at Scone on 24 September and acknowledged Edward III as his liege lord. Soon driven over the Border by the party of David II, Baliol sought the help of the English king. Edward III undertook a full scale invasion of Scotland, won the battle of Halidon Hill on 19 July 1333, and maintained Edward Baliol on the throne for some four years against a background of guerilla warfare from partisans. We can see that the chance of succeeding where his grandfather had failed must have spurred Edward III on to all-out exertions to win Scotland for good and all. He very nearly succeeded.

The chances of a permanent settlement in Scotland, and of a long peace in France, were disrupted by a combination of economic and political factors in Flanders. England's prosperity depended upon the export of wool to the great cloth towns of the Low Countries, mainly in the county of Flanders, an autonomous province of France on the same footing as Aquitaine, but without any complication of foreign sovereignty. The Flemish problems were internal, and the tension lay between the interest of the powerful cloth-weavers and that of the counts and their entourage, by this time entirely francophile and completely dominated by the influence of the French Court. The Flemings had a stubborn tradition of independence from France and, a generation before, had inflicted a crushing defeat upon a French invading army at Courtrai in 1302. Louis de Nevers, who succeeded as count in 1322, went to the opposite extreme against local feeling and repeatedly called in French help to repress the burghers and the growing influence of the weavers. To him the economic alliance between the weaving classes and England smacked of treason, and he took every step to make Flanders as much as possible a part of France.

Attempts by their count to put the Flemings down played directly into the hands of his opponents. Knowing that the power of the burghers came from the cloth trade based on English wool, Louis prohibited all trade with England. This brought a swingeing counterstroke from Edward III, who on 12 August 1336 stopped all exports of wool to Flanders and moved the staple – the only port through which wool might be sent into the continent – from Bruges to Antwerp. Antwerp, on the right bank of the Scheldt, belonged to the duchy of Brabant and served the markets of Brussels, Malines and Louvain. The Flemings found their own leader in the wealthy merchant Jakob van Artevelde, an extraordinary mixture of gangster and statesman. Froissart gives us a vivid picture of the man and his two faces.

> He had always with him going up and down in Gaunt (Ghent) sixty or fourscore varlets armed, and among them there were three or four that knew the secretness of his mind, so that if he met a person that he hated or had him in suspicion, incontinent he was slain: for he had commanded his secret varlets, that whensoever he met any person and made such a sign to them, that incontinent they should slay him, whatsoever he were, without any words or reasoning; and by that means he made many to be slain, whereby he was so doubted, that none durst speak against anything that he would have done, so that every man was glad to make him good cheer.

On the other hand, Van Artevelde had extraordinary qualities as a leader, for

> To speak properly, there was never in Flanders nor in none other country, prince, duke nor other that ruled a country so peaceably so long as this Jaques d'Arteveld did rule Flanders. He levied the rents, winages and rights that pertained to the earl throughout all Flanders, and spent all at his pleasure without any account making. And when he would say that he lacked money, they believed him, and so it behoved them to do, for none durst say against him: when he would borrow anything of any burgess, there was none durst say him nay.

By this time King Philip was stirring up the Scots of the Bruce party and it became evident that his purpose was to seek pretexts for the invasion of Gascony. On 24 August 1336 he virtually declared war by stating his intention to help the Scots, at the same time invading the English territory in south-western France. Seeing that he did this at the very time when he was being urged by the pope to make peace with Edward and to undertake the Crusade, there can be no doubt that it was the king of France who was the deliberate aggressor. War had actually begun and was no longer avoidable, though it is true that it might have been localized and kept at a low pitch. To a young man as spirited as Edward III was at 23, fired with the recent successes of his campaigns in Scotland, such an outcome was unthinkable. Put on his mettle he viewed the situation coolly and proceeded upon a well considered plan of alliances. Unsavoury as Van Artevelde might be, his aid was indispensable: he had already immobilized the legal government of Flanders by Count Louis, and the merchants and weavers who followed him were in the closest touch with the City of London and the English suppliers of wool.

Possibly the most remarkable feature of Edward's plan was his care for public relations at home. He did not simply demand grants of money and raise troops, but through the county courts told the whole country the story of his attempts to secure peace, and the reasons why he felt obliged to resort to war. The threat of invasion was no empty scare, for the French attacked not only the Channel Islands but also the Isle of Wight. Edward in reply proclaimed that 'our progenitors, Kings of England, were lords of the English sea on every side', and took steps to build up a strong naval force. Sacrifices were demanded from all, and food rationing was brought in: 'no man shall cause himself to be served at dinner, meal or supper with more than two courses, and each mess of two sorts of victuals at the utmost'. There is in this an implication that by 1336 the great mass of the English population was living in rude plenty and could well afford to tighten its belt. The result was a surprising enthusiasm for the war: the commons in parliament urged the king to undertake it for the common good. By 7 October 1337 he had made up his mind to play for the highest stakes and styled himself king of France in letters asking the assistance of his allies, the duke of Brabant, the count of Hainault and Holland, and others.

The young Prince Edward was only seven, and had been created duke of Cornwall in March 1337; he was not to be made Prince of Wales for another six years, and nine had yet to pass before he would be able to join in his father's invasion of France. Mediaeval warfare tended to be extremely slow, with long periods of local or general truce, with minor skirmishing, and lengthy diplomatic approaches to potential allies. Even so, the lapse of almost nine years from the moment of claiming the French throne to the first serious attempt to obtain it by force of arms is strange, and must have seemed so at the time. It is as though the process of unleashing the dogs of war had been put into slow motion by the hand of destiny, so that the boy Edward might grow to man's estate and have time to win his spurs. Yet the long, slow introduction, overture to an intermittent dance of death lasting for nearly one hundred and twenty years, had begun; the game was afoot.

The first essential was to secure a firm bridgehead on the other side of the Channel, and this was threatened by certain knights of the count of Flanders, who garrisoned Cadsand (now Cadzand in Holland, just across the Belgian frontier) and cut direct communications between England and the English emissaries in Valenciennes at the court of the count of Hainault. The English slipped home by a circuitous route through Dordrecht. When they informed the king of the garrison in Cadsand 'he said he would provide for them shortly'. The earl of Derby (Henry, afterwards first duke of Lancaster) was sent with Sir Walter Manny and other knights and squires, 500 men of arms and 2,000 archers. The expedition sailed from London: 'the first tide they went to Gravesend, the next day to Margate, and at the third tide they took the sea and sailed into Flanders'. The Flemish garrison in the French interest consisted of 5,000 men besides knights and squires, hand picked by the count to prevent the English from getting a footing. But the Englishmen 'took land and came and fought hand to hand'.

Froissart gives a spirited account of the fight: 'The earl of Derby was that day a good knight, and at the first assault he was so forward that he was stricken to the earth; and then the lord of Manny (Sir Walter) did him great comfort, for by pure feat of arms he relieved him up again and brought him out of peril, and cried, "Lancaster for the earl of Derby!" Then they approached on every part; and many were hurt, but more of the Flemings than of the Englishmen, for the archers shot so without ceasing, that they did to the Flemings much damage. . . . There was a sore battle and well foughten hand to hand: but finally the Flemings were put to the chase.' The first serious engagement of the Hundred Years War had been fought, and one of its most significant features was the fact that as the English landed, they called upon the name of God and St George: the patron of England, though a national saint for more than a century, only now came into his own.

And so the scene was set for one of the most extraordinary episodes in history. None of those who fought at Cadsand, none of those at home who heard the news of the victory, few or even none of any of their children, were to hear the end of the story then begun. One hundred and sixteen years afterwards, on 19 October 1453, the beleaguered English garrison of Bordeaux surrendered to the French. Even then the end had not come, for Calais, to be won in ten years time, was not lost until 20 January 1558, more than 220 years ahead or some seven generations. In the end the war was certainly won by France, but by a France sorely wounded, greatly impoverished. England, which had all but exhausted herself and came near to destruction in the civil wars which were perhaps the worst result of the French war, lost; but as so often happens, she won the peace. In the meantime the great campaigns were still to be fought, in which a young prince was to win for himself an imperishable fame. We may well deplore warfare at any time, feel that the Hundred Years War was unjustified in any case, that it should never have been fought. But we cannot deny the title of hero to the brilliant and spirited man – still a young boy at the time of Cadsand – who was to devote his whole adult life to the cause, his father's cause and his country's. We have to go back to the dim light of the dawning Middle Ages to find England's greatest hero, Alfred: the king who beat the Danes only to give them half of his kingdom at Wedmore in exchange for baptism. Before Alfred we have the legendary Arthur; after him the outlaw Robin Hood; but even if they represent historical originals, we know nothing of their lives. 600 years ago England not only acclaimed a patron saint: in the same struggle she found her typical hero, the Black Prince.

CHAPTER III

The Years of Youth

The great war had begun, but much else was happening, in England and elsewhere. Not least, the young Edward was growing up, from a boy of seven at the time of Cadsand to a young man of 16 when he accompanied his father to France on the campaign of Crecy in 1346. We do not know much of the detail of his life in those years, but it is certain that they included the crucial part of his education as a chivalrous man able to fight skilfully and to bear his part in war. Throughout his boyhood the predominent influence upon him was that of his mother, who had only reached her middle twenties by the time Edward was ten. By the summer of 1340 she had borne five more children: Isabella, at Woodstock in 1332; Jeanne, in the Tower of London in the following year; William, at Hatfield in Yorkshire, who died an infant and was buried in York Minster in 1336; Lionel, at Antwerp on 29 November 1338; and John at Ghent in March of 1340. These were the first half of her family: another six children were to follow: a daughter Blanche, born in the Tower in 1341, who died in infancy; Edmund, at Langley in June 1342; Mary, at Waltham in October 1344; Margaret, at Windsor Castle in July 1346; a second William, also at Windsor, who died in 1348; and after a much longer interval, Thomas, once more at Woodstock, on 7 January 1355, her only child to be born after the Black Death.

Of the large family, three died in infancy and Jeanne when aged only fifteen. The remaining eight all lived to marry, though Lionel, later duke of Clarence, died at 30; Mary, who was to marry John IV, duke of Brittany, when 16, died the next year; Margaret, who married the earl of Pembroke when only 13, died at 15. The Black Prince, as we know, died at 46; John of Gaunt at just under 59; Edmund at 60; Thomas, the youngest son, at 42, perhaps murdered in prison. Isabella, the eldest daughter, did not marry until she was 33 and died at 47, the wife of Enguerrand de Coucy who became earl of Bedford. Even in the royal family, the mediaeval expectation of life was terribly low, and it is striking that the females who lived a sheltered life did not on the average outlive their menfolk who were exposed to all the risks of campaigning and hand-to-hand combat. The Plantagenet line was fairly long-lived for the times: Henry III reached 65, Edward I passed 68, Edward II was murdered in his prime at 43; Edward III himself died in his 65th year.

Queen Philippa, in spite of her large family and the extent to which she followed her husband on his travels, survived until 55, dying after a long dropsical illness in 1369. Deservedly famous for her kindness and her ability to appease her husband in his fits of terrible anger, the queen was also a good woman of business and did a great deal to promote trade and industry. Philippa showed her tender heart as a young bride at York, when she heard that a girl under 11 years old had been convicted of a robbery at Bishopthorpe and had been imprisoned until she was old enough to have sentence passed upon her. The queen, herself a girl only three years older, succeeded in obtaining a pardon for the juvenile offender. Three years later she appeased the king's wrath when he would have punished the carpenters who had built a stand in Cheapside which collapsed during a tournament. The stand, in the form of a wooden tower, gave way beneath the queen and 'many other ladies, richly attired and assembled from all parts of the realm'. The framework 'brake in sunder, whereby they were with some shame forced to fall down' and the knights and others beneath were grievously hurt. On that occasion, as later on when she begged the lives of the burghers of Calais, Philippa knelt down before her husband to persuade him to grant pardon.

The queen's serious interests included the establishment of Flemish weavers at Norwich in 1331–35, and she encouraged coal-mining on her estates near Newcastle-upon-Tyne. She took her eldest son with her on some of her visits and the contacts with craftsmen, miners and merchants in early life must have helped to produce the gracious freedom of manner with persons of all classes for which the Black Prince was later noted. On one of the queen's northern journeys she joined her husband as a guest at the monastery of Durham and had already retired to bed when she was told that the misogynistic St Cuthbert could not abide women sleeping within the precincts. She obligingly got up and in her nightdress was escorted outside the gates to seek lodging in the castle for the night. Philippa was loyally attended by old friends who had accompanied her from her father's court in Hainault and who made a permanent home in England. Among them were presumably the William of St Omer and his wife Elizabeth who in 1336 were rewarded by the king with £25 a year for life on account of their gratuitous service in staying constantly with his son Edward and his daughters. William may have died soon after, for six months later another grant was made to Elizabeth of St Omer and her son Bertram. But the chief Hainaulter in the queen's retinue was Sir Walter de

Mauny or Manny.

Manny was a young esquire when he attended Philippa at the time of her marriage. He stayed on to carve for her and wait upon her at table, but it soon became evident that he had all the qualities of a great and heroic soldier. Knighted in 1331, he won great honour in the Scottish wars of the next few years and, as we have seen, covered himself with glory by his single-handed rescue of the earl of Derby at Cadsand. It was certainly Manny who was responsible for arousing in the young prince a boundless enthusiasm for feats of arms. Thrown into daily contact as they were, it is easy to picture the admiration of the boy for the heroic and dashing young knight. By the time that Edward was five years old Manny had made a splendid marriage, to the widowed Margaret, Lady Segrave, daughter of Thomas earl of Norfolk, the younger son of Edward I. Such a marriage was possible because Manny was himself related to the counts of Hainault and so a distant connection of the queen he served.

Once the landing at Cadsand had been consolidated with the help of the anti-French party of Flemings who adhered to Van Artevelde, the king could open negotiations for a much wider system of alliances. In July 1338 he crossed over to Antwerp with the queen, leaving the young Edward behind as the nominal regent of England. For more than eighteen months Edward III made his headquarters in the Low Countries, and as we have seen it was there that his second and third sons were born, Lionel at Antwerp in the autumn of 1338 and John at Ghent in the early spring of 1340. This foreign sojourn of queen Philippa explains an episode, apparently trifling in itself, but with unexpected consequences. While Philippa was at Antwerp her mother, the countess of Hainault, sent her as a valuable herbal medicine a supply of the plant rosemary, and a booklet telling of its remarkable virtues. It would, apparently, cure almost anything from gout to bad dreams and was written up by some herbalist who claimed the authority of the famous medical school of Salerno.

When the queen returned to England with her two young sons she must have brought in her baggage, not only the booklet but the plant itself, the first notably tender evergreen introduced as an exotic and requiring special treatment from gardeners. Probably a plant was taken to the great Infirmary Garden at Westminster Abbey, next to the palace. At any rate, it received very careful treatment over the next generation or so, for before 1400 copies of the booklet, translated into English, were accompanied by a series of remarkable cultural hints on how the plant might be kept alive in a northern climate. As an example of the practical science of the time, learning by trial and error over a considerable number of years, this horticultural treatise of rosemary has unique value. In spite of curious remains of superstition, it shows a genuine spirit of enquiry. Whereas it was traditionally held that the plant did not grow above the height of Christ, and that it stopped growing at 33 years, the supposed age of Christ, the master gardener was a thoughtful man and evidently found that his own observations could not easily be squared with this theory. So in one copy we find that in height it 'passeth not commonly in height the height of our Lord Jesu Christ while he walked as man on earth' with the parenthetic addition: 'that is man's height and half as man is now'.

Another of the manuscripts gives the date of introduction as 'about 1342' which may mean that, although the plant had reached Queen Philippa in Antwerp in 1338, it took three or four more years to get it established in English gardens. The remarkable thing is that careful records must have been kept of the behaviour of the plants over the next thirty or forty years, to account for the very detailed knowledge shown in the horticultural hints. One of the translators of the Latin medical treatise was the Dominican friar Henry Danyel, who flourished in 1379 and made translations into English of many scientific works. Danyel may possibly have been concerned with at least the writing down of the cultural guide; if he was, this might be in favour of experimental planting having taken place in the Queen's Garden at King's Langley, beside the friary. The earliest contemporary record of rosemary in England, as a green plant (rather than the dried flowers for medicinal use) tells of petty crime. In November 1364 a London alewife, Alice Causton, was prosecuted for selling by short measure. She had spread a thickness of one-and-a-quarter inches of pitch over the bottom of a quart pot and stuck sprigs of 'rosemaryn' in it to look like a bush. The idea of a herbal spray, such as borage, placed in the cup is no new one. Rosemary was one of fourteen ingredients in the recipe for a salad prepared by Richard II's master cooks shortly before 1400.

Translations into the vernacular became numerous during the fourteenth century, not only in England but on the continent. Edward III was probably one of the last English kings to have a conversational command of many languages: Latin, French, German and Spanish as well as English. In general the period was one of relapse from multilingual activities into the relative isolation which has tended to be the norm in this country ever since. Certainly the existence of the new translations proves that the reading public was becoming wider, and reached far beyond the limits of the clerical classes with their grounding in Latin. Quite ordinary men and women, particularly in the category of master craftsmen and city merchants, were beginning to ask for reading matter, some of it literary. Mannyng's verse chronicle has already been mentioned, but it was only the start of a tradition carried on by John Trevisa, who finished a version of Ralph Higden's *Polychronicon* in 1387, and by 1398 had produced the first encyclopaedia in English, based on the Latin *De Proprietatibus Rerum* compiled about 1250 by Bartholomew de Glanville. The translators often improved upon their originals and added new matter:

Trevisa, for instance, continued Higden's history from 1352 to 1360.

This rule not only applied to factual prose books but to works of the imagination including poetry. Chaucer took great liberties with the text of the *Roman de la Rose* in his English version, founding a tradition which was to culminate five centuries later in Fitzgerald's *Rubaiyat*. Chaucer, along with many other writers, knew very well where to draw the line between fact and fiction. In his scientific work – for he was a distinguished man of science as well as an efficient civil servant and a poet – Chaucer was precise and explicit, as in his treatise on the Astrolabe and its sequel on the Equatory of the Planets, another complex instrument. The short text on growing rosemary and the Constitutions of Masonry, based on a Latin original and dating from c. 1350–60, are examples of this completely new style of clear and expressive English treating of factual matters and addressed to the commonsense layman. What is particularly noteworthy about this prose is that, notwithstanding its almost complete lack of antecedents, it is quite 'modern' and thoroughly intelligible. Most of its obscurity can be removed by re-spelling, and the rest by a very slight glossing of words now obsolete.

The move towards vernacular languages did not begin here. Dante's great poem, the foundation of Italian, was written in 1314–21 and overthrew the then reigning school of literature written in French by Italians aiming at a lay public. There had been an extensive poetry in German since the twelfth century, but the language was anything but modern and it was not until the sixteenth century that vernacular German was revolutionized by Luther's Bible. By far the oldest 'modern' vernacular in the West was Spanish, which had as Castilian broken right away from the common Romance-Latin of the Peninsula as far back as the tenth century. But in spite of this respectable antiquity there had been no general literature in Spanish before the twelfth century, with its epic poems on the life of the Cid. Castilian prose, however, was launched on its triumphant way by the deliberate action of Alfonso X, who determined that the vernacular should be used for his great compilations on history (the *Cronica general*), geology and chemistry (the *Lapidario*) and the astronomical works for which he is most remembered. In Spain the most important serious literature was not in Latin but in Arabic, and it was doubtless this fact that had a predominant weight in determining that a single work of translation should bring the matter home to the public which was to make use of it. So we find that it was the treatises of Arab botanists on agriculture and gardening that were appearing in the vernacular of northern Spain around 1300: the books of Ibn Wafid (Abenguefidh) and of Ibn Bassal, successively chief gardeners of the royal – botanical – garden of the Moorish sultans of Toledo in the eleventh century. These were turned from Arabic into Castilian, but Ibn Wafid's other great work, a herbal on the medicinal properties of plants, was put into Catalan about the same time.

Science, at any rate in principle, knows no frontiers, and even in a period of slow and difficult transport learned men managed to communicate with one another, mostly in Latin. Even today this tradition is preserved in the natural sciences, where valid descriptions have to be put into intelligible Latin to be recognized. In the fourteenth century at least three different classes, apart from royalty, travelled considerably on business and had opportunities for exchanging ideas. The first was, obviously, the higher clergy, obtaining preferment in different countries and visiting Rome. Secondly there were the wealthy merchants who, aware of the risks of undue reliance upon subordinates, conducted their own business and met foreigners on their own ground. Such men belonged to international bodies like the fraternity of the *Feste du Pui* with its musical conferences at Le Puy in Auvergne, and with supranational monopolistic tendencies looking quite modern. A practical instance of its strength is seen in the fact that one of its members, Henry le Waleys, succeeded in being mayor of Bordeaux in 1275 and five years later mayor of London.

The third class of travellers consisted of the upper ranks of skilled artists and craftsmen, men in demand because of their special knowledge and abilities. The introduction of fresh industries might imply fostered immigration of substantial communities, and Queen Philippa provided an instance of this in her bringing of Flemish weavers to Norwich. Writing in 1331 to John Kempe of Flanders, a woollen weaver, she promised her protection and assistance if he would come and settle in England, bringing his own servants and apprentices of his mistery, and also dyers and fullers and others of related trades who would exercise their skills in this country. As is well known, Kempe and his fellows did migrate to Norwich and set up a flourishing cloth industry there, visited on several occasions by Philippa in person and accompanied by her son Edward.

In some crafts, notably that of stonemason, it was customary to insist upon the novice, after the end of his apprenticeship, wandering as a journeyman employee from job to job for a further three years. During these wanderyears some men, perhaps many, visited foreign countries and brought back with them the memory and possibly actual drawings of details and designs they had admired when abroad. In England we know of men with French, Flemish or German names getting employment, and a good many English craftsmen can be identified in French documents. German miners were induced to settle in England in considerable numbers in the fifteenth century, and some may have been here earlier. Even in the thirteenth we hear of the Spanish gardeners brought from Aragon to King's Langley by Queen Eleanor of Castile in 1289. Contacts between men from different nations but having relevant craft secrets must account for the diffusion of many specialized methods and processes. In some instances the knowledge may have come from higher up in the social scale. For instance, it is striking that the remarkable discovery of how to stain glass yellow with silver salts, known among the Arabs of the Near East for several centuries, suddenly appeared in England in windows made in York for York Minster about 1308–10, probably earlier than anywhere else in Europe. Part of the secret, however, had been set down in the *Lapidario* of Alfonso X compiled about 1276–79; and it seems an amazing coincidence that during the years 1276–82 an English clerk, Geoffrey of Eversley, was working both for King Alfonso in Castile and for his brother-in-law Edward I in England. There surely must in this case have been transmission by diplomatic bag, and subsequent experiment in England. It would be ironic if the chemical operations then carried out, resulting in glass of a glorious golden colour, should have given rise to the inexplicable myth that the great Catalan mystic Ramon Llull came to England as an alchemist and transmuted a score of tons of brass and copper into gold for 'King Edward' – who could only have been Edward I or Edward II, since Llull died in 1315 aged over eighty.

Orthodox science was once more advancing, largely as a result of the counterblasts to closed-circuit scholasticism from the Englishmen Roger Bacon in the previous century and William Ockham more recently. We have seen that both Richard de Bury the book-loving bishop of Durham, and Dr Walter Burley the student of Aristotle, were among the inner circle of churchmen at the court of Edward III. Another, also a member of Bury's household in the 1330's, was Thomas Bradwardine 'the Profound Doctor', the greatest mathematician of his time and one of the very few in the whole of the western Middle Ages to make any advance in arithmetic and geometry. Like Bury and Burley he was in the king's confidence and became his chaplain; indeed, he was probably confessor to the royal family for some years. He accompanied the English forces on the Crecy campaign of 1346 and in 1349 became archbishop of Canterbury, but died of the plague only a few weeks after his consecration. Even if there is little sign of any continuing progress in theoretical science in the next two centuries, minds of this stamp must have had considerable impact upon the temper of society. In particular one must attribute to Bradwardine as royal chaplain a particular influence upon the king and his children, notably his eldest son.

The international exchange of information and the furthering of technical progress depended not only upon the few individuals of high rank who travelled, as it were, on their own account. It has to be remembered that kings, queens, princes, lords, prelates and even business men were commonly attended by a considerable retinue. Both on military and on civil journeys kings and the higher nobility might often have with them skilled engineers, their master masons and master carpenters who were the architects of the time, and other artists including poets and musicians. It was usual for at least one physician to be in constant attendance, and some of these doctors were genuinely learned in medicine and in related subjects such as botany and chemistry. Although so many serious diseases were quite beyond the powers of the medical faculty, there was understanding of the importance of cleanliness and good sanitation. Not all cures were superstitious nonsense; not all physicians were charlatans, even though there must have been a lot of truth in Chaucer's gibe at the Doctour of Phisyk: –

> For gold in phisik is a cordial,
> Therfore he lovede gold in special.

Even this medical man was, according to Chaucer's description, genuinely learned in the works of the great classical and Arabic authorities.

Chaucer names three modern British authorities as well as the ancients: Bernard, and Gatesden, and Gilbertyn. Bernard Gordon was a Scot at the university of Montpellier and author of *Practica seu lilium medicinae*, written in 1307 and translated into French and Hebrew. Gilbertyn, or Gilbert the Englishman, had flourished in the middle of the thirteenth century and produced an extensive compilation from Italian and Arabic sources, though he is said also to have made useful observations on leprosy. Dr John Gaddesden was a fellow of Merton College, Oxford, in 1305 and M.A. by 1307. Within the next ten years he had written his lengthy and renowned book, *Rosa anglica medicinae*, and took his doctorate before 1332 when he became one of the king's clerks and on the king's special recommendation was made a canon of St Paul's. During the childhood of the Black Prince and the elder children of Edward III, Gaddesden was the family doctor and is known to have attended the princess Jeanne, or Joanna, in 1341. Later on he was attached to the service of the prince of Wales, who gave him at New Year 1346 the present of a rose made of gold, in allusion to his book, by that time famous. Gaddesden was an eminent consultant, called in by the monks of Abingdon and St Albans, and continued to attend the royal family until his death, probably of the plague, in 1349.

Less famous than Gaddesden, but perhaps a better doctor, was Nicholas de Tingewick, another medical clergyman. He had attended Edward I with great success, being described as 'the best doctor for the king's health', while the king himself in 1306 said that he owed his recovery from a long illness to Tingewick next under God. Tingewick travelled abroad on the king's business, apparently not medical, but was also a general consultant, being called in by the prior of Christ Church, Canterbury, Henry Eastry, in 1324. He held canonries at Salisbury from 1309 until 1337 and died a year or so later, but it is uncertain whether he remained one of the royal physicians to the end of his life. By the standards even of their immediate successors, these physicians were not outstanding, with the possible exception of Tingewick. But they must be given credit for amazing diligence in perusing and distilling the great authorities of Greek and Arabic medicine and republishing them. As we shall see later, genuine progress in medicine was very soon to follow, within the second half of the century.

Even if their science was antiquated and mostly second-hand, and their cures inadequate and infrequent, the doctors were at least trying to save life and improve the human lot. Real progress was being made in the opposite direction, the destruction of life and the maiming of men. For during the lifetime of King Edward III came the invention – or re-invention – of gunpowder, it is said by a German Grey Friar, Berthold Schwarz, in 1313. The English scientist Roger Bacon, by the middle of the thirteenth century, knew of the explosive character of a mixture of saltpetre, charcoal and sulphur, but he had the sense to hide the recipe in an anagram and may even have failed to realize the projectile possibilities of his discovery. The actual facts of the invention of guns are still obscure and all that can be said with complete certainty is that they were in existence by 1326. In that same year they appear in drawings in two English manuscripts, and were being made for the defence of Florence. Materials for making gunpowder were bought by the clerk of the chamber to Edward III in 1333 and cannon were in use by 1345 and probably sooner. Abroad they were employed by the French at Cambrai in 1339, and the Flemings of Bruges were making guns at the same time. On the other hand, the first major engagement in which cannon were used was at the siege of Algeciras in 1342–44, by the besieged Moors against the Christian host, which seems to have been taken rather by surprise.

For a very long time there had been use of igneous chemicals in warfare in the Near East, but the 'Greek Fire' used by the Byzantines was not an explosive but an incendiary bomb. Bacon's invention seems to have been a development from this, though it could have been used as gunpowder if the idea of firing it in a confined space had been present. Because of the novelty of guns and gunpowder, the early accounts tend to confuse them with the much earlier use of Greek Fire and incendiary devices, and are consequently ambiguous. But in view of the undoubted use by the Moors, and not by the Christians, of cannon at Algeciras in 1342–44, it is at least possible that an earlier statement of 1324–25 may refer to the use of real guns in southern Spain. The sultan of Granada, Abulwalid Ismail, was besieging Baza, and was said to have machines that cast globes of fire into the town. There is of course no certainty that the machines were not typical mediaeval catapults, and the globes of fire incendiaries of the ancient kind, but the association both in place and date is at any rate suspicious. It is now generally, though not universally, accepted that the true invention of gunpowder was in China and long before the fourteenth century, and it is inherently likely that in common with most other chemical processes it reached Europe in some form by way of the Muslims. At present it is impossible to assign precisely the credit or the blame.

What is certain is that by 1345 there was substantial manufacture of gunpowder and of guns going on in London, in readiness for the great expedition being mounted against France. On a very small scale at Crecy and at the siege of Calais, in 1346, the English were using artillery of a kind, small guns pushed around on hand-carts. This kind of field-piece was not impressive but it was, regrettably, the thin end of a wedge, destined to overshadow the whole world. In 600 years from that primitive powder-making and gun-smithing of 1345, the first atomic bomb was dropped in 1945 and the possibility of annihilation of the globe and of the human race with it clearly stated.

Such developments, and the fact that they could be even contemplated by civilized men, would have horrified the leaders of the nations when the Hundred Years War was about to break out. The brave Manny and his pupil Prince Edward had no part in such forms of combat, even though they accepted the necessity of archers and crossbowmen, and were to live long enough to see the use of gunnery – as a more effective form of archery – in the field. Edward III, the commander-in-chief of his own armed forces, in giving orders for the making of arms and ammunition, certainly never realized the revolutionary nature of what he was doing. His own chivalry was absolute: at the age of fifteen, when he first took the field against the Scots during their invasion of England, his troops were drawn up on the south bank of the river Wear. He sent over a flag of truce, offering to retire from the river so that the Scots might cross over and have adequate room to fight. In 1340 he made a sincere attempt to avert the war by offering to fight Philip of Valois hand to hand in person. When Philip declined the challenge, a wag in the English camp who had had a grammar school education produced the verse:

> *Si valeas, venias, Valois! depelle timorem,*
> *Non lateas; pateas; moveas. Ostende vigorem!*

which Agnes Strickland englished as:

> Valois, be valiant! vile fear can't avail thee;
> Hide not, avoid not, let not vigour fail thee!

The skit was shown to king Edward who swore that they were valiant verses and had them fastened to an arrow and shot into the French camp.

It was as a warrior of this school that the Black Prince was trained, and he lived up to its highest standards throughout his military career. Taking part in frequent jousts he learned to be not merely effective but brilliant, and to display all the force and skill that could be taught by his father, the greatest soldier of his generation, and by the bravest of the brave, Sir Walter Manny and Sir John Chandos. We know that at the age of 13 he took part in a tournament at Norwich during one of his mother's visits. They stayed with the prior of the cathedral and were entertained by the citizens at a cost of £37 4s. 6½d. This was in 1343 during the long years of delay leading towards the great expedition, but some time after the start of serious though sporadic hostilities. Before the war could be fought many difficulties had to be overcome, problems economic rather than military.

Between the young Edward's ninth and eleventh years his father was, as we have seen, based upon Antwerp and other cities in the Low Countries. His main purpose was to build up a system of alliances with the rulers of all those states that felt themselves threatened by the France of Philip de Valois. As we know in long-distance view, the threat from expansionist France was a very real one, and Edward III may be absolved from any accusation that he was indulging in a mere campaign of alarmist propaganda. The independence of the many small principalities on the fringe of the Empire but not adequately protected by the Emperors was threatened, and French influence and alliances were spreading across the frontier. The whole region had once been part of Charlemagne's united Empire, but had been dismembered and then reassembled along an artificial border which had little justification in physical geography. It was not surprising that the ruling families of the duchies and counties on either side should, in course of time, get possession of bits of territory opposite, by marriage or conquest or even purchase. The map of the greater Netherlands had come, by the middle of the fourteenth century, to look like a patchwork quilt, with odd separated bits of the same pattern recurring at widely spaced intervals.

At the time, 1338, the large area of the county of Flanders had already been secured; across the Scheldt lay Hainault, under Edward's friendly brother-in-law William II, ruler from 1337 to 1345; to the north-east of Hainault and Flanders and including Brussels, Antwerp and sHertogenbosch was the extensive duchy of Brabant, over 100 miles long and one of the richest of all the principalities. William of Hainault, like his father before him, was also count of Holland and Zeeland, holding the estuaries of the Scheldt and Rhine and stretching from the border of Flanders near Cadsand and Sluys up to the Zuider Zee, a distance of nearly 150 miles, and extending inland to a common frontier with Brabant south of the Maas and Rhine. East of Holland and Brabant was Gelderland, whose count Reinald II had married Edward III's sister Eleanor in 1331 and was in 1338 created a duke by the Emperor and granted East Friesland. The duchy of Limburg, south-east of Brabant, was already united with it under the same duke, in alliance with England. Virtually the whole of the Netherlands, a solid block of territory 200 miles across each way and the wealthiest industrial area in western Europe, was thus associated with England, either dynastically or by bonds of common interest. It remained to get formal approval of the state of affairs from the reigning Emperor, Louis IV the Bavarian.

Edward III undertook a tour from Antwerp across the principalities to the Rhine to meet Louis, and obtained an appointment as Imperial Vicar-General over the parts of the Empire on the left bank of the Rhine and an order to all the princes to follow him in war for seven years. At least in theory Edward was now in a strong position and it is easy to understand the cheerfulness with which he gave £67 10s. to the work of Cologne Cathedral, a sum which would now be equivalent to quite £20,000 of building. The king was still not 26 and had an exceptionally brilliant and charming personality. Popular everywhere he went, he was royally entertained by princes and prelates at every stop, but in Cologne stayed in the home of Heinrich Scherfgin a prominent citizen of great wealth. We know that, back in England, Edward was to get on close terms with the merchants of London, and he showed an awareness, unusual in mediaeval monarchs, of the importance of money and credit.

We cannot follow the complex details of the war of sieges and skirmishes which filled the next few years, nor the equally complicated relations between the king and his bankers in England. Shortage of coin and the need to impose war taxation provide a basis for long chapters in books of economic, constitutional and social history. Here we are concerned with a few decisive actions: notably the definite assumption of the title and arms of king of France by Edward III at Ghent on 25 January 1340, and his great naval victory at Sluys on Midsummer Day the same year. The French had for several years been making surprise attacks on the towns of the south coast, and in 1338 plundered Southampton and captured the king's ship the *Christopher*. Now a French fleet of exceptional size, with their prize the *Christopher* in the van, lay off Sluys to intercept Edward on his return from London to join the queen at Ghent. Though outnumbered by four to one the English won a crushing victory and recaptured the *Christopher* between morning light and noon. The king rode on to Ghent to see his infant son John for the first time, and to meet the rulers of Brabant and Hainault, and Jakob van Artevelde representing Flanders, in celebration of the alliance. In the meantime messages announcing the great victory went back to England where the ten-year-old prince was regent in his father's stead.

CHAPTER IV

A Share of Glory

The life of kings is not smooth. No sooner had Edward III returned safely to England at the end of November 1340 than he found himself faced with obstruction from his archbishop of Canterbury, John Stratford. Stratford and his brother Robert, bishop of Chichester, had been playing Box and Cox as alternate chancellors for several years and the king had come to rely on them as sound if mediocre ministers. Modern historians of the Whig persuasion, and notably Bishop Stubbs, have seen a 'crisis' in the ensuing political events of the next year or two, and have magnified the affair into a milestone of constitutional progress. In fact there was an undignified passing of the buck between rival magnates and ministers to evade responsibility for their failure to support the king's army in Flanders and to raise sufficient funds. Matters were made worse by the circumstances of the king's return. After a very stormy passage the royal ship tied up at Tower wharf and it was found that the constable had deserted his post to visit a lady friend in the city, abandoning the royal children, alone with their three nurses, in the Tower. The king's anger was, not surprisingly, unbounded, and the next day he removed from office the chancellor, the treasurer, and several judges.

Archbishop Stratford, brother of the dismissed chancellor, withdrew to Canterbury and refused to come to court when ordered to do so. He had in fact been bound as surety for the king's debts to some merchants of Louvain, who pressed that he should be surrendered and taken to Brabant pending repayment. The earl of Derby was already a prisoner in Flanders in respect of other debts of the king's, and Edward pointed out that if the archbishop did not go, he would himself have to redeem his honour by going to prison in Brussels. Stratford took up a line of impudent self-justification and implied that he was a second Becket, victimized by his sovereign. But when he went so far as to proclaim that he would suffer torture and die if need be in defence of his rights, the bubble was pricked by the king's chamberlain, Sir John

Darcy, who told him that nothing like that would happen: 'you are not so worthy nor we so foolish'.

Vastly more serious matters preoccupied the king than this storm in a teacup. The heavy load of debt had somehow to be discharged and in the meantime it became necessary once again to intervene in Scotland, where David II returned and for the last time succeeded in expelling Edward Baliol. For five years the public history of England contains little but parliamentary squabbles over taxation and the failure of the Florentine bankers, the Bardi and Peruzzi, from whom Edward III had been forced to borrow. It has been said, and often repeated, that the bankruptcy was due to the debt having been repudiated, but this is completely untrue. There was no repudiation, and the difficulties of the bankers were due not only to their over-extension in England but largely to the state of affairs in Italy. The problem of the king's debts was, after 1343, taken over by the English merchants and it was they who found the means to finance the great programme of rearmament which led up to the successful campaign of 1346–47. For some time before that the English star had seemed to be on the wane. In 1341 the Emperor Louis changed sides and made an alliance with Philip of France, while the party of Van Artevelde lost ground in Flanders. Better news came from Brittany, where another dynastic struggle for the dukedom was in progress, England taking the side of John de Montfort. A force under Sir Walter Manny had considerable success in 1341 and the English troops were reinforced by Edward III in person next year. The campaign in Brittany was on the whole successful, and the pages of Froissart are filled with the exploits of Manny and his companions.

It was probably about this time that the idea of founding an order of knight-hood took hold of King Edward's mind. The romantic land of Brittany, filled with legends of Arthur and the Round Table, may well have been the root cause of a determination to revive the practices of this fabled chivalry. The king arrived back in England in March 1343 and two months later in full parliament created his son Edward prince of Wales. North and South Wales, with all their castles and royal estates, were handed over to him to administer as his own. Though not yet quite thirteen, the boy had grown into a young man by the standards of the day, and his capacity to administer his lands and territories was thus recognized. There was probably a connection in the king's mind between his son's precocious 'majority' and its celebration by the founding of a permanent Round Table which would ensure a constant succession of tournaments as an encouragement to and preparation for knightly deeds.

From time to time individual tournaments on a grand scale had been called 'Round Tables', notably the one at Nevin to celebrate Edward I's conquest of Wales in 1284, when local excavators discovered what were accepted by the king as the body of Constantine the Great's father and King Arthur's crown. Again in 1302 Edward I called a Round Table at Falkirk when a truce with Scotland had been concluded. But there was no suggestion of any continuity of institution in these functions. Edward III, however, seems from the start to have intended to found a continuing society with its headquarters in Windsor Castle. Before Christmas 1343 he sent out invitations to knights, gentlemen and esquires of all parts to come and take part in tournaments and jousts to be held at Windsor for four days after 19 January 1344; and on 1 January he issued a general protection for every comer with his servants and goods. According to Canon Adam Murimuth, who was there, the king also

> had all the ladies of the south parts of England and the wives of the burgesses of London invited by letters. So when the earls, barons, knights and as many ladies as possible had assembled . . . in the said castle, the king kept a solemn feast, the great hall of the castle being completely filled with ladies and not a man among them except two knights who had come by themselves from France. At the feast were two queens, nine countesses, more wives of barons, knights and burgesses than can well be numbered, all of whom were conducted to their places according to their rank by the king in person. The Prince of Wales, duke of Cornwall; the earls, barons and knights, feasted together with everyone else in a tent and elsewhere, where food had been laid out and was handed to all liberally and without question. In the evening ring-dances and other dancing were properly organized. On the three days following the king with nineteen other knights held the lists against all who came from abroad. The king himself, by no favour but by his strenuous exertions and the good luck of those three days, bore off the prize among the defenders.

Murimuth went on to describe the concluding supper held on the Thursday, when the king wore his crown and his robes of state and took an oath, the whole company standing, that he would begin a Round Table in the same manner that had been appointed by Arthur, formerly king of England, of 300 knights to begin with and later to be increased. The earls of Derby, Salisbury, Warwick, Arundel, Pembroke and Suffolk, and many barons and knights took the same oath. The very next week work began on a noble building in which the Round Table was to be held, and the king ordered masons and carpenters to be brought to Windsor, with stone and timber. The chief architects of the royal works, the master mason William Ramsey and the carpenter William Hurley, were in charge. Large numbers of men were impressed and the works were carried on throughout the season until the end of November. The building was afterwards destroyed and all we know is that it consisted of a circular wall 200 feet in diameter. What had been built by the winter of 1344 was covered over against frost with a roof specially made of 40,000 tiles bought for the purpose.

It has never been explained why Edward III, having sworn to set up this permanent Round Table of 300 knights and upwards, should afterwards have abandoned the project in favour of the Order of the Garter. The remarkable building for the Round Table was presumably to have been hollow like a Roman amphitheatre or a Spanish bullring, with an open space for jousting in the middle. It is tempting to associate the basic idea of the building with the Arthurian concepts in the king's mind, and to see in it an attempt to realize the circular Temple of the Holy Grail described in the romance of the *Younger Titurel*. The hill on which Windsor Castle stands would serve for Montserrat, but it has to be said that the diameter, large as it was, amounted only to one-third of the hundred fathoms of the mythical Temple. Whether the circular building was to have chapels, chambers or ambulatories formed within it we simply do not know. Ramsey and Hurley, as we have seen, were concerned with other buildings of grand scale and the octagon at Ely has an internal span of about 68 feet. The dome of St Peter's at Rome is just over twice as large; that of the classical Pantheon is more than 142 feet in internal diameter. It cannot be imagined that the Windsor Round Table was to have a dome or vaulted roof in clear span on such a scale. None the less the building was for its time something quite out of the ordinary and shows that its royal projector was possessed of an unparalleled imagination.

The great festival of the Round Table at Windsor was doubtless a master-stroke of propaganda, but it was not merely that. We must not picture the king as calculating the political advantage to be reaped as the measure of success. There was a genuine ardour for the grand gesture and the very real risks of jousting, the greatest game in the world short of knightly warfare itself, in Edward's eyes. What is striking is that at the very same time that the great feast was being planned, the king was busy on a highly practical gesture of a different kind, the establishment of a standard gold coinage. First came the issue of a gold florin in 1343, worth 6s., and with half- and quarter-florins. The next year saw the employment of Italian moneyers who were to mint a whole range of money, based on the gold noble worth 6s. 8d., also with half pieces and quarters, and with new silver coinage as well, notably the standard silver groat valued at 4d. The importance of a standard coinage did not exclude from the king's mind the need for other standards, and on 14 July 1344 he gave orders to the keeper of the Tower of London to deliver balances and standard weights to the London merchants. This was not a fresh preoccupation, for as early as 1333 Edward had licensed the citizens of York to have a standard of weight tested by the standard of London, for use in the wool staple which he had appointed to be held in York. Although there was a multiplicity of different standards in use in different places, the royal standards of measure, weight and capacity had been fixed long before and were kept in the Tower for reference. Sealed measures and weights of the King's Standard could be bought, and a set was sold in 1391 for use in the Honor of Pevensey belonging to John of Gaunt's Duchy of Lancaster.

The new coinage in England was a success, and seems to have contributed to the renewed prosperity which was able to bear the great load of war expenditure and also the burden of Edward's programme of civil architecture. But his attempt a couple of years later to extend the English currency to Flanders, a sort of sterling bloc, failed to work. Still, the king should be given such credit as is due for envisaging a European Common Market with a single standard of money. If only there had been a more stable economic background Edward III might have pulled off a far greater achievement, no less than the hegemony of the West. His fame and reputation were steadily growing and when, a year after his great victories over the French, the German emperor Louis IV died, the electors offered the imperial crown to Edward. He had to decline, but we shall see that 50 years later Richard II was to return to the idea and by 1397 actually had several electors in his pay. The thesis of the kings of England as leaders of Europe, though destined never to be realized in practical politics, had a certain validity.

Before turning to the expedition against France which was to win both the king and his son, the Black Prince, their lasting fame, we must consider what they managed to achieve in the peaceful arts before the onset of the Black Death, a natural calamity which put an end to the older civilization of England and of Europe. Architectural work for the Crown came to a sudden stop late in 1326, when Edward II ceased to rule. After an interruption of five years the building of the exquisite chapel of St Stephen in the Palace of Westminster was continued – under the same architect, Thomas of Canterbury – and in three phases, 1331–34, 1340–44, and 1347–48, was structurally finished. After 1340 it was William Ramsey who was the responsible master mason. The best glaziers and painters were, as we have seen, employed to complete the decorative scheme after the Black Death. The Chapel, when all was done, represented the high-water mark of English royal enterprise and, fittingly enough, the paintings included a representation of Edward III and his sons being presented, on their knees, by St George to the enthroned Virgin and Child. The little figure of Thomas of Woodstock bringing up the rear shows that the design was completed after his birth in 1355. Fitting up and furnishing were at last ended in 1363, over 70 years from the start of the work under Edward I.

The prince's main residence was at Kennington in Lambeth, across the river from Westminster, though he had also a large house in the City at the upper end of Fish Street Hill. Extensive works were done at Kennington in the twenty years or so from 1342 and these, like his father's at St Stephen's, ended in 1363. This was the natural consequence of his appointment as prince of Aquitaine on 19 July 1362 and his move to Bordeaux in the following year. Little survives at Kennington, but excavations have shown that there was a hall standing on an undercroft, and at right angles to it a large block including what was called The Prince's Chamber, with his principal living apartments. There was also a separate kitchen, evidently regarded as a model, since as late as the 1430's it was inspected by the Guild of Merchant Tailors when they were proposing to build a new kitchen at their hall. In the years before the Black Death the prince employed a mason, Nicholas de Ailyngton, who had worked on his father's palace, and after Ailyngton's death other masons from the king's service. Highly significant is his employment, from the beginning of 1358 if not before then, of Henry Yeveley. Yeveley, who had come to London from the North Midlands in 1353, was already one of the principal masons in the City by 1356. By 1359 he was employed by the king and it may be that he owed his advancement to a recommendation from his first royal client, the Black Prince.

Outside the London area there was the abortive work for the king on the Round Table at Windsor in 1344, and in the next year there were relatively slight repairs at Dover Castle. More important works were carried out for the Black Prince by Henry de Snelleston, who had been in his pay by 1343 and who on 29 September 1346 was formally appointed master mason to the prince in Chester and North Wales. Snelleston designed the mediaeval bridge at Chester, begun in 1347, and in that year also made alterations to the great hall and other buildings of Conway Castle. Snelleston probably died in the Black Death, as by November he had been succeeded by Hugh de Huntingdon. Chester Bridge is the finest surviving mediaeval bridge in Britain, and one of the most beautiful of all bridges in spite of alterations and the rebuilding of some arches. The original spans employ a rather flattened type of four-centred arch strongly suggestive of the early Perpendicular period, and Snelleston had probably long been associated with the royal works. The bridge was not finished until some years after his death, in 1355.

In painting we know that the great Master Hugh of Saint Albans worked for the prince as well as for the king, and no artistic division can be drawn between the works carried out for different members of the royal family by the same artists. What can be said is that from the onset of the Perpendicular style in architecture, about the time of the Black Prince's birth, the subordinate arts also took on new life and a new type of stylization, and in painting in particular are seen borrowings from the latest Italian use of perspective. This is easily explained since English artists were working alongside painters from Italy in the new Palace of the Popes at Avignon between 1321 and 1341. There was a demand for artists of English origin and working in up-to-date modes from England: witness the extraordinary 'modernity' of the sculpture worked in Catalonia by the expatriate English master 'Reinard Fonoll' between 1330 and 1362. For once in the history of art it was a positive advantage to come from England.

What was the reason for this English vogue on the continent? We saw that the first symptom of an English artistic ascendancy was the adoption of the form of free jurisdiction of the English stonemasons by the lodge of Strassburg Cathedral in 1275, and that this came at a time when Edward I had won renown on Crusade as the hero of the whole of Christendom. Edward's later conquest of Wales increased English prestige, and his failure in Scotland was not so obvious as to diminish the lustre of his life when seen in retrospect. The reputation of England had perhaps never stood as high as it did at the old king's death in 1307. The generation born in the last few years of the thirteenth century and the first decade or so of the fourteenth was, then, in a position to benefit from political success and rode on top of a wave of national prestige. Why did this prestige not fall away when it became clear that Edward II was not a powerful and outstanding ruler in any way comparable to his father? The answer may lie in the momentum already won by England in a long reign of more than a third of a century. It certainly owed much to the short and broken reigns of the sons who succeeded to Philip IV of France: three within the brief period from his death in 1314 to that of Charles IV in 1328. There was no real opportunity for France to profit from England's weakness.

The main reason why English art was not just a flash-in-the-pan but continued to enjoy foreign esteem was that it was novel and full of fresh ideas. The classicism of French Gothic followed the pattern of French scholastic philosophy. Reduced to its simplest terms this rested on the argument: having reached perfection, why go further? It was this that stultified the living force which had produced French Gothic and maintained it in a state of dynamic progress for a century. A set of rules had been made, and for evermore the game must be played by them. It was not possible for English artists or craftsmen to think within such limiting terms, and on the plane of philosophy they had been rejected by Bacon and Ockham. Hence the phenomenon, in the first half of the fourteenth century, of a multiplicity of schools of English style, and its reinforcement by the readiness of Englishmen to adopt exotic features from lands of far-off fantasy. It might be, in the last years of the old century, the reversed ogee curve formed by playing with a pair of compasses, producing endless diaper patterns reflecting the geometrical art of Islam. Later it was the more specific motive of a four-centred arch inside a square surround, from

Persia; and the stiff hexagonal 'wire-netting' reticulations of the earliest Perpendicular tracery, copying the mosques of Cairo.

These oriental influences, strangely enough, made most appeal to the English themselves and were not re-exported. But the notion of the reticulated pattern formed by the continuous flexing of parallel lines in never-ending ogee curves – never-ending unless artificially brought to a close – seized upon the continental imagination. From Portugal to the Baltic and from Scotland to Venice the pattern spread far and wide, though abandoned for about a century after 1370 in its country of origin. There is no chauvinism in claiming that it was this English invention that, admittedly picked up and amplified abroad, made possible most of the later developments of mediaeval architecture. The whole of Central European *Sondergotik* as well as the Flemish, Italian and Spanish moves towards Flamboyant was due initially to the adoption of this English idea, and to the freedom which it gave from the static quality of French Gothic. But having let off steam by throwing away, as a free gift to the foreigner, this architectural plaything, and the graphic and sculptural babewynerie that accompanied it, England turned on its heel and developed its own national manner, indifferent for well over a century to what was going on outside.

As a matter of historical fact we now know that Prior was right in stating, in 1900, that 'had there been no Black Death and no One Hundred Years War, the coming of a new style was predestined – nay, already, before 1350, in accomplishment'. All the essential elements of Perpendicular and of its associated forms in the rest of the arts, had indeed come together by 1335 or 1340 at the latest. It may be that their general adoption was hastened by shortage of craftsmen skilled in the old traditions after the plague, but even this is far from certain. What then of the Hundred Years War? Had it not been fought it is quite possible that France might have invaded England successfully according to the plan of 1344, and later English Gothic might have lain under the heavy hand of French classicism. We shall see that, in line with Richard II's policy of peace and closer relations with France towards the end of the century, the so-called International Style did affect English painting, sculpture and the minor arts – though not architecture. The strength of later English art may have owed a good deal to the sense of sturdy superiority, and to the positive nationalism, engendered by the war.

To the prosecution of the war we must now return. The long delays that had followed Edward III's claim to the French throne had borne fruit. England by 1345 was better able to bear the cost of a grand expedition than it had been earlier, and this more than made up for the failure of the alliance with the Empire and the death of Van Artevelde, murdered on 24 July 1345. The financial failure of the Florentine bankers, the Bardi and Peruzzi, was shortly to take place in spite of the king's kindly efforts to help them out of their difficulties. He cancelled various payments which his ministers had attempted to claim from them, notably a special tax of £1,200 levied on them as aliens. The heavy deficit budgeting required by the preparations for the invasion of France was now backed by English merchants. It may even be said that from a theoretical viewpoint the war actually gave English banking a fillip by demonstrating what it could achieve in case of need. The disastrous effects of the Black Death could not well have been foreseen, and it was the plague alone that upset all calculations. An English body of capitalists, rather than a capitalist 'class', rose from out of the general mass of commercial craftsmen who both made and sold their wares.

For nine years, since the invasion of English Aquitaine by Philip of Valois in 1336, there had been a serious risk of being driven back on Bordeaux and even of losing that foothold on French soil. To guard against this possibility the earl of Derby had been sent out with Sir Walter Manny and was steadily making headway. In 1345 Derby was able to take the offensive and on 21 October won a major engagement at Auberoche in Périgord, about 80 miles east of Bordeaux. This victory re-established the English in a wide stretch of country where they had lost control. According to Froissart's account, French prisoners taken included nine counts and viscounts and so many lords, knights and squires 'that there was no English man of arms but had two or three prisoners'. The occasion offered a display of chivalric good feeling, for 'the Englishmen dealt like good companions with their prisoners and suffered many to depart on their oath and promise to return again at a certain day to Bergerac or to Bordeaux'. Many towns were taken back from the French, including La Réole. There Manny was able to discover an old man who told him where his father, murdered while on a pilgrimage to Compostela, had been buried years before. Manny was able to have his father's body exhumed and sent to Valenciennes for honourable reburial among his kindred.

The French staged a counter-attack in the winter of 1345–46, and recaptured several important towns. It was this renewal of the threat to Bordeaux and to the whole of the English possessions that determined the course of events. Edward III decided upon an expedition in such force that it could march overland through France, cutting the French lines of communication and taking their armies in the rear. A descent upon Normandy had the further advantage that it would punish the Normans for their spontaneous offer of 1344, which had now leaked out, that they would invade and capture England for the French king as Duke William had done in 1066. The monstrous insolence of this boast put King Edward, and the whole of England, on their mettle. The expedition which resulted has been reckoned superior to any that left these shores subsequently until the last years of the nineteenth century.

As was to be expected there were great difficulties in getting everything ready and there were several false starts through the early summer of 1346. On 25 June the Prince of Wales reached Portsmouth with a contingent of 3,500 Welshmen, half of them armed with spears and the rest archers. There were also 50 picked archers from Chester and a corps of sappers consisting of 40 professional miners from the Forest of Dean. The total force to be moved is said to have amounted to 20,000 men, of whom 7,000 were cavalry. At length on 11 July the fleet, which had been standing off the Isle of Wight, set sail, and the next day a landing was effected at St Vaast-la-Hougue in the Cotentin, some 18 miles east of Cherbourg. The hero of the day was the young earl of Salisbury, William de Montague, who led the attack on the beach-head and was knighted by the king on the spot, along with the prince, Roger lord Mortimer who was later to be a founder Knight of the Garter, and several others. Less than a week later, after consolidating their position, the army moved forward on 18 July, with the prince in command of the vanguard.

In spite of the long time that had elapsed since the intention to invade had become known, King Philip seems not to have credited that the English would really land, so that he was by no means ready to oppose them with a substantial army. While he sent messengers far and wide to his allies, Edward III and the prince were marching unchecked southwards, first to St-Lo which was robbed by the troops without opposition, and then east to Caen. Caen, the capital of Lower Normandy, was said at the time to be larger than any English city except London. On 26 July the army reached the river Orne and forced the town with serious loss of life. No quarter was given to the defenders as a result, and the French leaders, the counts of Eu and Tancarville who were respectively constable and chamberlain of France, surrendered to Sir Thomas Holand, a one-eyed English knight with whom they had served on crusades against heathen Prussia and Muslim Granada. Their lives were spared, along with those of a number of other lords and knights who had taken refuge in the castle. The English troops got out of hand, and Holand and other knights had a hard job riding through the town to save ladies and girls from assault and also the clergy. Fortunately the worst excesses were restrained, and Caen was not destroyed but was in three days despoiled of great riches sent down to the English fleet at Ouistreham on the estuary of the Orne. The king bought the counts of Eu and Tancarville from Holand for 20,000 nobles, and this great sum laid Holand's fortune. He became a founder Knight of the Garter and three years after the Crecy campaign married Joan, daughter of the earl of Kent. After Holand's death in 1360 she was to be the wife of the Black Prince.

The taking of Caen was a savage episode, one of the most horrifying in the history of British arms. It was not in fact a sack in the accepted sense, but this was mainly due to the brave efforts on behalf of discipline made by Holand

1   Edward of Woodstock, the Black Prince (1330–1376), from his effigy in Canterbury Cathedral

3   Edward III (1312–1377), in the choir of York Minster

2   The Black Prince, from his father's tomb in Westminster Abbey

4   The Black Prince, in the choir of York Minster

5   Joan, 'The Fair Maid of Kent' (1328–1385), from the Black Prince's Chantry, Canterbury Cathedral

6   The effigy of the Black Prince in Canterbury Cathedral

7   The Wilton Diptych (left)

The Wilton Diptych (right)

8 Joan of Kent (1328–1385)

9 John of Gaunt (1340–1399)

10 Henry, duke of Lancaster, K.G. (d. 1361)

11 William, lord Latimer, K.G. (1330–1381)

12 Thomas de Beauchamp, earl of Warwick, K.G. (1313–1369)

13 William de Montague, earl of Salisbury, K.G. (1328–1397)

14   William of Wykeham (1324–1404), bishop of Winchester from 1366.
The great statesman of his time, he was Lord Chancellor 1367–1371 and
1389–1391, and founder of Winchester College and of New College, Oxford

15 Richard II
(1367–1400)

16 Henry, earl of Derby, later
Henry IV (1367–1413)

17 Richard II's quadrant, made for his
personal use in 1399, from the British
Museum

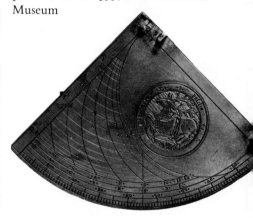

and other knights on their own initiative. It can only be supposed that the exceptional barbarity of the English troops was directly due to the Norman plan for the invasion of England. Many of the men no doubt came from Portsmouth, Southampton, and other English towns which had suffered severely in the French raids of recent years, and we have to remember that these cruelties were not one-sided, but part and parcel of the whole war. There is not an atom of evidence for the suggestion, which has been made, that the Black Prince at his first battle opened his military career with a sack and massacre, to close it in 1370 with another at Limoges. A boy of sixteen, taking part in his first battle, the prince acquitted himself bravely, but had no responsibility for the conduct of the action. The marshal and leader of the host was Sir Geoffrey de Harcourt and it was to him that Caen owed its survival. The king was so enraged at the number of his men killed by the resistance of the civilian citizens that he gave orders that next day the population should be put to the sword and the town set on fire; but Harcourt urged him to exercise restraint and succeeded in getting the answer: 'Sir Geoffrey, ye are our marshal, ordain everything as ye will.'

On 31 July the English forces left Caen, moving still eastwards as the objective had now been determined: Calais. It is not clear whether the strategic plan of taking Calais and holding it as a continental bridgehead had yet been formed, or whether it was regarded as the best place for evacuating France after doing a maximum of damage to the French war effort. At Lisieux the king was met by two cardinals empowered to offer the whole of Aquitaine, but Edward declined to treat with them. The line of march was deflected towards Paris, following the south bank of the Seine, through Pont de l'Arche, Louviers and Vernon. All the bridges had been destroyed, so the line of least resistance was followed. Mantes was captured and then on 13 August the army reached Poissy, where the engineers were able to repair the bridge. The invasion had reached to within sixteen miles of the heart of Paris, and it is fascinating to wonder what might have happened if Edward had pushed on to assault the city, taking advantage of the element of surprise. Given the king's nerve and ambition it seems astonishing that no attempt to strike at the capital was made; probably Harcourt again restrained the courage of his master and counselled the safer course. The die was cast, and the English force turned due north and made across country for Beauvais and Amiens.

A distance of 70 miles was covered in only six days, a great rate of speed for such a large army. Evidently spies had brought in news of the French outflanking movement which, Philip hoped, would encircle the English and result in their crushing defeat. The invaders were, of course, living off the country and had comparatively few of the problems of supply which would normally be faced. It was part of the custom of mediaeval warfare, for which all had to be prepared, that the enemy would requisition the food and supplies that they needed, and those were reckoned merciful who did no wanton damage to life and property beyond that limit. Booty from towns and cities captured after resistance was officially recognized and, as happened after the assault on Caen, was carried off to England in ships of the king's fleet. Nevertheless, a strict line was drawn between what was and what was not permissible. Assaults upon those of gentle blood by the common soldiery, apart from the legitimate hazards of battle; attacks upon women; and any aggression upon the clergy or the property of the Church: these were sternly discountenanced. Edward III, who took after his grandfather Edward I in his rigid sense of justice, had given strict orders that there should be no destruction of churches or monasteries upon pain of death. Consequently, when he found that his troops had set fire to the abbey of St Lucien near Beauvais, he had 20 men hanged as an example, and afterwards took more stringent precautions against arson and unnecessary damage to the towns the army passed through. The route lay to the west of Amiens itself, through Grandvilliers and Poix to Airaines in Edward's own inheritance of Ponthieu. At Poix the two daughters of the lord had been left alone in the castle, and were saved from assault by Sir John Chandos and then at the king's command taken in safety to Corbie where they wished to go.

The passage of the Somme presented the same difficulty as that of the Seine had done: the bridges were broken down or held by strong French forces. For three days attempts were made to cross, from as far up the valley as Picquigny down to the estuary between St Valery and Le Crotoy, but eventually a countryman named Gobin Agace was found who revealed to the king how to ford the estuary at low tide. Although even this passage was stoutly contested by the French, the army got across and before evening on Friday 25 August was encamped at Crecy. Ever since reaching Airaines King Edward had been in Ponthieu, by right his own feof, but at Crecy he had come near to the northern border. It was this factor that determined his stand, for he said: 'I have good cause here to abide them.' He was not only fighting for the throne of France, but for his own ground. His whole future hung upon the outcome of a single pitched battle, for he knew that his forces – of the order of 20,000 men all told – were vastly outnumbered by the French and allied troops under Philip of Valois. Although the suggestions that Philip had from six to eight times as many men as Edward are certainly exaggerations, there are not likely to have been fewer than 60,000 engaged on the French side, an immense army by the standards of the age.

Let us leave it to the military historians to fight over again the details of the field of Crecy: the numbers, the cannon, the emplacements, the dead. The essentials are soon told. King Edward could choose his ground, and drew up his forces with their backs to the sea. Whether this was due to skill or good luck, it proved of vital importance, for the attack did not come until the afternoon and the sun shone into the eyes of the French from behind the Englishmens' backs. Tactical brilliance was undoubtedly shown in the way the army was drawn up, with two divisions in front and the third, under the king himself, placed centrally in reserve. Each division consisted of dismounted men-at-arms flanked by archers, armed with the longbow. The French sent in their mercenaries, Genoese crossbowmen, who were put to rout by the fast and continuous firing of the longbows, a weapon to which the continent was unaccustomed. The Genoese turned tail and were cut down on King Philip's orders by the mounted French knights. The result was utter confusion. But the French launched attack after attack, not doubting to win by sheer weight of numbers. The battle continued until after nightfall, fiercely fought and with appalling losses on the French side.

The right-hand or southern division of the English was commanded by the prince, who had with him the earl of Warwick, Sir Thomas Holand, Sir Reginald Cobham, Sir John Chandos and several other of the most famous captains on the English side. The king was determined that his son should, though only just turned sixteen, have the chance to prove himself and to win the honour of the day. At the peak of battle, after the second division had come up to aid the prince, things none the less began to look very serious. The prince was unhorsed and was saved in the nick of time by his standard-bearer, Richard de Beaumont, who stood over him, covering his body with the standard of Wales. Warwick sent Sir Thomas Norwich with an urgent message to the king, who was surveying the field from the vantage point of a windmill mount. The king declined to advance, sending back Norwich with word to suffer the boy to win his spurs that day: 'If God be pleased, I will this journey be his and the honour thereof, and to them that be about him.'

CHAPTER V

The Days of Fame

Prince Edward had become a man upon the field of the hardest fought battle that men could remember. It was not merely a victory but one of the few classic fights of history. The overweening power of France, leader of the West, had been humiliated by an army apparently in full retreat and not more than a third the size. The English had lost but fifty men of note, whereas of the French the dead amounted to over 1,500 of coat-armour, counted by heralds, and included the duke of Lorraine and more than half-a-dozen counts, as well as Philip's courageous ally King John of Bohemia who, though almost totally blind, had been led into battle by his faithful knights with their reins tied together, and so fought until all had fallen. The ostrich feathers which have ever since been the badge of the Princes of Wales were not, as fable reports, won by Prince Edward from the dead king of Bohemia. On the contrary, they came from the county of Ostrevant, an appanage of his mother's homeland of Hainault, and the motto 'ich dien' is Flemish rather than German though the meaning, 'I serve', stays the same.

The prince had no need to snatch a badge from the dead. His father's generous wish, that he should get the honour of the day, was fulfilled. From that time onwards it was Edward, prince of Wales, whose name was on the lips of all soldiers, and of many civilians too. His father's stature was not diminished, but rather increased by his fame. King Edward was for the time being the arbiter of the West, and gloried not merely in success of arms and a prosperous kingdom, but in having a son who sought and ensued glory on the field, whether of battle or tournament. From then on, it seems, the French knew him as 'Edouard le noir', possibly from his having worn a suit of black armour at Crecy, but of this there is no direct evidence. It might be thought that 'black' was used in the metaphorical sense of sinister or harmful, but there is good evidence that the Black Prince was as highly regarded, in his character of a chivalrous knight, by his enemies as by his friends. His intensely scrupulous honour was well known, to the extent of being played upon, and certainly he was not reproached by his contemporaries. In a shadowy way his heroic memory survived in folklore and even until about 1900 French children were singing a song that began: '*Le Prince noir ne connait pas la haine*', a remarkable tribute to character to have lasted more than half a millenium.

One of the strangest contrasts between mediaeval and modern attitudes of mind concerns the dead enemy. Modern hatred, at least among politicians and civilians though probably not among many professional servicemen, outlasts the grave. In the Middle Ages, whatever might have been the degree of enmity in life, all bitterness was cancelled before God. It was the English king who, after his dead enemies had been identified and counted, saw to it that the bodies of those of high rank should be suitably buried in consecrated ground, and had a truce of three days called to enable the men of the countryside to bury the rest. The usages of chivalry, so different from those of modern warfare, also emerge from Froissart's anecdote of Sir Walter Manny's journey across France at this time. Manny, in the south-west at the time of Crecy, captured a knight from Normandy and asked what he would pay for ransom. The Norman said he would be happy to pay 3,000 crowns. Manny then offered that if the knight would go to the duke of Normandy, who was his relative, and obtain for Manny and twenty of his men a passport to enable them to cross France to Calais, 'paying courteously for all our expenses' – no requisitioning – he should go free without ransom; otherwise he was to return as a prisoner within a month. The Norman knight went to Paris, obtained the safe-conduct from the duke, brought it back to Manny at Aiguillon and was set free. Manny and his twenty men were able to ride across enemy territory, showing their passport, until they reached Orleans, where they were arrested and taken to prison in Paris. King Philip threatened to kill Manny, for he thought him his great enemy; but the duke of Normandy said that if the king did so, then he would never again bear arms against the king of England or serve in Philip's forces. Eventually Philip was persuaded to release Manny, paid all his expenses, and treated him to dinner before sending him on his way, to Valenciennes first and then to King Edward at Calais.

The fortress of Calais was practically impregnable, so Edward resolved to starve it out. The French governor, anxious to conserve what stores of food he had, sent out 1,700 or more poor men, women and children. Although it was to the disadvantage of the besiegers to let them out, they were allowed to pass and what was more, given food and drink and twopence sterling each, 'for the which divers many of them prayed for the king's prosperity'. The contrast between this generous treatment of peaceful civilians and the ferocity brought out by citizens' resistance has to be understood. Kings and princes had no quarrel with the common people and were prepared to treat them well, regardless of their belonging to the enemy. If they joined the forces they took their chance of booty if their lords won, or sudden death in the contrary case. But as long as they remained private men it was their business to get on with their work, earn a livelihood if possible, and take no interest in high matters.

This is the real point of the famous story of the burghers of Calais at the end of the siege next year, in August 1347. Calais had been summoned to surrender, and had the citizens who remained then laid down their arms, their lives would, by the laws of mediaeval warfare, have been safe. What the rules provided, however, in case of an obstinate defence was that the lives of all defenders were forfeit. In practice this was greatly mitigated by the showing of mercy on the part of a magnanimous victor, but everyone knew what the rule was. Sir Jean de Vienne, the Burgundian knight in command of Calais for King Philip, had orders to hold out and await a relief, and he and the citizens heroically obeyed these orders for nearly a year until famine forced them to sue for surrender. By that time so many English lives had been lost in the siege and so much money spent, that Edward III was beside himself with rage. He insisted that there must be unconditional surrender to his pleasure to do as he would with everyone captured. Froissart tells the whole story of how Manny went backwards and forwards to negotiate, and how he slowly persuaded the king to demand six of the chief citizens only 'bare-headed, bare-footed and bare-legged, and in their shirts, with halters about their necks, with the keys of the town and castle in their hands'. We all know that six volunteers were found, but probably few remember their names: Eustache de Saint-Pierre, Jean d'Aire, Jacques de Wissant and his brother Pierre, Jean de Fiennes and Andrieu d'André.

The king would have had them beheaded on the spot but all his courtiers besought him to have mercy. The prince pleaded with his father to spare their lives, and Manny made a most eloquent case for clemency. All was, apparently, to no avail when the queen knelt down in tears and begged for mercy with success. Philippa received the six men as a gift, took them to her chamber, had them fitted out with new clothing, gave them a dinner and six gold nobles apiece, and then set them free. The sequel was in its less obvious way dramatic. The knights who had defended Calais were taken prisoners of war to await ransom in the normal manner; the common soldiers 'that came thither simply to win their living' had to pile their arms in the market and were then free to leave. The whole of the remaining civil population except one priest and two old men learned in the customs of the town was then ejected, to make way for new English inhabitants who were brought from London. Calais, taken at such heavy cost, was to be made safe for ever, so far as human ingenuity could secure that end. And if we think it a harsh settlement we must remind ourselves of the many equally sweeping transfers of population in Europe and elsewhere within the last sixty years.

In October the king, with the queen and their infant daughter Margaret and the Black Prince, sailed for England. The great expedition had lasted fifteen months, in which the prince, now turned seventeen, had held his first command and been one of the victors in a pitched battle of exceptional ferocity and danger, and had played his part to the full in the greatest siege of his time. His father's position as the most renowned monarch in Europe seemed assured, and he as eldest son and heir to the throne of England was held in high esteem. Along with his parents he made a triumphal entry into London and went in procession to the palace of Westminster. In thanksgiving for the success vouchsafed him, he made costly gifts to the shrine of Becket at Canterbury, and then entered into a round of jousts and magnificent entertainment. His open hand and purse led him deeply into debt, but he was incapable in a real sense of counting the cost.

The months that followed the royal family's return to England were possibly the happiest, certainly the most glorious, of the whole reign of Edward III. During his absence David the king of Scots had been captured as well as Charles of Blois, the French claimant to the duchy of Brittany. Many other distinguished prisoners had been taken in the course of the expedition and at Calais. Tournaments and jousts alternated with other festivities, put on in such splendid style that 'it seemed as if the Golden Age was returned to England'. The prince was one of the principal challengers in tourney and won fresh laurels in these combats of peace. The smiths and armourers, the tailors and the herald-painters of London were kept busy: the arts and crafts of luxury had seldom been so richly patronized. For the king's plays at the manor of Guildford, at Christmas 1347, the costumes included 84 tunics of coloured buckram, 42 vizards – grotesque masks – of different shapes, 14 each of painted cloaks, dragons' heads, white tunics painted with peacocks' eyes, and swans' heads with their wings. The Court spent much of the year in the conditions of a fancy-dress ball or a garden party.

When not at Westminster or Windsor the prince kept up his own state at Berkhamstead Castle, and busied himself with the administration of his immense estates: not simply Wales, Cheshire and Cornwall, but lands spread over many counties. His favourite recreation was hawking on the downs, and he was also a keen huntsman. Though deeply in debt, there is little evidence that this preoccupied him unduly, any more than it did many other leading figures of the age. Somehow the money was found to put in circulation, and circulate it did to amazing purpose. The very few remaining objects of the art of the Court display an exquisite quality but rarely equalled. The crowning glory came with the founding festivities of his father's Order of the Garter, substituted for the Arthurian Round Table, probably held on and about St

George's Day, 23 April 1348. It was then that robes and garters with the famous motto: *Honi soit qui mal y pense* were first issued. The prince was one of the founders, at the head of one of the two 'teams' of twelve knights which, along with the sovereign and his heir, comprised the Order of 26 persons in all. During the Middle Ages it was the custom for the queen, wives and daughters of the knights, and sometimes other ladies of quality to be admitted as Dames of the Order. In November 1348 the prince gave 'twenty-four garters to the knights of the Society of the Garter', probably on the occasion of some special festival then held.

It is singular that there should be no public record of the precise date when the Order of the Garter was founded; no explanation of the completely changed character of the new foundation of – probably – 1348 when compared with the vow to found the Round Table four years earlier; not even any certainty as to the meaning of the garter itself nor the motto. Few now believe the romantic story of the king's attachment to the countess of Salisbury, and it is considered far more likely that 'Shame be to him who thinks evil of it' refers to Edward III's claim to the throne of France. Three centuries ago Ashmole took the view that the colours of the Garter, gold upon blue, were an heraldic allusion to the golden fleurs-de-lis on the blue ground of the arms of France, and this view has been reinforced by the authority of the present Garter King of Arms, Sir Anthony Wagner. It does indeed seem likely that the founding of the Order was the direct outcome of the great and successful expedition into France, which had taken place after the vows of 1344. In some way the merely romantic devotion to the legendary figure of King Arthur had given place to a strictly military loyalty, through the sovereign and his heir, to the national patron St George. Faithful allegiance to the king and a bond of unbreakable fellowship among the twenty-four knights were the guiding principles of the brotherhood.

Very soon after the start of the Order the king founded in connection with it an enlargement of the old college associated with Henry III's chapel of St Edward in the lower ward of Windsor Castle. The former institution had eight chaplains, but the new one was to have 24 canons and also 24 poor knights, and was dedicated to God, the Virgin Mary, St George the Martyr, and St Edward the Confessor. The establishment was by letters patent of 6 August 1348, the same day on which Edward III also founded St Stephen's College in the palace of Westminster, in connection with the magnificent chapel which his craftsmen had just completed. Confusion between the two foundations of the same day, and the wording of their respective charters, has occurred, so that an unnecessary mystery regarding the dates of building has been introduced. In fact the two charters are quite explicit: at St Stephen's the king referred to the structural completion of the chapel; at Windsor he spoke of having devoted a sum of money to the intended completion of the collegiate foundation of Henry III. This agrees perfectly with the known date of works on the Vestry (1350–51), Chapter House (1350–52), Canons' Houses (1352–53), Porch (1353–54) and Cloister walks (1353–56). The only question is why there should have been a delay of two years between the issue of the charter and the start of works in fulfilment of it.

The question is no sooner asked than it receives an overwhelming answer. At the very time that Edward III in Westminster was sealing the charters of his two great religious foundations, a dreadful epidemic was setting in down in Dorset, where about the beginning of August an infected ship had loosed upon the unsuspecting countrymen the fleas which carried the germs of bubonic plague. Although news of the great mortality, spreading westwards through the Mediterranean and across the continent for the past two years, had been received, the appalling reality burst upon a country quite unprepared. No effective quarantine regulations nor any medical skill to deal with the infection existed. Until early in the present century not even the cleverest physicians knew the true causes of the disease, and even now it is not clear why it has historically spread out from China in waves at some periods, and receded eastwards again in others. In 1348 it began in southern Dorset in the first days of August and moved all over the country and reached Scotland, gradually dying away, for about two years in all. The worst period was the summer of 1349, when it might be said that the clergy – whose names are largely on record – were dying like flies. Within three or four weeks several priests might successively be instituted to the same church. The heroism of the ordinary parish clergy cannot be overpraised: faced with a horrifying and almost infallibly mortal illness, they stuck to their posts and stepped into the houses, the shoes and – alas – the fleas of dead men.

The extent of the mortality due to the first great pestilence, in Europe and in England, is quite uncertain. Estimates have varied between one-quarter and three-quarters of the total population. It is most unlikely that less than one-third of all the men, women and children were wiped out. Among the clergy and in many monasteries the percentage was certainly far higher and it may well have been only about one-third that remained alive. Even a conservative estimate of the deaths in Europe stands at 25 millions. It was as though a direct judgement of God upon evil and corrupt mankind had been made manifest; men's faith was tried to breaking point and, though more on the continent than in Britain, became distorted. Fanaticism of every kind was let loose, from the exaggerated penances of the Flagellants to massacres of the Jews who were alleged to have spread the plague by poisoning wells. As was said by contemporaries, the world never afterwards returned to its former condition. All the landmarks had been washed away, and human nature – far from having been purged and strengthened by suffering – took a pronounced turn towards selfishness and the greedy enjoyment of anything that a short life could offer in the way of material pleasures.

The direct consequences of the Black Death in England, reinforced by the murrain in cattle and sheep which followed, were to produce an extreme shortage of labour and, within two or three years, practically to double wage rates. It was not possible for Parliament to meet, the king proroguing it from time to time. He had rightly deduced – as his writs to all the sheriffs and to members indicated – that there was great danger of spreading the disease in large assemblies. On the other hand, he and the prince of Wales set a good example by continuing to live, as far as was possible, their normal life. The business of the law courts was halted by the deaths or absence of the judges. The thousands of dead animals all over the country added further infections to that of the plague; there was neither meat to eat nor wool to sell. The loss of so many breadwinners, added to the other concurrent factors, ended in a grave food shortage and in many parts of the country people came near to starvation. There was little to relieve the gloom of the situation, except the creditable fact that the nobility and gentry on the whole were generous in their remission of customary rents due from their tenants. The new national spirit which had been fostered in the war did not altogether disappear from the country struck by the visitation of nature.

What was in the long run to have the worst effects on the country was the unleashing of a forerunner of trades unionism in a hostile form. In the hope of checking runaway inflation the king made ordinances in June 1349 to deal with the new problem of those who 'refuse to serve unless they receive excessive wages' and of others who 'prefer to beg in idleness than to get their livelihood by labour'. All victuallers were to sell food at reasonable prices 'so that they shall have a moderate not excessive profit'. The work-shy were not to be encouraged to live unemployed and nothing 'under colour of pity or alms' was to be given to encourage them in idleness, 'so that they may be compelled to labour for their living'. When Parliament was once more able to meet, in 1351, statutes were passed in greater detail, but by 1360 it was found that many craftsmen were making 'alliances and conspiracies' to demand excessive wages. They were also becoming skilled in the practice of demarcation disputes and 'leap-frogging' so that it had to be laid down that, for example, 'each mason . . . be compelled by his master whom he serves to do all work that pertains to him, of freestone or rough stone'. Wycliffe a few years later inveighed against all such practices and declared that the curse both of God and man would fall on 'new fraternities or guilds made' by men who 'conspire together that no man of their craft shall take less on a day than they set'.

Once the bubonic plague had reached England it tended to break out at intervals, and during the latter part of the fourteenth century there were serious second and third epidemics in 1361–62 and 1368–69, as well as more restricted outbreaks in certain districts. The country was never to be free of this terrible menace until after the great plague of London in 1665. For well over three hundred years men were accustomed to the ghastly scenes of mass burial in pits, new grounds covering acres of land having to be consecrated in haste. In spite of heroism on the part of many priests and some doctors, afflicted families were often shut up by themselves to take their luck of the outcome. Most of the philosophical and religious breakdown of those ensuing three centuries can be attributed to the plague and the resulting depressive effect on men's minds as well as the indirect effect upon the economy. It was no longer possible to view life as a progress from relative darkness towards light, as on the whole it had been for the two centuries between the accession of Henry II in 1154 and the coming of the Black Death in 1348. We can well appreciate this from the analogy with the century of peace coupled with amazing progress of 1815–1914, and the maelstrom of misery which has followed the outbreak of the first World War and the failure to combat inflation in our own century.

Most of the royal family survived the plague, but the princess Jeanne, or Joanna, who had been betrothed to the Infante Pedro of Castile and was on her way to marry him, caught the disease and died near Bordeaux on 2 September 1348. Her father's noble and resigned letter of condolence to the disappointed groom has survived and shows that Edward III was both affectionate towards his children and deeply religious. The second prince, William of Windsor, also died in 1348, but in infancy and perhaps not of plague. The thwarting of the intended close alliance with Castile was to have serious consequences: in the near future the clash between Spanish and English fleets in the Channel in 1350, and in the longer term probably the civil war in Castile which involved the Black Prince and led to his long illness and death. For had Pedro been known to have the close support of Edward III the rebellion of his bastard brother Henry of Trastamara might well never have broken out: the aid given to Henry by the English companies as well as by Du Guesclin and the French, would have been inconceivable had intervention of the English court on Pedro's side been obvious.

No sooner had the pestilence abated than the war in France once more became serious. Intelligence reached the king of a plot to deliver Calais to the French. The captain of one of the castles guarding the town was a Genoese, Americ of Pavia, who was paid 20,000 crowns to admit a French force led by Sir Geoffrey de Chargny from St Omer. English reinforcements, led by Manny, were secretly sent to Calais and the king, the Black Prince and a group of their most trusted knights served incognito. When the first party of French was treacherously admitted they found themselves ambushed by the English and a desperate struggle followed. Manny's party is said to have been reduced to 30 men when the king leapt into the fight 'gnashing his teeth like a wild boar' and shouting 'Hey St George! Ha St Edward!'. The enemy were pressed back with great loss and Calais saved. The king singled out one of the attackers, Sir Eustace de Ribemont, and took him prisoner after a hard fight. De Chargny and most of the other Frenchmen too were taken, and the king later gave his knightly prisoners supper, when 'the prince, lords and knights of England served the king at the first mess'. After supper the king took off the chaplet of pearls he was wearing on his head and gave it to his opponent De Ribemont as a prize for his prowess as 'the best doer in arms in this journey past of either party'. Said the king: 'I desire you to bear it this year for the love of me. I know well ye be fresh and amorous, and oftentimes be among ladies and damosels. Say wheresoever ye come that I did give it you, and I quit you your prison and ransom and ye shall depart tomorrow.'

King Edward was undoubtedly unrivalled in his judgement of knightly qualities and martial prowess, and it has been remarked that in his choice of the first twenty-four knights who, under himself and the prince, were to constitute the Order of the Garter, he showed wonderful discernment. It was not primarily eminence of blood or social position that he required, but prowess and skill in tournament and war, and the promise of such qualities by the younger men. As time went on the great captains became members of the Order, but they were not all among the founders. In spite of their contemporary fame, many of the founder knights remain little more than names, but several were among the most famous men of their time, continuously mentioned in the history of the war. Such were Henry earl of Derby, later the first duke of Lancaster; Thomas Beauchamp earl of Warwick; William Montague earl of Salisbury; the Gascon Jean de Grailly, Captal de Buch; Sir Bartholomew Burghersh; Sir Thomas Holand; and several of the Black Prince's closest friends and companions in arms: Sir John Chandos; Sir James Audley the younger; and Sir Nele Loryng. Chandos was the prince's chamberlain; Loryng had been with him since 1342. Another of the founders who served the prince was Sir Henry d'Enne who came from near Cambrai, close to Queen Philippa's home.

The sea fight between Edward III and the Castilians returning from Flanders was one of the more remarkable episodes of the war. The Spanish fleet consisted of 40 ships and had on board 10,000 men including Flemish mercenaries. Froissart tells a circumstantial story of the day, 29 August 1350, which he must have had from someone present. King Edward stood on the prow of his ship, the *King's Hall*, wearing a black velvet jacket and a black beaver hat, 'which became him well'. He had his minstrels play on horns a German dance brought back by Sir John Chandos who had just returned from a mission to the Empire, and then persuaded Sir John to sing to the minstrels' accompaniment. When the Spanish vessels had been sighted the king and his knights drank wine and then put on their helmets. The king laid his ship against an enormously bigger Spaniard, and so did the ship bearing the young prince of Wales. The prince's vessel was holed in many places and almost ready to sink when the duke of Lancaster's ship grappled the other side of the great Spaniard. Lancaster cried 'Derby to the rescue' and swept the whole Spanish crew into the sea in time for the prince and his men to scramble on board as their own ship sank. At least 14 of the Spanish fleet were taken, the English trumpets sounded, and the victors with their prizes returned to Rye by nightfall.

The war in France was quiescent for several years, but a severe winter in 1352–53, ending in a great storm, caused widespread damage and led to famine conditions in some parts, notably Cheshire. There was a serious revolt there which had to be put down by the prince in person. He was adjudged a fine of 5,000 marks from those who had taken part and put one-tenth of this towards the completion of Vale Royal Abbey, begun by Edward I in 1277. The work undertaken for him, by the mason William Helpeston, was to have an unusual plan suggesting influences from Spain. By 1354 the French were again on the offensive in Aquitaine, and had retaken a great deal of territory. The English reply was a double expedition: the king and the duke of Lancaster crossed to Normandy, and the prince sailed from Plymouth to Bordeaux in September 1355. On 21 September the Black Prince was invested as duke of Aquitaine in the cathedral, and in October he left on a major expedition aimed at Narbonne, which he reached on 8 November, then returning to Bordeaux by 9 December. His army of 60,000 men had proved irresistible and met with no serious opposition, but served only to restore English prestige.

No doubt by agreement with his father, the prince issued new gold coins from Bordeaux similar to the king's coinage, and this will have helped to restore confidence and to bring over those of the Gascon nobles and merchants whose loyalty might have been wavering. Great efforts were made to conciliate local feeling in the provinces in dispute, and Edward III actually sent his son a letter pointing out the value of avoiding reprisals against areas recovered from the French and which might be supposed of dubious allegiance. Sir John Chandos, who had won a reputation mainly by his bravery and romantic deeds, now proved himself a wise diplomat and serious strategist. He was for all practical purposes the prince's prime minister of Aquitaine, and most worthily filled the office. It was probably Chandos who promoted the great scheme for a synchronized two-prong attack on France from Brittany and Bordeaux at the same time. Unfortunately the poor communications of the time did not allow this to be effective. The duke of Lancaster started to advance from Brittany too soon and had to retreat before the king of France – by now Philip's son John II – with his full army. The Black Prince marched out of Bordeaux on 6 July but was slowed up by local skirmishes in the Dordogne. On 4 August the army left Bergerac and in the next three and a half weeks covered three or four leagues a day, reaching Bourges and Vierzon. Bourges was too strongly defended to be worth attacking, and intelligence was received that all bridges over the Loire had been destroyed.

King John massed all his forces at Chartres and by 10 September had crossed the Loire and was marching in full strength to seek out the Anglo-Gascon army and destroy it. In the meantime the prince had been besieging the castle of Romorantin and took it after five days in which he behaved with great gallantry, exposing himself to the enemy's fire. After spending a few days encamped before Tours, the prince heard that King John was rapidly advancing and realized that discretion was the better part of valour. He broke up the camp and retreated southwards to Chatellerault, making directly for Bordeaux. A few days later, on 17 September, the scouts of the vanguard made contact with the rear of the great French army which had outflanked and outdistanced the prince's force and was already between him and Gascony, in the neighbourhood of Poitiers. The next day the English reached the village of Maupertuis, seven miles beyond the city to the south-east. The French sent out a reconnoitring party under the gallant Sir Eustace de Ribemont – of the pearl chaplet – who reported that the prince's army had 2,000 men-at-arms, 4,000 archers, and 1,500 light troops; but was in a strong position. The French army had at least 20,000 men and King John had no doubt of being able to destroy the English once and for all. It seemed to him that the long story of a foreign region cut out of France was over.

The king of France had the great advantage of being advised by Sir William Douglas, a Scot who had fought against the English on the Border with much success. It looked as though, with an enormously superior army which had already shown that it could outmarch the prince and bar his passage, and with this inside information on English tactics, victory was assured. It was obvious to all observers who appreciated these factors favourable to the French, but also knew the fantastic and desperate courage of the Black Prince, that the resulting battle would be appalling. The local clergy made earnest efforts to mediate and prevent the dreadful loss of life bound to ensue if conflict could not be averted. The Cardinal de Périgord went from one camp to the other, but his utmost endeavours were only able to secure a truce until sunrise. The task of the peacemakers was made impossible by two irreducible factors: on the one hand the king of France felt absolute certainty that he had at last got the English in his grip and that a crowning victory that would finish the war was his; on the other side, the Black Prince felt bound in honour to his father not to conclude any truce on terms that might bind Edward III in an unacceptable way. To the prince this would have been a betrayal of trust and complete dishonour.

King John 'the Good' was himself a deeply chivalrous man, even though he would take advantage of anything allowed by the rules of war. He was, for instance, resolved to crush the English power, and gave orders that no quarter was to be given and no prisoners taken. On the other hand, he was determined to venture his own life and those of his lords, knights and troops rather than accept the shrewd counsel of De Ribemont and Douglas, that he should bottle up the English and starve them out, without risking pitched battle. Such canny advice, even though it came from proven soldiers who had long experience of fighting the English, he simply despised. Like his father at Crecy, he felt such confidence in the overwhelming superiority of his numbers and equipment that he never seriously considered the possibility of defeat. It seems singular to us in the light of after knowledge that the French high command should have learned little or nothing from Crecy or from many lesser episodes of the war, but this seems to be an historical constant of French psychology. Long before the kings of France had lost Aquitaine to England by underrating their opponents; centuries later the same defect caused the leadership of France to overreach itself under Francis I, Louis XIV and both Napoleon I and Napoleon III.

This mental obstinacy, though in what seemed a good cause, was to be John's undoing. Not prepared to let go what he thought was in his grasp, he lost all. He failed to reckon on the united spirit of his opponents, and above all he was blinded to the amazing, indeed almost unbelievable, ascendant star of the prince. What is perhaps stranger is that he attempted to apply to his massed attack the methods of infantry deployment which the English had successfully used on the defensive at Crecy. This condemned his heavily armed troops to weariness before they reached the battle. Once again the value of trained archers used to the longbow was disregarded, and the conduct of the fight from the French side shows desperate valour but little generalship. The prince's quality as a captain in the field was ahead of his time and rendered him almost unbeatable. Although we are not told the details, it is clear that he had made a serious military study of history and of the battles of comparatively recent years in Britain and in continental Europe.

Military skill allied to the highest personal courage are in themselves not enough; the human approach to the men, the right word in season, are essential too. Perhaps for the first time a royal commander on the field made two separate addresses to his army, neatly gauging the distinct psychological needs of the lords and knights on the one hand, of the archers and common

soldiers on the other. It is likely, of course, that the speeches which have come
down to us in Latin were, that to the knights spoken in French, and the other
in English. To the chivalrous knights his comrades the prince appealed, to win
the friendship of every manly fellow-soldier, making their names for ever
famous by contributing to the victory of a few over a multitude with their
accustomed valour. 'Constantly ensuing justice, as is our wont, whether we
live or die we are the Lord's. He who is steadfast unto death shall be saved and
they who suffer in a just cause, theirs is the kingdom of heaven.' To the
archers he spoke in a deeper and more personal tone: 'To me your bravery and
loyalty are known well enough, you have shown yourselves in many dangers
the undegenerate sons and kinsmen of men for whom, under my father and
my ancestors the kings of England, no task was insuperable; no rough place
impassable; no steep hill unclimbable; no strong tower unconquerable; no
army impenetrable; no enemy in arms too terrible. . . . Honour, love for your
country, and the splendid booty of the French urge you to take after your
fathers more than anything I can say. Follow the standards, obey attentively
the commands of your officers in body and spirit. So, if life with victory be
granted us we shall make lasting friendships "always of the same mind". But
if an unkind fate – perish the thought – compel us to go the way of all flesh,
your names will suffer no disgrace of an ignoble end, but these gentlemen my
companions and I as well will drink of the same cup with you.'

   As Froissart was to write, many deeds of arms were done on that field which
came not to knowledge. The battle of Poitiers, or more strictly of Maupertuis,
fought on Monday, 19 September 1356, was one of the hardest fought and
most complex of the whole war. The decisive factors, apart from the military
genius of the Black Prince, were the good ground he had chosen for defence;
his disposition of the archers behind a hedge overlooking lower ground in
front; and his arrangement of diversionary forces in reserve able to attack the
French on the flanks at crucial moments. The repeated assaults of the bodies of
French troops were thus held off and beaten piecemeal until the fourth and
last division under King John himself joined battle furiously. When sheer
weight of numbers was at last overwhelming the English, one of the prince's
staff cried out: 'Alas, we are overcome', but the prince called to him that he
lied like a coward, 'for thou canst not say we be overcome while I live'. In the
last resort the French nerve broke when they were assailed in the rear by a
small company under the Gascon Captal de Buch, who had ridden round the
flank. The fight became a rout, though the French king with magnificent
personal bravery laid about him with a battle-axe until he was overcome by
weight of numbers as his own men melted away and fled towards Poitiers.
His son Philip, a boy of 14, fought by his side.

   The Black Prince's own news letter to the mayor and citizens of London has survived to give a straightforward account of the raid into France and the events leading up to the battle, with the peace negotiations beforehand. Of the actual fight, his modest account runs: 'battle was joined two days before the feast of St Matthew and, praised be God, the enemy was defeated, the king and his son taken prisoner, a multitude of other great men captured or slain'. Upon the field, when the outcome was sure, the prince had opened his heart in giving thanks to the almighty: 'This is the work of God, not mine; we should thank Him and pray to Him with all our heart that He may give us His grace and pardon us this victory.'

CHAPTER VI

Castles in Spain

Poitiers was in some senses the turning point of the Middle Ages so far as England was concerned. The particular cause for which it was fought was to become ancient history, a dead issue, in less than a century; but the principles upon which it was fought were to underlie the creation and maintenance of the British Empire over the next six hundred years. Commanded in the field by the heir to the throne, now a mature man of 26, the victory was no accident in the sense that the success of Crecy might be regarded as accidental. At Poitiers the prince, ably advised and seconded by Sir John Chandos and supported by a brilliant body of picked knights, won by showing superior generalship. In every sense of the word this was deserved. It was not simply the reward of having learned the right answers to a set of military, strategic and tactical questions. It was won firstly by personal courage; the prince's words to Chandos at the start of the fighting were amply redeemed: 'John, go forward; you shall not see me turn my back today.' It was won by deploying his forces with a just assessment of each man's capacity. Sir James Audley the younger, of Cheshire, a knight errant of Arthurian stamp, asked to be allowed to fulfil a vow to be foremost in the fight, and got the prince's handshake and: 'James, God give you this day that grace to be the best knight of all other.' The dashing Gascon Jean de Grailly, Captal de Buch, and, like Chandos and Audley, a founder K.G., was sent to lead the risky flanking movement with a handful of men that, at the crucial moment, was to break the French nerve.

What seems astonishingly modern, in contrast to the panoply of mediaeval warfare and the chivalric personal encounters between knights who, though enemies, were members of an international caste, is the prince's subtly psychological appeal to the common soldiers. He carried on what his father had begun. Whereas Edward III, in times of peace, would stay with wealthy burghers or take a drink with London merchants, his son at war positively identified the blood royal and the knights of England with their fellows in the same cause, common soldiers of mean degree. The new national cult of a patron of all Englishmen was invoked in the word of command to the standard-bearer, Sir Walter Woodland: 'Banners advance, in the name of God and St George!' Notwithstanding this proclamation of the comradeship of all ranks, the Black Prince rigidly adhered to the highest standards demanded by the rules of war. Finding that one of the enemy dead was Sir Robert de Duras, a nephew of the Cardinal de Périgord and member of his staff, who should therefore have remained neutral, he ordered that the body be taken to the Cardinal with the contemptuous greeting: 'I salute him by this token.' Another of the Cardinal's household was captured and would have been beheaded on the spot, had not Chandos interceded.

In spite of this insistence on fair play and the rigour of the game, the prince set a splendid example of humanity after victory. Though he knew of the French king's orders to give no quarter, he attempted no reprisals after the fight was won and his men took twice as many prisoners as their own total numbers. 'The prisoners found the Englishmen and Gascons right courteous; there were many that day put to ransom and let go all only on their promise of faith and truth to return again between that and Christmas to Bordeaux with their ransoms. . . . Every man made good cheer to his prisoner.' The captured foodstuffs of the French commissariat were particularly welcome, as many of the English and Gascons had had little to eat for three days, but the prisoners got their share, and the captured king and prince, with the archbishop of Sens, 14 counts and many French knights and squires, were entertained by the prince to a sumptuous supper. The prince would not sit with his captured guests but waited personally on King John 'as humbly as he could'. He tried to cheer his prisoner, saying: 'Sir methink ye ought to rejoice, though the journey be not as ye would have had it, for this day ye have won the high renown of prowess and have passed this day in valiantness all other of your party. Sir, I say not this to mock you, for all that be on our party, that saw every man's deeds, are plainly accorded by true sentence to give you the prize and chaplet.'

The result was a dreadful blow to French pride as well as costing terrible loss of life, some 2,000 knights and men-at-arms as well as about 500 of lesser rank. The losses in killed and taken prisoner were at least a quarter of the whole force of the French. The English had not merely justified their raid into France in a purely military sense, but by the capture of King John had obtained a bargaining counter of incalculable value. It must have seemed that in such circumstances the war was as good as won outright. A mocking joke swept France, having regard to the supposed friendly neutrality of the Pope, Innocent VI, towards the French: 'The Pope is French but Jesus is English; judge which of them is stronger.' In spite of Edward III's claim to the Crown of France, his real aim was actual sovereignty over Aquitaine, freed from any allegiance to Paris. The tables had been turned and it now seemed certain that this goal could be attained. So, for the time being, it was. After four years of protracted negotiations, the Peace of Bretigny was concluded on 8 May 1360 and ratified at Calais in a definitive peace treaty on 24 October. France was to be permanently divided into two countries: while Edward III and his successors were to have an enlarged Aquitaine, Ponthieu and greater Calais in full sovereignty, he and his son released all claims over Normandy, Anjou, Maine, Brittany and Flanders.

After the battle the prince gave handsome rewards to his principal lieutenants Sir John Chandos and Sir Nele Loryng. Besides his personal congratulations he gave to Sir James Audley, severely wounded in the fulfilment of his vow, 500 marks a year. Audley shared this among his four esquires, who had accompanied him faithfully throughout the fight; the prince insisted on Audley accepting a second annuity of 600 marks. Among others who obtained pensions was William Linch who had lost an eye in the battle, and was granted £20 a year and the ferry at Saltash in Cornwall, a valuable source of revenue for a veteran with a disability. Many awards were made on the field, but as soon as possible the prince began the homeward march to Bordeaux, taking all precautions against the escape of King John, whose rescue would have thrown away most of what had been won. In fact the army reached Bordeaux in safety and the winter and early spring were spent there. Notwithstanding the expectation of a serious effort by the French to intercept the convoy, a fleet set sail in April with the king under heavy guard in one ship and the prince in another. After a voyage of twelve days Sandwich was reached on 4 May 1357. Two days were spent there to recuperate and the journey overland to Canterbury and London then took four days. The captive king and the prince both made offerings at Becket's shrine while spending a day in Canterbury.

The entry into London was the culmination of the Black Prince's triumph, but he modestly rode on a small black pony while King John bestrode a white charger. From London Bridge they passed through the streets of the city between the serried ranks of the liverymen of all the companies in their distinctive clothing. By midday they reached the palace of the Savoy, where the French king was lodged during the first part of his captivity, and was visited by Edward III and Queen Philippa at frequent intervals. Later he was taken with all his household to Windsor and with his son Philip spent his time in hawking and hunting. The other prisoners stayed in London but were put on parole and allowed to visit King John at Windsor without restrictions. A truce had been arranged in April, to last for two years, but negotiation of a definite peace proved extremely difficult. With Scotland, on the other hand, a treaty was made at Berwick in October 1357 and King David II, who had been a prisoner in England for eleven years, was set free against a promised ransom of 100,000 marks.

Just as the Black Prince had been unprepared, before the battle of Poitiers, to commit his father, so the sons of the French king would not accept the terms which Edward III wished to impose. He demanded a ransom of four million gold crowns for King John, and Aquitaine in full sovereignty. When unable to get French ratification of these proposals, he asked for still more, nothing less than the restoration of the Angevin Empire, including Normandy, Anjou, Maine and Touraine, with suzerainty over Brittany. This at last made the French negotiators see reason, and they were ready to compromise, but only after another English expedition in the winter of 1359–60. The king was accompanied by the prince and by his younger sons Lionel, John of Gaunt, and Edmund of Langley, who had now reached 17 and was ready to play his part in the war. The army of 30,000 men was able to march through northern France almost to the gates of Paris without hindrance, but an attempt to take Rheims by siege was called off after seven weeks. The king moved on in the direction of Chartres, sternly rebuffing the French negotiators who tried to get better terms. It seemed that he had returned to his old plan of demanding nothing less than the crown of France itself, when a dreadful thunderstorm with a tempest of hailstones suddenly devastated his forces. It was reported that 6,000 horses and 1,000 men were struck dead on the spot. King Edward knelt down on the ground and prayed to Our Lady of Chartres, making a vow that he would grant peace.

This campaign in France was marked by the enormous baggage train of 6,000 carts laden with tents, mills, forges for shoeing the horses, and a great deal of provisions. To enable the king and his companions to get fresh fish, a few collapsible leather boats were provided and used on any lakes or ponds by the way. Thirty falconers rode with the king and his huntsmen brought sixty couple of hounds and as many greyhounds. War itself was made a continuation of the noble life which had been led in peaceful England. The pace had not slackened during the years of truce, and the presence at the court of two kings as prisoners had served as the excuse for a great tournament at Windsor called especially in their honour, before David's return to Scotland. In 1359, some months before the expedition sailed for France, John of Gaunt's marriage to Blanche, daughter of Henry duke of Lancaster, had served as the occasion for jousting in London. Edward III with the Black Prince and several of their closest friends held the lists, but what particularly marked the occasion was the costume of the king as mayor of London, and the prince as senior sheriff.

Prince John was ten years younger than Edward of Woodstock yet he married at 19, two years before his elder brother, who was over 31 at his marriage to Joan of Kent. This very protracted bachelorhood is puzzling and almost unparalleled in the annals of mediaeval royalty. The prince was quite a normal young man and is known to have had several bastard children: a son Edward old enough to be given a pony by New Year 1349, and two others who were later knighted as Sir John Sounder and Sir Roger Clarendon. The only probable explanation of the long delay is that the prince had fallen irrevocably in love with his cousin while she was the wife of Sir Thomas Holand. Joan was about two years older than the prince and was his cousin: strictly speaking, his first cousin of the half-blood once removed. Her father, Edmund of Woodstock, earl of Kent, had been the youngest son of Edward I by his second marriage to Margaret of France. The Black Prince was the great-grandson of Edward I, descended from Edward II who was his eldest son by his first marriage to Eleanor of Castile. Because of their close relationship a papal dispensation had to be obtained for the marriage, and as a condition they agreed to found a chantry in Canterbury Cathedral. The chantry chapel was formed within the crypt of the south-eastern transept of the cathedral, in or soon after 1363.

Apart from the fact that love matches were not at all encouraged in the Middle Ages, particularly in royal circles, Joan's career as a married woman had been a very singular one. Her first marriage to Holand took place when she was only about 11 years old, and a year later she went through a ceremony of marriage with William de Montague, earl of Salisbury. In 1349, when she was 21, this second marriage was annulled and her position as the wife of Sir Thomas Holand confirmed. It is hardly surprising that Queen Philippa is reputed to have opposed her marriage to the prince after Holand's death on 28 December 1360. Evidently both parties were determined upon marriage and the king and queen were sensible enough to give way. The pair were devoted to one another and the marriage was genuinely happy. There was a formal ceremony of espousal at Lambeth on 6 October 1361 and the wedding itself was celebrated in the chapel of Windsor Castle four days later.

On 19 July 1362 Edward III invested his eldest son as prince of Aquitaine, granting to him to hold in full sovereignty the newly enlarged area handed over to him by the treaty of Bretigny. The prince was to set up his court at Bordeaux and rule the country with his own officers and an administration completely independent from English control. This was a wise and highly intelligent step to take, for all too often the heirs to the throne have had too little to occupy their time. The Black Prince, fond of his father and completely loyal to him, could safely be trusted with this great region. There may too have been some personal feeling that it would be easier for the young married couple to make their home in another country rather than have to compete with the royal splendour of Windsor and Westminster. Whatever reservations the king and queen may have had over the marriage, they accepted it with a good grace, and before the prince and princess left Berkhamstead to take ship for Gascony the whole royal family visited them at Berkhamstead Castle.

Froissart recorded a curious reminiscence regarding this visit, which was during his first year in the service of Queen Philippa at the age of 24. 'There I heard an ancient knight, Sir Bartholomew of Burghersh, devise among the ladies and said: "There is a book which is called *le Brut* and it deviseth that the prince of Wales, eldest son to the king, nor the duke of Gloucester, should never be king of England, but the realm and crown should return to the house of Lancaster." . . . I saw, and so did all the world, Richard of Bordeaux twenty-two year king of England, and after the crown returned to the house of Lancaster.' This was not the only fulfilled prophecy of the age, for before serious hostilities began in 1340 the countess of Hainault, Queen Philippa's mother, had interceded both with her brother Philip of Valois and with her son-in-law: she had heard from her kinsman King Robert of Sicily (Naples). He was a keen astrologer and had cast the horoscopes of both kings, predicting that if they fought it would be Philip who would get the worst of it.

Before leaving the prince handed over his manor of Vauxhall to the monks of Christ Church, Canterbury, to pay for the chantry chapel in the crypt of the cathedral. By October 1363, a little over a year later, chaplains were appointed and the structural work had probably been finished. The details of the little chapel – later used as the French Huguenot church in Canterbury – are very fine and the design must have been by a leading architect, presumably Henry Yeveley who was already the prince's mason. He may well have had a local collaborator such as John Box, who worked as chief mason for Christ Church priory between 1350 and 1375. Not enough of the accounts of the prince have survived to enable all his craftsmen to be identified, but he retained a number in his service, such as John Cokard his minstrel, and the London goldsmith John de Thopisfeld who was described as his yeoman. Among the gifts which he presented to his relatives and friends were gold and silverware enamelled and jewelled, altar cloths and vestments, armour and horses. In 1349 he gave the bishop of Winchester, William Edington, a tabernacle of gold silk with an enamel picture of Daniel between two lions beneath a seated figure of the Virgin and Child.

The prince and princess sailed to La Rochelle in February 1363 and were met by Sir John Chandos, lieutenant in Aquitaine and the constable, in charge of home affairs of the principality, in the administration soon formed. After visiting Niort and Poitiers the royal party arrived at Bordeaux and it was in the cathedral that the greater nobles swore fealty to their prince in July. In another ceremony held a week later he received the homage of 180 municipal officials – mayors, jurats and consuls – from the towns and cities. The English dominions had been vastly increased by the treaty and now measured some

300 miles from north to south – as much as Holland and Belgium together – by 250 from the sea to the eastern frontier beyond Rodez. To govern this the prince set up a new body of permanent officers responsible to him: Sir Thomas Felton as seneschal, in charge of finance; Chandos the constable as virtual prime minister, and John Harewell, later bishop of Bath and Wells, as chancellor presiding over the courts of law.

What struck contemporaries was the fact that the Black Prince kept his court with a magnificence that threw the majority of the kings of Europe into the shade. Every day at his table were more than 80 knights and 320 esquires. Jousts and revels were held at Bordeaux and Angoulême on the pattern of those at London and Windsor. When the king of Cyprus, Peter de Lusignan, came to Europe to promote a crusade he visited the courts of France, England, Burgundy and Flanders, but declared that he 'had done little until he had seen the prince of Wales'. He was given a tour of Aquitaine, personally conducted by Chandos, and was at Angoulême to attend the celebrations for the birth of the prince's first son Edward 'of Angoulême'.

The Black Prince in his rule over Aquitaine faced a fundamental difficulty. The great nobles, who had been only too glad to exchange the exacting rule of a king at Paris for remote control from London, were now thrown into the French camp by the prospect of strong government centred on Bordeaux. The mercantile class, on the other hand, responded to the prince's encouragement of trade, and this is reflected by the fact that Bordeaux remained English to the bitter end, in 1453. It has often been claimed by modern historians of the anti-royal school that the prince failed in Aquitaine because of his personal extravagance, but this is to apply the criteria of nineteenth-century budgets. Far more serious factors intervened to make it impossible that the settlement of Bretigny should succeed, under any government. The fact was that the influential inhabitants of the new territories had grown used to being French for some two centuries, and resented willy-nilly transfer from one power to another. What was decisive was the combination of growing national sentiment among the French generally, and the coincidence of determined efforts by Paris to undermine the peace once the Black Prince had become a sick man.

Another very serious problem was posed by the free companies. The Peace of Bretigny for the time being put great bodies of soldiers out of work and out of prospect of booty. Ready to serve as mercenaries, they at first found no paymasters who would employ them, and roamed the country looting and burning. It was the great success of the prince that he rapidly put down the companies within Aquitaine and refused to tolerate such behaviour, even by English troops who in former times had served him well. The effect of his stern rule in the English-held lands was to drive the freebooters into French France, with consequent exacerbation of the residual difficulties left by the peace. The ransom for King John had not been raised, and it was evident that the interim government in Paris hoped to avoid payment and meant to procrastinate. Under pressure two-thirds of the first instalment, 400,000 crowns, was raised, and Edward III generously allowed his royal captive to depart when this was paid. Among the hostages who stayed in London was his second son Louis, who having been allowed to visit Boulogne on parole, met his young wife there and broke his word. His father, stricken in his tenderest spot, returned to England, giving himself up on 4 January 1364 with the memorable remark: 'If good faith were banished from the rest of the earth, it should still be found in the hearts and mouths of kings.' Three months later, on 8 April, he died in the Savoy, aged only 45.

The new king of France, Charles V, was a very different man from his father. He had never intended to be bound by the peace, and was prepared to take advantage of any pretext to overthrow it and the English power in France. Well served by the brilliant Breton soldier Bertrand du Guesclin, Charles was able in his reign of sixteen years to undo almost the whole of the fantastic English successes of the two previous reigns. He was well styled 'the Wise' in that his policy was one of playing a quiet waiting game, letting the other side make mistakes, and refusing to be drawn. In this he was, of course, the complete antithesis of the Plantagenet temperament so well exemplified by Edward III and the prince. Although captured by Chandos at Auray on 29 September 1364, Du Guesclin was able to survive the downfall and death of his patron, Charles of Blois the French claimant to Brittany, and after being ransomed joined the service of King Charles. He got rid of the companies from French soil by leading them to Spain – Frenchmen and Englishmen alike – to fight for the bastard Henry of Trastamara against Don Pedro. It was this successful rebellion by Henry in Castile that was to provide an opportunity for the Black Prince's last, and perhaps greatest campaign.

We have again to remind ourselves that geographical Spain during the Middle Ages was divided into several separate kingdoms, independent and often at war with one another. In the north and centre was Castile, by now stretching down to the south coast at Algeciras, between Portugal on the west and Aragon on the east. In the north, straddling the Pyrenees some way into geographical France, was Navarre. Though a small kingdom in itself Navarre was important for two reasons: it held the only practicable pass from western France into Spain, at Roncesvalles; and dynastically its sovereigns held many substantial feofs in France, some of them of great strategic importance. Navarre tended to be in alliance with England, just as Scotland aided and abetted France. For some years after the treaty of Bretigny the attitude of Navarre was crucial, since there were considerable Navarrese armies stationed in France to defend the holdings of the king, Charles II 'the Bad', including the counties of Evreux in Normandy and Brie east of Paris, as well as Cherbourg and other channel ports handed over by John II in 1354 to compensate the king of Navarre for the province of Angoumois.

The state of affairs in Castile was unusual, largely because of the highly idiosyncratic temperament of the king Don Pedro, commonly called 'Peter the Cruel' but by sounder historians the 'Justiciar' from his strict putting down of crime throughout his wide realms. His father Alfonso XI had set an example in this respect and managed to repress the unruly nobles, but laid up a store of trouble for Castile by his private life. He neglected his queen Maria of Portugal and showed great favour to the eldest of his illegitimate children by his mistress Leonora de Guzmán, Henry, whom he created count of Trastamara. Alfonso's eldest legitimate son, Pedro, was some months younger than Henry, who felt bitterly aggrieved by Pedro's succession in 1350 and by the resulting murder of his mother Leonora to satisfy the injured pride of Pedro's mother, Queen Maria. For some years he lived a precarious life in Castile, but fled to France in 1356 and spent the next ten years there. It seems all but certain that the campaign of the companies under Du Guesclin, which in 1366 put Henry on the throne, was part of a brilliant French strategy designed by Charles V to take the English in the rear. Not only did the expedition get the freebooting mercenaries out of France, its success smashed the alliance of 1362 between Castile and England. Furthermore, the preponderant political weight of Castile in the Peninsula would also restrain Charles's Navarrese enemies.

It came as no surprise to the Black Prince that Don Pedro, forced out of his own country by this usurpation with foreign backing, should seek his aid. He must, indeed, already have been made most uneasy by the coalition of many great English soldiers of fortune, along with the free companies of archers and spearmen under their command, with the French inspired invasion of Castile under Du Guesclin. Still more, he must have felt some personal responsibility for Du Guesclin's English colleague Sir Hugh Calveley, not only a Cheshire warrior from his own county, but one of the heroic survivors from the romantic Battle of the Thirty fought in Brittany in 1350. Calveley's assistance to Henry of Trastamara was in direct disobedience to Edward III's orders that every precaution must be taken to maintain the alliance with Castile which was, by mediaeval custom, in the strictest sense an alliance with its king, Don Pedro.

While King Pedro was still in Spain he received messages from the Black Prince promising support and offering asylum in Aquitaine. Taking ship from Corunna and touching at San Sebastian, Pedro reached Bayonne on 1 August 1366 and soon left for Bordeaux. The prince came out to meet his guest and insisted on giving the king due precedence as to a reigning monarch. He was lodged, alongside the prince's own household, in the great abbey of St-André.

There was considerable opposition in the prince's council to his espousal of Pedro's cause, for agents of Henry of Trastamara had been busy spreading slanders across Europe. The prince, however, took his stand on principle and disregarded arguments founded on estimates of the private characters of the two contestants. He very plainly told his officers and advisers: 'It is not convenable that a bastard should hold a realm in heritage and put out of his own realm his brother, rightful inheritor to the land; the which thing all kings and kings' sons should in no wise suffer nor consent to, for it is a great prejudice against the state royal.' He also pointed out that his father, Edward III, was already in close alliance with King Pedro and that he was thus in duty as well as in honour bound to succour him.

With astonishing speed when we consider the delays of any diplomacy, a tripartite treaty was sealed at Libourne on 23 September, between Don Pedro, the Black Prince, and King Charles II of Navarre. The prince had already managed to get his father's answer approving of his commitment and, to avoid diplomatic repercussions with France, that it should be not in the name of England but of Aquitaine. John of Gaunt, by this time duke of Lancaster in right of his wife, was being sent out with a large force in support, and it was made clear that in all but name this was a venture in which England was fully engaged. Another prophecy of Merlin from the *Brut* was being quoted, that 'The Leopards and their company shall spread themselves to Spain'. The treaty stipulated for important territorial and other concessions to Navarre and to the prince. The king of Navarre, who claimed the restoration of the ancient Basque territories which had long ago been taken from his ancestors by Castile, was to get the whole of the provinces of Guipúzcoa, giving access to the sea at San Sebastian, and Álava, as well as a whole range of strategic fortresses along the west bank of the Ebro: Haro, Logroño, Calahorra, Alfaro and others. The Black Prince was to have the province of Biscay (Vizcaya) with the important ports and shipbuilding arsenals of Bermeo, Bilbao and Castro Urdiales. Important trading privileges for the English and Gascons were added and all English pilgrims and travellers to Castile were to be altogether free from tax. To show his gratitude to Edward III, Pedro undertook that he and his heirs should always have the right to lead the van of the armies of Castile and that even when absent their standard of England should be borne alongside that of Castile.

Charles of Navarre, in addition to opening the passes for the grand army to enter Spain, would provide an allied contingent to be paid for by the Black Prince at the rate of 36,000 florins a month. Don Pedro gave his promise to repay this and all other costs out of his revenues when Castile had been recovered, and left his daughters at Bordeaux as hostages for his observance of all undertakings. Apart from the official terms of the treaty there is some evidence that Pedro also gave the prince the kingdom of Galicia, either for himself or for his son Edward of Angoulême. He had, most appropriately, made the prince a magnificent gift of a gold and jewelled Round Table on his arrival, but it is not clear whether he had brought it with him among his valuable collection of jewels, on his flight from Corunna. Organization of the expedition was placed in the capable hands of Sir John Chandos, and he was personally rewarded by King Pedro with a grant of the lordship of Soria when it should be recovered. In the meantime, money for equipping the troops ran short, and the prince had his own household plate melted down, sufficient to provide for all that was needed and to pay the army for months ahead.

Just before the expedition was ready to move, a second son was born to the Black Prince, Richard of Bordeaux, on the feast of the Epiphany, 6 January 1367. On 8 January he was baptized in the cathedral, his godfathers being the titular king of Majorca, James III, and the bishop of Agen. Froissart was in Bordeaux at the time and later set down: 'I was in the city of Bordeaux and at the table when king Richard was born, about ten of the clock. The same time there came thereas I was, Sir Richard Pontchardon, marshal as then of Aquitaine, and he said to me: "Froissart, write and put in memory that as now my lady princess is brought abed with a fair son on this Twelfth day, that is the day of the three kings, and he shall be a king. He is son of a king, for his father is king of Galicia. King don Peter hath given him that kingdom and he goes to conquer it." This gentle knight said truth, for he was king of England twenty-two year; but when this knight said these words, he knew full little what should be his conclusion.' At the time Richard's elder brother Edward was alive and would in the normal course have succeeded to his father, as he to Edward III. Whatever we may think of Pontchardon's prophecy, it was in any case remarkable that, on the feast of the Three Kings, there should have been three kings in Bordeaux at the time of Richard's birth: Don Pedro of Castile, Charles II of Navarre, and James III of Majorca, even though he and Pedro had lost their kingdoms.

A week later the prince went to Dax to meet his brother John, effecting a junction of all the contingents of the army. On St Valentine's day, 14 February, the great body of 30,000 men left the town of San Juan del Pie del Puerto, 'St John at the foot of the pass', and began the long climb of nearly 20 miles to the summit, about 3,500 feet above sea-level. By Tuesday 23 February the whole army was through the passes and had bivouacked near Pamplona. This completely successful crossing of the Pyrenees at the worst time of year was an amazing feat and fully justifies the Black Prince's reputation as a great commander and not merely a chivalrous knight errant. Credit must also be given to Chandos, his chief of staff, for organizing the details of one of the outstanding operations of history.

While the army marched south-westwards towards Castile, envoys arrived from the usurper Henry. He sent a letter of protest at the prince's intermeddling in Spanish affairs, to which the prince replied, urging Henry to see the error of his usurpation: 'You ought to understand in your heart that it is not right that a bastard should be King; nor should men agree to the disinheriting of a rightful heir who is of lawful wedlock.' He offered to act as mediator if Henry were to restore what he had taken, and secure his pardon from Pedro. Henry was not to be deflected from his career, even by the warnings sent him by King Charles V of France, and given by Du Guesclin, who begged him to remember 'the great army that the Prince brings. For truth there is the flower of chivalry, there is the flower of bachelry: these are the best men-at-arms in the world alive.' Besides, even with the French auxiliaries brought by Du Guesclin and a number of Aragonese, Henry's force was much smaller than the prince's army. He had moved south across the Ebro to block the main road into Castile at the little town of Nájera, where the great east-west pilgrimage road to Compostela crossed the river Najerilla, a southern tributary of the Ebro. There he deliberately chose to fight with his back to the river, reckoning that he had the advantage of the prince, who would have to advance in a narrow column along the road to make a frontal attack.

The prince naturally did nothing of the sort. He turned off the road north-wards several miles short of Henry's position and appeared from behind a hill just as dawn was breaking on Saturday 3 April 1367. Although his experiences at Crecy and at Poitiers had been of defensive battle against overwhelming superior forces, the prince was here equally successful in attack. Once again the firing power of the English archers, stationed on the flanks, broke the cohesion and the morale of the enemy. By noon they were in full flight; many were drowned in the Najerilla, coming down in spate; others were caught later trying to conceal themselves in the town of Nájera. The prince, in a letter to his wife, put the enemy dead at between 5,000 and 6,000 and said that 2,000 prisoners worthy of ransom had been captured. The losses on his side were four knights, only one English, with two Gascons and a German; with 40 men-at-arms and about 20 archers. The disparity between the losses on the two sides proves his consummate generalship as well as the unbeatable tactics which the English had been perfecting for the last thirty years and more.

The battle of Nájera and its aftermath were notable for several personal actions. Shortly before the battle was joined, just at sunrise, the veteran Chandos came to the prince who was riding with Don Pedro, and asked to be made a banneret, that is to display a square banner instead of the pointed pennon of a simple knight. He produced a banner of his arms rolled up: 'Then the prince and king don Peter took the banner between their hands and spread it abroad, the which was of silver a sharp pile gules, and delivered it to him and said: "Sir John, behold here your banner. God send you joy and honour thereof."' Chandos returned with the banner to his company and gave it to his esquire William Alery, who bore it through the day. Later on Chandos was himself felled to the ground by a giant Castilian, Martin Ferrant, famed for his prowess. Chandos managed to save himself with his dagger in single combat before his men could come to his aid. After the fight was won Don Pedro came to the prince and would have knelt down to thank him, 'but the prince made great haste to take him by the hand, and would not suffer him to kneel. Then the king said: "Dear and fair cousin, I ought to give you many thanks and praises for this fair journey that I have attained this day by your means." Then the prince said: "Sir, yield thanks to God and give him all the praise, for the victory hath come by him all only and not by me."'

CHAPTER VII

Downhill

There is a strange, perhaps intentional, irony in the Black Prince's recommendation to Don Pedro to give thanks to God alone for the victory of Nájera. Consciously or unconsciously he was paraphrasing the Arabic commonplace: 'The praise be to God' and the motto of Pedro's feudatories, the sultans of Granada: 'God alone is Conqueror.' Few non-Muslims can have known as well as Don Pedro these classical propitiations of the almighty, for he was notorious for his arabizing tendencies and for the magnificent palace at Seville that he had had built and decorated by Moorish craftsmen within the previous three years. It was indeed Pedro's complete tolerance of and friendship for both Muslims and Jews that were largely responsible for the intensity of the opposition that Henry of Trastamara had been able to foment against him. Pedro had set himself to return to the policy of his predecessors Alfonso VI and Alfonso VII as a 'king of the three religions' and in the audience which he granted to Ibn Khaldun in 1362 had offered to take the famous Tunisian into his service and give him all the great estates in Seville lost by his ancestors at the Christian reconquest of 1248.

The day after the battle Pedro demanded that the prince should surrender to him the lives of the Spanish traitors who had been captured. With the exception of the bastard Henry himself, the prisoners comprised almost all the leading opponents of the legitimate king, and it was natural that he should seek to put it out of their power to rebel again. The Black Prince, who was both chivalrous and statesmanlike, persuaded him to take a more humane course of action: 'I counsel you for good, if you wish to be king of Castile, that you send tidings everywhere that you have bestowed pardon on all who have been against you; and that if through ill will or by evil counsel they have been with king Henry, you pardon them, provided that of their own accord they come to pray you mercy.' He also reasonably pointed out that the allied captors had a very large financial stake in the ransoms which the traitors must pay. After consideration, Don Pedro agreed to pardon everyone except his arch-enemy Gómez Carrillo, who was forthwith put to death. Another of Pedro's bastard half-brothers, Don Sancho, already in his power, was allowed to live, which argues in favour of the view that the king's cruelty had been greatly exaggerated by Trastamaran propaganda, as he claimed.

This was an occasion when clemency did not pay, and no sooner were the captives freed than they once more joined Henry in his second and successful revolt. It is tragic that Pedro's defeat and murder in 1369 were due directly to his having allowed the prince's persuasions to outweigh his own estimate of the irredeemable treachery of these men. Yet we cannot regret the noble effort of the Black Prince to heal the wounds of Castile by moderation and forbearance. His chivalry added to his superbly successful campaign set him at the very peak of his renown. Not Englishmen alone but Germans and Flemings acclaimed him, saying that 'such a prince was well worthy to govern all the world'. This third personal victory, 21 years after Crecy and 11 after Poitiers, showed that his hand had not lost its cunning and that there was nothing merely accidental about his genius. The masterstroke which filled the cup of good fortune to the brim was the capture of Du Guesclin by Chandos.

The apogee of the Black Prince's career was reached at Burgos, where the allied armies kept Easter and all Spain rendered homage to Don Pedro. This extraordinary and rapid change of fortune, as everyone knew, was due to the prince alone. Housed in the royal nunnery of Las Huelgas, two miles beyond Burgos, the Black Prince was master of the situation and was able to send to his father in England a full account of the battle and, as a trophy, the usurper Henry's captured charger. It seemed for the moment that all was well, but within a few weeks confidence had been replaced by uncertainty. The restored king was unable to repay the enormous sums he owed to his allies, and seemed to be ever more reluctant to hand over to them the provinces guaranteed at Libourne. Even the grants to individual commanders, of Soria to Chandos and of Carrión to Calveley, were not made effective. The difficulties were not due to bad faith by Don Pedro, who did raise taxes and loans to pay his debt, but to the unavoidable delays. Clearly, too, there were serious local objections to the transfer of the Basque provinces to Navarre and to the Black Prince. In the course of the summer matters became ever worse and worse, and the prince was forced to consider even a drastic realignment leading towards the forcible partition of Castile.

Don Pedro had gone south to Seville to raise money, leaving the prince and his other allies at Valladolid, and there they spent the summer. The army grew restive and 'the heat and the infective air of the country of Spain', as Froissart put it, took their toll. The king of Majorca became very seriously ill, and it seems that it was about the same time, the end of June, that the Black Prince picked up the disease which was to render him an invalid and to kill him after a very painful illness of nine years. The hero of his age, repeatedly proved invincible by man, was overcome by an invisible micro-organism – from the symptoms very likely the dysenteric amoeba. Among the English and Gascon troops there were many deaths of disease during that long hot summer, and eventually the only course of action was to withdraw from Spain altogether. Before the end of August the prince had crossed the Pyrenees and early in September was back in Bordeaux. An ill man, but not incapacitated, he was met outside the city by the princess Joan who came out with her little son Edward, now three years old. 'Very sweetly they embraced: the gentle prince kissed his wife and son. They went to their lodging on foot, holding each other by the hand.'

The prince was just turned 37 and, even by mediaeval expectations of life, might well have lived as long again. In fact, nothing was to go right for him. It was not his debilitating illness alone: finance, political pressures, a wretched crop of failure and death for him and his had still to be reaped. The army had to be paid, and to do this there was no alternative to fresh taxation in Aquitaine. The assembly of the three estates at Angoulême in January 1368 voted a hearth-tax of ten sous for five years, which has been described as the most unfortunate act of the prince's administration; but he had no choice. The revolt of some of the Gascon barons, led by the count of Armagnac, though using the tax as a pretext, had no justification and was procured by King Charles of France. Charles went even further: completely ignoring the fact that Aquitaine by the treaty of Bretigny no longer owed fealty to France, he impudently cited the Black Prince to appear at Paris to answer complaints made against him. The prince replied that he would go with his helmet on his head and with 60,000 men, but soon afterwards became so ill that he could no longer ride a horse. The spies of the French king reported the prince's symptoms which were put before the leading Parisian physicians and surgeons, who gave as their opinion – all too correct – that the prince would never recover.

Another grave misfortune resulted from the release of Du Guesclin, who played upon the prince's chivalry by saying that he dared not set him free. The prince replied that he set his ransom at 100,000 francs and, although his council protested, gave this most dangerous enemy his liberty once the sum was paid. Du Guesclin rejoined Henry of Trastamara and was the principal instrument of Henry's success. Pedro's troops were defeated at Montiel and some days later the king was induced to visit Du Guesclin's tent, where he was murdered by his bastard brother on 23 March 1369. The foul deed has echoed and re-echoed from that day downwards, but has never been better remembered than by Chaucer:

O noble, o worthy Petro, glory of Spain
Whom fortune held so high in majesty,
Well oughten men thy piteous death complain!
Out of thy land thy brother made thee flee;
And after, at a siege, by subtilty
Thou wert betrayed and led unto his tent,
Whereas he with his own hand slew thee,
Succeeding in thy reign and in thy rent.

In less than two years the tables were turned and the whole object of the prince's last great expedition defeated. The crushing burden of debt had been incurred for nothing. For a time Chandos was successful against the French in the north of Gascony, but Sir Simon Burley was defeated at Lusignan and later on taken prisoner. The Black Prince was greatly distressed by this capture, since Burley was not only one of his closest friends, but one of the few outstanding and courageous leaders able to take the field while he was tied to his bed. On 21 May Charles V declared war on England and in June Edward III replied by resuming the title of King of France. Still worse was in store: on 14 August died his beloved queen Philippa. The king was in tears at her bedside when she put her hand in his, reminded him of their happy life together, and asked him to grant her three wishes: that he would pay all her debts, fulfil her legacies, and be buried beside her at Westminster. A week or so later Sir James Audley died in Gascony; so did Sir Bartholomew de Burghersh; and, worst of all, Sir John Chandos was fatally wounded near Lussac on 31 December and died the next day.

There was only one minor English success in 1369, the capture of the dowager duchess of Bourbon, who was exchanged for Sir Simon Burley, though such warring on women caused the prince serious qualms of conscience. The times were out of joint with a vengeance: the third of the great plagues was raging and claimed as a victim his charming sister-in-law Blanche of Lancaster, John of Gaunt's wife. Froissart, who had known her well at the English court, regarded her, next after the queen, as his patroness, 'who died fair and young at about the age of 22 years; gay and glad she was, fresh and sportive; sweet, simple and of humble semblance, the fair lady whom men called Blanche'. French successes in the war and treachery and defection had become the norm of existence by the summer of 1370. The treason of the bishop of Limoges was the last straw, and in spite of his completely unfit condition the prince took the field effectively for the last time. We already know the terrible and controversial nature of his final victory.

Still fate did not spare him any misery: just after New Year 1371 his elder son Edward of Angoulême died, and he was too distressed to remain for the boy's funeral. He embarked for England and before the end of the month had reached Southampton, whence he slowly moved on to Windsor and to his own home at Berkhamstead Castle, suffering fits of intense pain and at times fainting. He could no longer joust or indulge in any of the manly amusements he had so much enjoyed. One of his few consolations in leaving Aquitaine was that his favourite brother John of Gaunt could take over there as his efficient lieutenant. Even this was taken away for, neither money nor aid reaching Bordeaux from England, John resigned in July. In September Gaunt married Constance of Castile, Don Pedro's daughter, and through her claimed the throne of Castile. Another bizarre episode of Anglo-Spanish relations was launched.

The next year, 1372, saw no improvement. On 13 January Sir Walter Manny died in London. The French were sweeping forward on a wide front and took Saintes, La Rochelle, and Poitiers, along with other towns. Thouars had to undertake to surrender if no relief had arrived by 30 September, and this spurred the king and his eldest son to one more effort. The prince swore that he would go with his father even if he were to die on the voyage, but after sailing at the end of August dreadful storms prevented the fleet from rounding Ushant and the expedition had to return to England after five weeks at sea to no purpose. For all this time the prince was on board, very seriously ill. As no succour came, Thouars had to surrender. Humiliated by his failure to help the principality and seeing that it was impossible for him to make Aquitaine pay its way, the prince surrendered it back to his father. The prince of Wales had also been prince of Aquitaine for just over ten years.

Edward III was 60, but had rapidly aged after Queen Philippa's death. Though not suffering from any specific disease he was becoming senile before his time. The end of the reign forms the saddest of contrasts with its beginning. For years nothing had gone right; his son incurably ill, there can have been nothing to look forward to; Philippa, his good angel, was gone. The conquests in France which had cost so many lives, so much gold and effort, were shrivelling away and at any moment might be altogether gone. We can see that the unbelievable strangeness of this reversal of fortune must have been one of the most insidious aspects of the attack on the ageing king's health. Nor was even this enough: the three plagues and the crisis of inflation into which they had landed the country produced symptoms of the class war which, under his grandson in 1381 was to burst out in the Peasants' Revolt. There was, too, a major crisis brewing up in the relations between church and state. The francophil pope, Gregory XI, was interfering more and more in English clerical affairs and received considerable support from many of the clergy. The last years of the Black Prince's life were made miserable by the attempts to involve him in the sordid political schemes and corruption in progress.

Ostensibly he was placed in opposition to his father and to his brother John of Gaunt, but it is by no means certain that any such political animus existed within the royal family at the time. It was, all the same, the fact that while Gaunt was intensely unpopular, the Black Prince remained a national hero.

Negotiations with France started again and John of Gaunt secured a truce at Bruges to run for a year from 27 June 1375. The terms were most unfavourable and in effect left the English with little more than Calais and the coastal strip from Bordeaux to Bayonne. The erosion of influence and territory since the prince's return from Spain was almost unbelievable. The Spaniards under Henry of Trastamara were themselves successful against the English, winning fights at sea and taking important prisoners. Only the treaty of Windsor made with Portugal in 1373 offered some chance of a Peninsular foothold which might in course of time enable John of Gaunt to win the throne. This was a mere gambit, and nobody foresaw that this alliance was to be the longest lived in English history, lasting for more than six hundred years.

The so-called 'Good Parliament' met on 28 April 1376, and was involved both in attacks upon the king's administration and upon the rich mercantile interests in the City of London. The most notoriously corrupt of these Londoners, Richard Lyons, was a Fleming by origin and in 1381 was murdered along with other Flemings unpopular with the mob. Lyons had tried to get support from the dying prince with a bribe of £1,000, but it was indignantly declined. Out of the confused proceedings all that seems clear is that the prince's main support came from the wise bishop of Winchester and former chancellor, William of Wykeham. Personages around the court were taking advantage of the old king's senility and were feathering their own nests, chief among them perhaps Alice Perrers, one of the late queen's ladies. In spite of insistent rumour it is far from certain that she was the king's mistress, but she certainly had an eye to the main chance. As long as the prince lived it was impossible for these hangers-on to get things all their own way.

The prince was dying, possibly hastened to the grave by the perpetual quarrelling and bickering of the palace – for he had come to Westminster to his own apartments within the royal precinct and not far from his father. This was probably to be within reach of the best doctors in the country who were available there. Their skill, such as it was, could do little for him, though it may well have prolonged his life beyond what might have been expected. When it was clear that he could not survive more than a day or so, he made his will (see Appendix) on Saturday 7 June 1376. Like so many mediaeval men he worried lest his wishes might not be fulfilled and called in his son Richard, not yet ten, and 'commanded him upon pain of his curse, he should never change or take away gifts that he at his death gave unto his servants'. True to the symbolic pattern of his life, he was to die on Trinity Sunday, at 3 o'clock in the afternoon.

The Prince was most anxious to take leave of all his servants and of every one of his friends and acquaintance, and gave stringent commands that his door should be shut to none, 'not to the least boy'. He made one single exception: he was not ready to forgive Sir Richard Stury, who had been his irreconcilable enemy in Parliament, and whom he regarded as a traitor. To Stury he said: 'I would not suffer thy excuses in the evil counsel thou oft suggested to the King, unpunished, and truly so it would have chanced if God had granted me life, and thou would have found that to have been true, evil counsel is the worst councillor.' The bishop of Bangor, his confessor, was horrified at this outburst by a dying man and besought him to ask forgiveness of God and of all men whom of set purpose he had offended. The prince twice answered only: 'I will'; but after the bishop had asperged the room with holy water to drive out the evil spirit which he believed was impeding repentance, the prince's manner changed and he clasped his hands and said: 'I give thanks, O God, for all thy benefits and with all the pains of my soul I humbly beseech Thy mercy to give me remission of all those sins which I have wickedly committed against Thee; and of all mortal men whom willingly or ignorantly I have offended, with all my heart I desire forgiveness.'

So died Edward of Woodstock, the Black Prince, after nine years of painful and wasting illness which, several years before his end, had so weakened him that his own servants often thought that he was dead. 'Notwithstanding, he bore all those things with such patience that he never seemed to offer unto God one mutinous word.' In this long and hopeless battle with death, unaided by any of the successes which had borne him up during the earlier years of his worldly combats, he displayed the same fundamental quality of courage. It was this that so impressed the herald of his old friend and companion Sir John Chandos that, in concluding his life of the prince in French verse he wrote:

et ci fyn lui ditz
Du tresnoble Prince Edward
Qui navoit unqes coer de Coward

'here ends the lay of the most noble Prince Edward, who had never a coward's heart'.

Edward of Woodstock was undoubtedly a truly brave man, not merely on the field where many thousands, of high or low degree, have conquered fear; but through the hours, days and years of the sheer tediousness of humiliating sickness and weakness, of inability to do the things which so obviously needed to be done. Accustomed to success and to a smoothed path from the cradle, so worthily rocked by Maud Plumpton; through gilded youth and learning,

from the two Walters, the wise Burley and the valiant Manny; he had spent
twenty-one years of adult life, from 16 at Crecy to 37 at Nájera, in winning
battle after battle, skirmish after skirmish. Nothing in those thirty-seven
seasons could have led him to suppose that the full span of his life would not
be equally successful, spent on top of the wave until, perhaps, he fell in hand-
to-hand combat leading his men. The strange reverses and overturnings of the
Wheel of Fortune were a commonplace of the Middle Ages. No well-educated
man, least of all a member of the English royal family at home in palaces and
castles whose walls were decorated with the famous Wheel, could fail to have
in mind the thought of mutability and the falls from high fortune of men and
princes. Yet it was common for such a downfall to be sudden: great kings were
murdered, like Alexander or Don Pedro of Castile. A few were imprisoned,
but seldom for long before they too were murdered, like the prince's grandfather Edward II. It was rare and strange for a man with his activity and bold
spirit to be reduced for years on end to a state of bedridden invalidism. If any
man ever did, Edward of Woodstock deserved the epithet of bravest of the
brave.

He had towered, spiritually by head and shoulders, over the outstanding
men of his time, even above his remarkable father, Edward III. The unanimity
of acclaim from his contemporaries is amazing. Most public figures remain
enigmatic and are seen in very different lights by friend and foe, and by
objective outsiders. In his own time the Black Prince seems never to have met
with detractors or slanderers. He was never, like Don Pedro, the victim of
adverse propaganda, whether well or ill founded. Even his bitterest enemies
acknowledged his nobility and superb fair play, and regarded his Court in
Aquitaine as a high-water mark of chivalry. It would have been unthinkable,
given the opportunity, not to send a boy of good breeding to Bordeaux to
seize the chance of viewing the fountainhead of civilized manners. In his
personal contacts with men of all stations he displayed not just a surface charm
but a real kindness, a courtesy that came from the heart. He won men by sheer
personality, and he never lost a friend except – and that all too often – by death.

Looking back from the sober standpoint of the twentieth century, the life
of the Black Prince in the fourteenth seems to be a fairy tale. In a sense that is
exactly what it was: from earliest youth he had been brought up on the values
expressed in the great romances of the Arthurian Cycle. We can appreciate
this best from the version which has come down to us as a living work of
literature, the *Morte Darthur* of Sir Thomas Malory. Although in Malory's
and Caxton's version the words we read come to us from a hundred years later
than the prince's death, their lessons are precisely those which the young
Edward imbibed in his childhood and youth. For him, as for his immediate
ancestors and for most of the men who were to be his constant companions

through life, the Arthurian Oath was a living reality that governed behaviour more strictly than any precept in the Bible, but in the same way that medical men still are ruled by the etiquette of the Hippocratic Oath.

> The king stablished all his knights, and them that were of lands not rich he gave them lands, and charged them never to do outrage nor murder, and always to flee treason. Also, by no mean to be cruel, but to give mercy unto him that asketh mercy, upon pain of forfeiture of their worship and lordship of king Arthur for evermore; and always to do ladies, damsels and gentlewomen succour upon pain of death. Also, that no man take no battles in a wrongful quarrel for no law, nor for world's goods. Unto this were all the knights sworn of the Table Round, both old and young.

Malory thus put the commandments of chivalry into splendid English of the late fifteenth century, but he did not invent them. As far as human imperfection permitted they had been actively pursued between the reigns of Henry II and Richard II. Edward I, told by his judges that he might show mercy to a criminal, exclaimed: '*May* show mercy! why, I will do that for a dog, if he seeks my grace!' Those who failed to find mercy were usually those too proud, or too determined on their evil courses, to seek it. Obduracy in a bad cause, and the evident lack of repentance or regret on the part of the guilty, were indeed passports to sudden death or to condign punishment in accordance with the rigour of the law. On the other hand, enemies who fought bravely by the rules and bore themselves nobly, were very rarely slain in cold blood. Once the battle was over, courtesy and good cheer were the order of the day. Even traitors such as the Castilians who had supported Henry in his rebellion against Pedro were, in the eyes of the Black Prince and of the best knights of his time, worthy of pardon in principle. It is sad to know that this clemency after Nájera was ill rewarded by almost all of the prisoners again taking up arms against their lawful king before the year was out.

We have seen that the Arthurian attitude to women was adopted in real life by the prince and his knights. Holand, the princess Joan's first husband, risked his own life to save ladies and damsels at the siege of Caen; Chandos guarded the two daughters of the lord of Poix and saw them safe to Corbie, 30 miles away beyond Amiens. The avoidance of treason was the over-ruling principle in the prince's mind when, contrary to his own economic interests, he decided to give the fullest support to Don Pedro. Treason was the abandonment of a lawful and legitimate superior, especially a sovereign. The prince's readiness to aid the king of Castile against treachery cost him his life, not in the short term in the heat of battle, but in the terrible, slow fight against the disease which struck him down in the unfamiliar air of a Spanish summer. He was, no less than his grandfather Edward II or his son Richard, a royal martyr in the cause of sovereignty and legitimate rule. Unlike them, he was a sacrifice to the cause of another, not his own.

Counting the cost, whether financial or other, was utterly foreign to the prince's character. He was not and could never be a calculating machine. Like the fabled Arthur, to those not rich he gave lands or some other adequate support. To those already able to maintain themselves he gave horses, noble chargers and destriers fit for knightly combat. To the clergy and to members of his family he gave splendid articles of plate and works of art. While courage, not only physical but moral, was the keystone of his personality, it was his generous largesse that provided one of its main supports. The other was his spirit of adventure, his readiness to undertake any deed however desperate. In this he had been well taught by his elders in youth. Once, in later years, when Sir John Chandos counselled prudence in action, he cried: 'Chandos, Chandos! I've seen the time that you would have given me other advice, whether the cause was right or wrong.'

What is remarkable in such a man, devoted to daring deeds rather than to caution or calculation, is that he should have been one of the few commanders of the whole mediaeval period to show a clear appreciation of the organizational needs of warfare. His masterpiece, the crossing of the Pyrenees in 1367, worthily stands beside Hannibal's passage of the Alps in military history. The capture of Limoges in 1370 after its treacherous defection was due to his brilliant use of the corps of engineers he kept with him. Their patient and skilful work lasted a month and yielded the desired result. It is possible that the prince's master mason and chief architect, Henry Yeveley, had a hand in this, for he had been concerned with the army which crossed to France in 1359, and in 1369 and 1370 was impressing masons for overseas service. Much later Yeveley was to be a pioneer in the design of defences to be used with guns rather than bows. It was, however, the prince himself who must take the lion's share of the credit at Limoges, in that his great lieutenant Chandos was dead and it is specifically recorded that he personally directed the work of the miners and sappers.

Few men in history have been more sincerely mourned than the Black Prince. Even his crafty enemy King Charles of France did honour to him 'because of lineage' according to Froissart, for though enemies they were of course also relatives. At any rate, mass was reverently said for him in the Sainte Chapelle 'and there were many of the prelates and nobles of the realm of France'. His state funeral had to wait until the autumn so that it might be more honourably accomplished after the assembling of Parliament. On the feast of Michaelmas, 29 September, the hearse drawn by twelve black horses left Westminster Palace, followed by the whole Court and the members of both Houses. Along the Strand, through the City, over London Bridge and for sixty miles through Kent the sad procession moved to Canterbury. All that such pomp may do to soften anguish or to allay a sense of guilt was accomplished. But in the meantime the most poignant tribute to the Black Prince had been paid elsewhere. His noble Gascon subject and companion in arms, Jean de Grailly, the Captal de Buch, a prisoner in the Paris Temple since 1372, had steadfastly refused his freedom, for he would never swear not to bear arms on behalf of the king of England against France. He was resolved to spend his life in gaol rather than be untrue to his personal allegiance. When he heard of the prince's death his spirit was at last broken. He refused food, and within a few days was dead.

CHAPTER VIII

The Young King

The Black Prince was dead, but his spirit was to haunt England for another quarter-century. His amazing personality, the epitome of an era of romantic chivalry with roots going back far beyond his own age, overshadowed the activities of lesser men. Now that he had left the scene it is not surprising that the careers of his own surviving brothers should have taken on a new prominence. For the next 23 years, until 1399, John of Gaunt was to remain the elder statesman of the royal family, as was the Black Prince's friend Wykeham among the clergy. Wykeham, who did not die until 1404 at the age of 80, was in his early fifties. Though this was old by the standards of the time it was in his case the prime of life. Gaunt, born 16 years later, was still young enough to be filled with great ambitions, to become king of Castile and a dominant figure in European politics. He dreamed of succeeding where both his father and his brother had ultimately failed. Lionel of Clarence had died in 1368, leaving an heiress through whom the legitimate descent to the Yorkist line was later to be claimed. Edmund of Langley, though he had married Isabel, another of the daughters of Don Pedro, in 1372, was not ambitious. Thomas of Woodstock, youngest of the family and to be the evil genius of his nephew's reign, was still only just come of age.

The death of the great prince, preceded and followed by those of most of his companions, and by that of his father only a year later, marked the end of a remarkable generation. This was true not only in England but in Europe. The emperor Charles IV died in 1378; Charles V of France in 1380. In 1378 the great schism in the Church began, with two rival popes at Rome and Avignon respectively, obeyed by the countries allied to England on the one hand and on the other those in league with France. Nor was it the outstanding sovereigns and warriors alone whose lives had come to an end. In Italy the two great glories of fourteenth-century literature died within eighteen months: Petrarch in July 1374, Boccaccio at the end of 1375. The renowned French poet and musician, Guillaume de Machaut, was to follow them in 1377. In England it was also the turn of a group of artists and scientists to disappear.

Hugh of St Albans, the great painter, had already given place to Gilbert Prince in the royal service; the sculptor William Patrington is last heard of on 24 May 1372 when he was leaving for Scotland to make the monument for King David II at Holyrood. William Herland, who had succeeded William Hurley as Edward III's chief carpenter in 1354 and made the roof of the great hall at Windsor, died in June 1375; Philip of Lincoln, responsible for the wooden vault of York Minster nave, soon followed. John Bullok the king's tapestry-maker was another victim of that summer. Robert Horewode, the king's plumber, died in the spring of 1376 and John Geddyng the chief glazier by the beginning of 1378. Among the medical men were some of our first experimental scientists, notably the surgeon John Arderne, born in 1307 and last heard of as consultant to the Infirmarer of Westminster Abbey in 1378; and Master John Bray, physician to the king, to John of Gaunt and to the earl of Salisbury, until he died in 1381. Arderne had a European reputation after his service with the English forces of Henry earl of Lancaster at Algeciras in 1343. A brilliant operator, he effected many cures on patients given up by others as desperate cases, practising in Wiltshire and from 1349 to 1370 mainly at Newark-upon-Trent. He then moved to London and attended on the Court while writing his important surgical treatise, finished in 1376 when he was 69. He may be considered the earliest English surgeon to make fresh advances in knowledge, as well as in practical skill.

Both Arderne and Bray were botanists of importance, learned in the habitats and identification of the plants needed for medicine. Neither of them produced a herbal, but Arderne included in his writings many notes on herbs, and Bray compiled an excellent vocabulary of the names of plants and other substances used in medicine, in Latin, French and English. Arderne's knowledge and observation can be judged from some of his notes such as that on the juniper tree: 'Juniper is an evergreen tree and always in fruit, having slender leaves with a sharp point, and it bears berries which turn black when ripe . . . It grows in Kent on Shooter's Hill by the road to Canterbury, also at Dorking in Surrey and in several other places in that part of the country, as well as at Beddington near Croydon, where the local people call it "Gorse" because they do not know its real name.' ' "Volubilis" (Great Bindweed, *Calystegia sepium*) is a herb that grows in the fields and among bushes, in gardens and meadows, and is quite common; it twines round the trees and hedges where it grows and has round white flowers, undivided, in the form of a bell.'

Bray for the most part confined himself to dictionary entries, but included enough comments to show that he had a wide practical knowledge and was not compiling simply from earlier written sources. Thus he remarked that what was then called 'Acacia' was 'the juice of the little small wild sloes the which be not fully ripe'. He anticipated the binomial practice of Linnaeus by four centuries in stating: 'When it is y-write simply of "Lapacium", *acutum*, it shall be understood "*Lapacium acutum*", Little Dock', and '*Lapacium rotundum*' was similarly Much Dock or Great Dock, and '"*Scariola silvestris*" is wild lettuce'. Even a single name might serve for the identification of the commonest plants in some clearly defined cases: '"*Radix*" – when it is put simply of *raphani* – that is Radish, it shall be understood' and likewise '"*Rubus*" – wit it well that there be many brambles, but when *Rubus* is simply y-set of the bramble that beareth black berries, it shall be understood'. In listing the varieties of narcotic juices under the generic heading of Opium, Bray listed '*Opium theobaicum*' as the juice of White Poppy. 'It is good for men that may not sleep, to be anointed therewith about the temples, and in the palm of the hands and on the sole of the feet. When *opium* is y-put simply by himself, of *Opium theobaicum* it shall be understood evermore.' Of that old remedy Senna he wrote: 'the seed of a senna tree, and it is laxative'.

This older generation, which included also many practical inventors and introducers of new processes, had served England well, and in spite of the misfortunes of recent years it was a country rich in knowledge and in culture that was inherited in 1377 by the boy Richard II. His grandfather had lived long enough to celebrate his Jubilee after reigning for 50 years on 25 January, and died on 21 June after suffering a serious stroke. The facial paralysis caused can be seen on the death-mask taken for his funeral, and from which the later effigy was made as a stylized copy. The old king's advanced senility even before 65 is puzzling. It has been common among historians, following the hostile *Chronicon Angliae*, to adopt the accusation of sexual excess, but it seems far more likely that Edward III was worn out by the unprecedented series of misfortunes which loaded him with responsibility and nervous strain. Ever since 1348 the epidemics of the Black Death and their widespread economic consequences had given preoccupation enough. On top of that the reverses in France so unexpectedly following soon after the success of Bretigny, the illness and death of Queen Philippa, the hopeless decline in the health of his eldest son for nine whole years were an intolerable burden. Considering all things he did well, and in spite of being hamstrung throughout his career by inadequate finances, his new coinage and his promotion of trade laid the foundation for future national prosperity.

We have seen that many of the famous commanders in the war had left the scene before the Black Prince himself. It was a very different world that surrounded his young son at his coronation on 16 July 1377. Almost all the founder Knights of the Garter were gone, as well as many of their successors. The one great magnate who survived from the days of glory was William de

Montague, the younger earl of Salisbury who had succeeded his father in 1344 and was to live on until 1397. Of the Black Prince's close associates, Sir Nele Loryng lived until 1386; Sir Simon Burley, the young Richard's tutor, became the tragic victim of the embittered plotting of Thomas of Woodstock, the king's youngest uncle, in 1388.

The fundamental question posed by the history of the reign of Richard II is: why should the son of the Black Prince, who had been the most universally popular and beloved member of the Plantagenet family, have been continuously opposed and eventually forced to abdicate? We must remember that it was not only his father who had been well liked; so was his mother. Joan 'the Fair Maid of Kent', whatever her marital adventures may have been, was never the object of dislike. It was certainly Richard's misfortune that his mother died at 57 in 1385, after the Peasants' Revolt but before the first great crisis involving the supposed 'advice' by which he governed. It is at least possible that she might have exerted some restraint over the overweening attitudes of the Lords Appellant of 1387–88. Ever since Edward III had disposed of Mortimer in 1330, for well over half a century, political crises had been the merest storms in teacups. Under the old king, whether in his youth or age, nobody dreamt of challenging the right of the sovereign to retain loyal ministers and to rule as well as reign.

The answer to the question must contain two factors: an envious spirit, external to the king and anxious to condemn him; and a quality in the king himself that called forth opposition. We know perfectly well who it was that had the envious spirit: Richard's uncle Thomas of Woodstock, earl of Buckingham and from 1385 duke of Gloucester. He undoubtedly had a vicious and vindictive personal temperament and was possessed of a sense of his own importance verging on megalomania. The conversation reported by Froissart, in which one of the courtiers commented to the king himself on Gloucester's manner, is revealing: 'When your uncle cometh to you, which is not often, we dare not lift up our eyes to look upon any person, he looketh so high over us. He thinketh we do him much wrong that we be so near about you as we be.' Gloucester, by far the youngest of Edward III's family, had acquired a deeply seated inferiority complex, and fancied that Richard's companions of less than royal birth implied an insult to himself.

What was the quality in the young king that, by the time he was twenty, aroused such bitter opposition? It can have been no less than his central characteristic: the fact that when he spoke it was as one having authority. Richard, well taught in the philosophy of kingship and its duties by Sir Simon Burley and by his Dominican confessors, was not prepared to brook bullying dictation from anybody, least of all a member of his own family for whom he cannot have felt respect. Undoubtedly he did respect John of Gaunt, 15 years older than Gloucester and a whole generation senior to himself. This discrimination between the two uncles must again have infuriated Thomas. There was, however, another and subtler factor in the relationship between Gloucester, who represented that side of the blood royal which identified with the magnates and higher baronage, and the king, whose aspirations moved away from the material interests of the grandees and from the war as an instrument of national aggrandisement.

It is precisely this enlargement of Richard's philosophy of life that distinguishes him from all his predecessors on the English throne. Even Henry II and Edward I, who were certainly averse from unnecessary warfare, found themselves continually embroiled in political wars. Edward III and the Black Prince had been so romantically devoted to knight errantry that they did not stop to consider the effects of war upon the nations and upon civilization as a whole. Not that they were oblivious of the loss of lives: Edward III's personal challenge to Philip of Valois specifically made the point that by single combat they could avoid 'great destruction to the people of the country, which thing every good Christian should eschew, especially princes and others who have the government of the people'. He went on to stress that 'it is very desirable to . . . avoid the mortality of Christians, since the quarrel is between you and us only'. Edward III was indeed perfectly aware of the principles at stake, but when it came to the point he – and the same is true of Edward of Woodstock – was unable to avoid war.

Both Edward III and his eldest son were devoted to jousting and were prepared to risk life and limb in mimic, as in real combat. It is an indication of Richard's more refined sensibility that he was never a jouster, though he was equally prepared to risk his life in direct confrontation with the rebels of 1381 or, in later life, against the Scots or Irish if a peaceful solution were put out of his reach. It is impossible not to see in Richard II an improvement upon the Plantagenet stock, though it may have been an atavistic hark-back to his remote ancestor Fulk II the Good of Anjou, notorious among the rulers of the tenth century for the fact that he waged no wars. The Way of Peace had reality for Richard, alone among his contemporaries of the fourteenth century: he was seriously trying to grope his way out of the impasse of the Hundred Years War and its appalling losses without any redeeming benefits. In this object he might conceivably have succeeded, had he not tried to do more. The crisis of the Peasants' Revolt of 1381 into which he was flung at the age of 14 brought him face to face with the realities of life for great masses of his poorer subjects. He was forced to grasp, on the instant, that he was king over many more peasants and labourers than magnates and knights.

We need not credit the boy king with any impossibly deep appreciation of the political, social and economic problems of the time. It was enough that he brought the well equipped brain and resilient spirit of a mediaeval – and there-fore precocious – prince to cope with the immediate issue of the day. What he clearly did understand was that upon him alone depended the being – for well or ill – of several millions of souls. His strict Catholicism seems unimpugned, and we cannot credit him with any understanding of what it meant to be a Lollard or a Muslim or a Jew, or one of the heathens of Lithuania or the remoter lands. We do know, all the same, that in later life he was to resist the pressures from the papacy and from the higher ranks of the English clergy, in favour of a statute for the burning of heretics. It was reserved for his cousin Henry, as soon as he had usurped Richard's throne, to pass into law this infamous statute 'De Heretico Comburendo' which was in the course of two centuries to manufacture hatred and horror to a degree unknown before.

Richard did not reject the values of his father and his grandfather. His was not the attitude of the pacifist who, to demonstrate his sincerity, finds it necessary to spit on military medals and to object to war pensions. On the contrary, he could appreciate the genuine nobility of their lives, so closely linked to his own. He was, after all, over nine when his father died, and 18 at the time of his mother's death. From Joan he must have learnt to honour his father's memory, even if he did not do so already. He certainly meditated upon the strange scene by his father's deathbed, the Black Prince's curse upon him if he should subvert any of his father's gifts to his servants. Even a boy of nine might be aware, in the contemporary climate of opinion, that executors were commonly untrue to the charge laid upon them. But he may well have pondered upon the doubt in his own father's mind, that he might conceivably be so disloyal. This, and perhaps other factors, made him aware very early in life of the crucial importance of loyalty. In modern times we have become horrifyingly inured to the regular subversion of trust funds, by legal decree, from the purpose to which they were destined by the donor. It is a singular dishonour to England, a supposedly Christian country, that in this respect it falls below the scrupulous behaviour of Muslim lands, where government departments administer in perpetuity the charitable bequests or *waqfs* set up centuries ago. We have to struggle to remember, what was manifestly present in the mind of Richard II, that all charities and all bequests by the dying were given to God in perpetuity.

The life and reign of Richard II were then, not a reversal of his grandfather's policies or his father's values, but an attempt to transcend them. By fulfilling the good intention and discarding the defects of execution he must have hoped to build a new England, more closely subjected to God's laws as he understood them. For we cannot, if we follow his deeds or read his own will, think that Richard sought power for his own glorification. He was not an Alexander, a Caesar or a Napoleon. He saw himself as truly the servant of God upon whom a tremendous burden of responsibility had been laid. It was not just the law of England that lay in the king's hand, but the law of heaven itself. The lives and fortunes of every man, woman and child in England, Wales and his other dominions depended, under God, upon him. He could not, as a matter of duty and conscience, allow encroachments from any quarter upon his freedom of action to rule. The purpose of his being was government.

In every respect Richard's aims transcended those of his forerunners. It is of the highest significance that he should have visited Ireland twice, seeing in his lordship of the western island the supreme test of his capacity. It was not in France, Flanders or Spain that he should seek to impose his will; but to attempt to govern the ungovernable realm with whose lordship he was invested. Henry II and John had been to Ireland when it was taken over by the English crown with papal approval; but no subsequent monarch had shown any interest in the country. English influence there was steadily diminishing as the native lords pressed in upon the Pale and English governors progressively became less and less effective even within a reduced jurisdiction. With remarkable acumen, Richard appreciated that there were two distinct causes of trouble in Ireland: the real Irish themselves who had never been tamed, and the Anglo-Norman settlers who had grievances. On his first visit in 1395 he wrote back to his uncle the duke of York, regent during his absence, remarking that these latter 'Irish rebels' were perhaps 'so rebellious by reason of the grievances and wrongs done unto them, . . . and that redress hath not been made to them'. He had grasped the lesson of the Peasants' Revolt, that a generous clemency might conciliate even rebels in arms. This had been, of course, his father's argument to Don Pedro after Nájera, ill-fated though that instance of clemency had been in the upshot.

Another aspect of Richard's Irish policy indicates his attitude towards unruly members of the propertied class. He noted that there were already, half a millenium before the days of Boycott, absentee landowners who drew revenues from Irish estates but lived at ease in England. Such drones he ordered back to their lands in Ireland, setting a precedent for the much later policy of Charles I towards the English gentry. Both Richard and Charles lost their thrones and their lives because, as governors of the whole people, they saw that no category of the population must be granted privilege devoid of responsibility. The equity of the apportionment of Ship Money throughout the country was an equivalent to Richard's determination to reduce the over-mighty to reasonable proportions. Obviously the self-interest of the magnates with really great estates exploded in antagonism. Though the biggest single factor in opposition, it was not the only one. There was distrust by the warrior lords, used to rich pickings in France, for a policy verging on pacifism. Obstinate emotions were aroused by a young king who did not joust and actually opposed the values of those who did.

Before 1381 Richard was a mere boy but from the Revolt onwards, because of his decisive personal intervention, he became the most significant individual in the country. An indelible mark was left on his spirit by the bad faith of his seniors, who rescinded the pardons he had given to the peasants and forced him to witness the proceedings. The pardons were obtained under duress but the king had meant to honour them. He did succeed in moderating repressive measures and prevented the social counter-revolt from becoming a draconian reduction of the labourers to slavery. Executions were mostly limited to notorious conspirators and detected murderers. Spiritually the king had, before he was fifteen, shown himself a leader of men and saved a situation virtually lost by the cowardice and ineptitude of his councillors and courtiers. From then on he was conscious of his own powers and could only be held back by brute force.

In this early and impressionable phase of his life Richard must often have felt overshadowed by the name and fame of his father. Though an exceptional boy, he would have had to be quite abnormal had he not taken great pride in the prince's amazing exploits. After the death of his elder brother Edward of Angoulême when he was himself just four, there had been over five more years in which to get to know his father. By the talk of the Court and from his mother he would derive the whole romantic history, almost a fairy tale, from the winning of spurs at Crecy on to the patient sapping of the defences of Limoges, nearly a quarter-century of prowess unrivalled in modern history. By temperament he was unable to emulate this pattern of chivalry who had successfully emulated and even excelled *his* father's exploits in the same field of action. The mighty deeds of the Black Prince loomed over the scene to an extent that put a premium on adventurousness, even if of another kind and exercised in a different direction. The confrontation with the rebels of 1381 has to be seen as the first of a series of 'feats' conceived of by Richard (perhaps subconsciously) as his answer or equivalent to the record set for him. Where the Black Prince, exercised in combat, had overcome his enemies in one hand-to-hand fight after another, his son was to practise moral authority which, in its own way, would yield him the victory.

The origins of the Peasants' Revolt have occupied much of the time of several generations of historians, and no simple account is possible. What emerges from the study, both of the contemporary statements and the patient researches into the records made in the last century, is that as usual there were both genuine and bogus grievances. In any land at any time there will be some injustice, some will naturally be envious of the relative prosperity or luxury of their neighbours. Such envy, and the complaints based on it, do not constitute a genuine grievance unless the inequalities are gross beyond measure, or result from corruption, or involve oppression of the weak, the aged, widows and orphans. The continuous struggle for power, on the other hand, puts a premium upon the artificial fomenting of a sense of grievance by the agents of an 'out' faction engaged in a campaign against the 'in' establishment of the day. At different times the opposed parties are variously polarized: Pagan v. Christian, Orthodox v. Arian, Catholic v. Protestant, Anglican v. Nonconformist, Royalist v. Republican, Capital v. Labour, White v. Black and so on *ad infinitum*. Such issues involve both genuine principles, such as the maintenance of good faith or of law and order, and minutiae which amount only to the battles of frogs and mice.

Good government consists in an impartial restraint imposed from above upon all contending interests, so that men of all conditions may enjoy their lives and a reasonable amount of property without undue interference. Nobody has ever expressed this ideal better than the Roman Emperor Marcus Aurelius: 'a polity in which there is the same law for all, administered with regard to equal rights and equal freedom of speech, a kingly government which respects most of all the liberty of the governed'. It was this which formed the basis of the concept of monarchy in which the kings of the Middle Ages were educated, and notably among them Richard of Bordeaux. Where Richard differed from most sovereigns, of his own and other ages, was in degree rather than kind. He took a more exalted view of his responsibilities and conscientiously believed that he must not palter with his bounden duty. As sovereign, he had been delegated by God to exercise supreme and unfettered control over the English for term of his life.

Like most princes, Richard II had been trained to take an objective view and to look to the interests of all his subjects without prejudice. He could see that at one end of the scale there were the unduly rich and powerful, lords or merchants; at the other the sowers of sedition who made the most of genuine grievances and whipped up bogus wrongs. In between and suffering or liable to suffer from the harm and provocation were the great mass of his people, the flock whose shepherd he was, not by personal ambition but by the decree from above. It was his tragedy that the resolute enmity of a few men, some of them of his own blood, was to render him in the end powerless to continue the work which he had begun in furtherance of the ideal government of his people as a whole.

There were at least four main causes, or sore points, which contributed to the outbreak of the Revolt in 1381. Two of these lay in the background as general or predisposing bases of discontent: the inflation which had resulted from the Black Death and subsequent plagues; and the return of soldiers from the wars, necessarily disappointed of any further booty. The two other causes were much more specific: the impatience of many of the country people at the irritating restrictions put upon them by their status as customary tenants of the manorial lords; and the imposition of the necessary but naturally unpopular poll-tax that spring. In England, as in the Black Prince's Aquitaine when the hearth-tax of 1368 had to be collected, it was impossible to convince the ordinary man that demands for money were not the direct result of mis-government. After all, taxes very often are just that.

There was, however, a precipitating cause which embraced all these and various minor and local annoyances. This was the deliberate plotting of a small group of agitators. Even without the subsequent confessions of some of these men, the fact can be deduced from the simultaneous outbreaks in many parts of the country. No theory of spontaneous ferment can adequately account for the accuracy with which the revolts coincided in time, even though the grievances proclaimed by the various regional bands differed greatly. Most of the ringleaders seem to have been known by false names, but the renegade priest John Ball is an historical character who had been noted for his extremist views fifteen years before the rising and was said to have preached sedition for more than twenty years. His most famous political speech or 'sermon', to 20,000 assembled on Blackheath, began with the text

> When Adam dalve and Eve span,
> Who was then a gentle man?

and went on with the predictable rigmarole to the effect that all men were created equal. His recipe for action was to kill the great lords of the realm, then all lawyers, justices and jurors, finally anyone else whom they knew to be harmful to the community. Although the ostensible causes of the Revolt may have been quite distinct from those which had led to the Jacquerie of 1358 around Beauvais and Meaux, it is evident that Ball derived a good deal of his propaganda from that or a common source.

Moreover, cryptic letters were found, sent out to some local ringleaders, and Ball is said to have admitted that he wrote many more. Presumably there had been a substantial period of preparation in which agents had been told to await the arrival of letters, not themselves unduly specific, and then move on London. The surviving text, omitting some doggerel in conclusion, runs: –

'John Sheep, sometime St Mary priest of York, and now of Colchester, greeteth well John Nameless and John the Miller, and John Carter, and biddeth them that they beware of guile in borough, and stand together in God's name; and biddeth Piers Ploughman go to his work, and chastise well Hob the robber, and take with you John Trueman and all his fellows, and no more, and look ye shape you to one head and no more.'

The confession made by 'John Straw' who, whatever his real name may have

been, was one of the main leaders taken in the act, said that the plan had been
to kill all the knights, esquires and gentlemen who came with the king to
Blackheath; to lead the king around the country as their authority, murdering
all the lords who could oppose the movement, and notably the order of
Hospitallers of St John; then kill the king and drive out all bishops, monks,
canons and rectors of churches. 'Since there would be no one left who was
senior, stronger or more knowledgeable than ourselves, we would have
founded laws at our own pleasure by which all subjects would be ruled. These
were our aims, as God will help me on the point of death.'

This confessed programme, recorded at the time, corresponds far too closely
with the aims of extremist revolutionaries of all periods to have been a
fabrication. Besides, the accomplished deeds of the revolt confirm not only the
main aims, but the ruthlessness with which they were pursued. Arriving in the
London suburbs on Wednesday 12 June the rebels in the next three days
murdered the archbishop of Canterbury, Simon Sudbury; Sir Robert Hales,
who was treasurer of England as well as prior of the Hospital of St John of
Jerusalem; the Franciscan friar William de Appleton because he was the
physician and friend of John of Gaunt; one John Greenfield for no better
reason than that he spoke well of Appleton; Richard Imworth, marshal of the
Marshalsea, dragged from sanctuary in Westminster Abbey in the king's own
presence; Richard Lyons and 35 Flemings found taking refuge in the church of
St Martin Vintry; and about 150 other persons in the City alone. They
released all prisoners in the Marshalsea and the Fleet; sacked Lambeth Palace
and burnt the rolls and registers; completely destroyed John of Gaunt's palace
of the Savoy; sacked the Temple and burnt the books and rolls there; burnt
part of the buildings of the Hospital of St John at Clerkenwell and destroyed
as much of the houses and property of the Hospitallers as they could identify.

On Thursday, the feast of Corpus Christi, they laid siege to the Tower of
London where the king was. Richard 'anxiously and sadly, climbed to a little
turret facing St Katherine's, where many of the commons were'. He sent them
a tactful letter, which they mocked, then sending out parties to burn more
houses. The king 'went up to a high garret of the Tower to watch the fires;
then he came down and took counsel of the lords. But they did not know how
to advise him and were surprisingly abashed.' Richard then sent out proclama-
tions to all the companies of the rebels saying that he would meet them next
day at Mile End, and on the Friday he was there by 'seven of the bell', the
seventh hour or 1 p.m. After the king had left the Tower a band of the rebels
burst in, and this was when the archbishop and Hales were killed. It has never
been clear how the Tower came to be taken, but it shows incredible ineptitude
on the part of those left to guard it. There is also a good deal of doubt as to
precisely who accompanied Richard to Mile End, but it seems reasonably

certain that he had with him Sir Thomas Percy and Sir Robert Knollys, veterans of his father's wars, William Walworth the mayor of London, and as his sword-bearer Sir Aubrey de Vere, the uncle of his great friend Robert de Vere earl of Oxford. The mob awaiting him numbered about 100,000 and few of his companions can have expected to get away alive.

All the way to Mile End the king was beset by a disorderly crowd, some of its leaders making vociferous demands to which he gave diplomatic answers. In the eventual confrontation he asked to be told the rebels' petitions, which mainly concerned the abolition of serfdom. This he granted, with an amnesty for those who returned home at once. He promised to give his banners to all such parties leaving London, and charters of freedom and pardon. To the repeated pressure to give up the 'traitors' such as the archbishop, Richard said that they must first be proved traitors by due process of law. Meanwhile, of course, vengeance had been wreaked on these men in his absence, as he was to discover on his return. His mother had been taken to the Wardrobe in the City for relative safety, and he joined her there for the night. The hard core of the rebels had not left London and atrocities were continuing. On Saturday morning arrangements were made to meet Wat Tyler and his band at Smithfield later in the day, but the king first went to Westminster Abbey with a retinue of perhaps 200 all told. There he witnessed the dreadful incident of Imworth being torn from sanctuary and hustled off to death in Cheapside. The king confessed to the anchorite of the Abbey, received absolution and took the sacrament at the high altar. The party then rode for Smithfield by passing outside the suburbs of London to the north. It has been pointed out that it would have been easy to escape to Windsor by making a bold dash at this stage, and the fact that no such attempt was made proves the determination of the king to see the affair through to the end. He may have been buoyed up by a resolution to acquit himself well in the company of several of his father's knights, De Vere, Knollys and Percy.

Though details vary, the outline of what happened at Smithfield is clear. Mayor Walworth summoned Tyler to the king: Tyler familiarly made a mocking reverence and hailed him as 'Brother'; asked why all rebels had not yet dispersed, he began to string together more demands; called for water and rudely rinsed his mouth. At this point one of Richard's retinue, possibly Sir John Newton the keeper of Rochester Castle, called out that he recognized Tyler as the greatest thief and robber in Kent. Tyler attacked Newton with a dagger but was warded off by Walworth the mayor, who was stabbed by Tyler without effect as he was wearing a mail shirt under his clothes. Walworth drew his sword and seriously wounded Tyler, who was then dispatched by Ralph Standish. Walworth and Standish were later knighted for their courageous and effective action, which has been strangely described by some historians as 'the murder of Tyler'.

As soon as the surrounding mob grasped what had happened they bent the bows with which they were armed and began to fit arrows to the strings. Within seconds the whole of the royal party would have been annihilated. King Richard, two years younger than his father at Crecy, at once spurred his horse forward towards the rebels and waved them back. There is no precise record of his words, but what he said was in effect: 'Stop! Would you fire on your king? Do not grieve for the death of that traitor and ruffian; I am your king, your chief and leader. Follow me to the fields and you may ask what you will.' This drew off the crowd northwards into Clerkenwell Fields, while Walworth galloped back into the City for help and called out the trained bands of which Knollys took command. For about an hour the king kept the rebels, whose ranks still included fanatics like John Ball, in parley, until the rescue of some 7,000 men arrived. Knollys was for summary massacre but Richard refused: 'three-fourths of them have been brought here by fear and threats; I will not have the innocent suffer with the guilty'. He commanded them to depart, and this time all their companies melted away. With the old earl of Salisbury, who had supported him against Knollys in his clemency, and the rest of his loyal party he returned to the Wardrobe where his mother greeted him with: 'Ah, fair son, what pain and great sorrow I have suffered for you this day!' The king replied: 'Certainly, madam, I know it well; but now rejoice and thank God. I have this day recovered mine heritage and the realm of England, the which I had near lost.'

CHAPTER IX

Brittle Glory

The king's extraordinary success in quelling the unruly mobs of the 'Hurling Time', contrasted with the total failure of the magnates and councillors – other than Salisbury – increased the psychological resistance to his personality. For several years Richard was repressed and kept in leading strings. In compensation he made a happy marriage which had noteworthy results for English art. The bride was Anne of Bohemia, daughter of the emperor Charles IV and so grand-daughter of the heroic King John who died at Crecy. Charles himself had been wounded there but escaped. He was educated in France and devoted to the French alliance, utterly opposed to Edward III. By truckling to the papacy he had reversed the policy of his imperial predecessors, but in Bohemia where he was born and died he left his mark. The marriage between Richard and Anne broke the frozen attitudes of combat and began to build a bridge towards understanding with France. Through the queen's entourage England discovered the new world of art which owed as much to Rhenish, Bohemian and central European sources and contacts with Byzantium as to Paris. English art had, as we have seen, stolen a march on France in its closer relations with Italian painters during the first half of the century. In the years towards 1400 it was able to become an equal partner in the short-lived triumph of International Gothic while at the same time bringing the wholly English architecture of the Perpendicular style to a triumphant climax.

Unlike his father's late marriage to the lady of his heart, Richard's match was arranged, but we do not know to what extent he was able to promote the arrangement himself. Since he was scarcely turned 15 at the time, and had been only 13 when it was first mooted, it seems unlikely that he could have had much say. What is beyond doubt is that he fell in love with Anne quite as profoundly as his father with the Fair Maid. While it lasted it was an ideal marriage except that there were no children and thus no direct heir to the throne. The rage and despair with which the king was filled at his wife's death, causing him to have the palace of Sheen where she died razed to the ground, was a true index of what their union had meant. Nothing was ever to be the same again, and the king's intent changed subtly. Until 1394 Richard in his private capacity saw himself as repeating the idyll of true love which had united his grandfather and Philippa, his father and Joan. He very likely had realized as a boy something of the desolation of his widowed grandfather, maybe even knew that it was a major factor in the old king's premature dotage. The Black Prince had at any rate had the solace of his affectionate wife with him to the last.

The marriage of Richard and Anne lasted from 20 January 1382 until the queen's death, apparently from the plague, on 7 June 1394. The great crisis of the reign, the conspiracy and dominion of the Lords Appellant in 1387–89, came in the middle of this period and sharply divided five years of relative placidity and happiness from five of tension. In the years from the fifteenth to the twenty-first of Richard's life he was feeling his way towards real statesmanship and developing a philosophy. Gradually he freed himself from the tutelage of the older men who had shown themselves wanting in 1381. By 1387 he was starting to interest the pope in his plans for the canonization of Edward II, a sure sign that he had by the time he was 20 already matured the view of legitimate monarchy which he afterwards made his own. He was probably thinking ahead when, in October 1382, he granted a licence to William of Wykeham to found his College at Winchester. Wykeham's great plan for a double foundation, of which the senior part at Oxford was already under construction, envisaged the training of men especially for the civil service of the sovereign. No idea could have been more welcome to the king, and it was Wykeham that he appointed chancellor when he rid himself of the Appellants in May 1389. He associated himself still more closely with Wykeham's great school by granting it unusually wide privileges in 1395.

It was in the course of the first years of his marriage that the king was able to build up a group of personal friends and supporters who have been called the 'court party' or curialists. There is little to suggest that they formed a party in the ordinary sense of the word: they were alike in placing loyalty to the person of the sovereign above their own interests. Among them Robert de Vere, earl of Oxford and later duke of Ireland, was the closest friend, though five years older than the king. The most significant politically was perhaps Michael de la Pole, earl of Suffolk, chancellor from March 1383 to October 1386 and a statesman of integrity. As time went on it was Richard who became more and more his own first minister, so that it is misleading to accept the view that he was 'advised' by his courtiers. On the contrary he was decidedly independent, but courageously defended his friends and ministers from repeated attacks. By 1385 the king was in effective control and able to strengthen the hold of his central government over the counties and to restrain the undue privileges of mighty subjects. Here again was cause for annoyance, if not worse, on the part of the greater baronage.

One difficult problem was that of Richard's relationship to his eldest surviving uncle, John of Gaunt. Gaunt had become a strangely controversial figure. In the revolt of 1381 he was the most hated man in England, so far as the Home Counties rebels were concerned. Yet news came from the North that he had been freeing the serfs on the Lancaster estates, and it was true that he and his family were popular among their own tenants, as was demonstrated in 1399 when Henry of Lancaster landed in East Yorkshire to claim his father's inheritance. John of Gaunt, moreover, protected the outspoken 'protestant' John Wycliffe, which naturally made him unpopular with many of the higher clergy, yet might have endeared him to men who thought of the archbishop of Canterbury as a traitor. Always on the closest terms with the Black Prince, in spite of the political cleavage leading up to the Good Parliament, Gaunt seems to have had an affection for his nephew and there is not much to support the rumours that he had designs on the throne. It may be that Richard was affected by such tale-bearing, for Gaunt's influence declined in the early '80's. This may or may not have decided him to leave the Court and prosecute his own ambitions in Spain. At any rate he went, in July 1386, and it was not until late in 1389 that he returned at the king's command. By that time his senior authority was needed to maintain Richard's ascendancy over the dissidents, and for the remaining ten years of his life he can be regarded as the king's friend.

As things turned out it was Gaunt's absence that opened the way to Richard's most deadly opponents. The unambitious character of Edmund of Langley, earl of Cambridge (the later duke of York), left the field free for his youngest brother Thomas, at the time earl of Buckingham but best known by his later title of duke of Gloucester. Around Buckingham gathered a group of malcontents: Richard FitzAlan, earl of Arundel and his brother Thomas bishop of Ely, later archbishop of York and, twice, of Canterbury; and Thomas Beauchamp earl of Warwick, son of the Warwick who fought at Crecy. Later on this party gathered to it Henry of Bolingbroke earl of Derby, Gaunt's son and eventually king Henry IV; and Thomas Mowbray earl of Nottingham, later duke of Norfolk. The inclusion of Warwick is the one unlikely factor, for his father had been among the closest friends and supporters of Edward III and of the royal family.

After several years of truce with France, the renewed threat of a great French invasion caused the government to take defensive measures. Castles were built, rebuilt or repaired in Kent and Sussex, and for a time there was a state of alarm. The invasion did not materialize, but it became necessary to deal with the Scots, and in the summer of 1385 it was decided that invasion of

Scotland was the best form of defence. A great muster was summoned to Newcastle-upon-Tyne for mid-July and the king went north to take command. On the way a dreadful incident occurred which was destined to have serious repercussions. Richard's half-brother Sir John Holand (later earl of Huntingdon and duke of Exeter) killed Sir Ralph Stafford, son of the earl of Stafford and a member of Queen Anne's household. One of Holand's squires had been murdered by Stafford's men, who fled to sanctuary at Beverley. The king forbade his brother to take personal revenge, but a chance meeting near York between Holand and young Stafford led to a bitter quarrel in which blows were struck, from one of which Stafford fell dead. Richard would have placed his brother on trial for murder, but his mother pleaded for her favourite son John. Matters were still in uncertainty when she died, it is said of grief at the sad affair, early in August.

The death of the princess Joan in such circumstances of family tragedy broke the last personal link which tied Richard to the older generation in his family. With his uncle John he was on uneasy terms during the campaign in Scotland. The Scots, with French help, carried out a raid on Cumbria but made no attempt to hinder the English, who reached and occupied Edinburgh without serious fighting. Gaunt wished to pursue the enemy, if necessary into the Highlands, but Richard was the wiser general. He declined to sacrifice his men in pursuing a will-o'-the-wisp foe through barren mountains and, with considerable moral courage, retired into England again after spending only a fortnight on Scottish soil. By some singular conjunction, while King Richard was momentarily holding the Scottish capital, the independence of Portugal was won at Aljubarrota with the help of a contingent of English and Gascon troops. Fought on 14 August 1385 the battle against the invading Castilians under Juan I, son of Henry of Trastamara, was one of the most absolutely decisive in the history of Europe. On the Portuguese side was a total of some 7,000 men, the Anglo-Gascon support forming perhaps one-tenth; against them was a Spanish army of nearly three times the size, with much larger numbers of Frenchmen than the opposed force of Anglo-Gascons. Castile also had supporting cavalry, which the Portuguese had not, and 16 light cannon under a master artilleryman.

The news of this success was possibly the determining reason for Gaunt's Spanish expedition. Now was the crucial time to overthrow the bastard house of Trastamara once and for all and rule Castile in right of Don Pedro's daughter. The duke of Lancaster, as his rash proposals in Scotland might well suggest, was not the great general his elder brother had been, and his military schemes in the end came to nothing. We must not overlook, however, the remarkable dynastic effects upon history of this venture into the Peninsula. The king of Portugal married the duke's eldest daughter Philippa and their children included not only the future king Duarte (Edward) but Henry the Navigator, father of exploration, and Fernando the Constant Prince who preferred to die at the end of ten years in a Moorish prison rather than have Ceuta given back as his ransom. Philippa was Gaunt's daughter by his first wife, Blanche of Lancaster; her sister Elizabeth married the controversial John Holand; and their younger half-sister, the duke's daughter Catherine by his Spanish second wife, was in the end to marry Henry III, son of John (Juan) I, and so bring back to Castile its legitimate royal line.

Next year John Holand, who had been on the run, was pardoned at the intercession of Gaunt, whose son-in-law he was about to become. He was also appointed constable of the expedition leaving for Spain, and so was conveniently got out of the way for a long time. What was less fortunate was a second threat of French invasion as soon as Lancaster's force was safely on its way to Galicia. The likelihood of a defensive war played into the hands of uncle Thomas, by now duke of Gloucester, and his bellicose friends the Arundels. They were not ashamed to ally themselves to a majority of the Commons in the 'Wonderful Parliament' of October 1386, and forced through demands that the king should dismiss his ministers, particularly Michael de la Pole earl of Suffolk, his chancellor. Richard, from Eltham, sent back the message, justified but possibly rash, that he would not dismiss the meanest scullion from his kitchen on the advice of Parliament. He was, however, prepared to meet a commission of forty knights at Eltham. The rumour was put about that the king intended to murder them, and Parliament instead sent Gloucester and bishop Thomas Arundel. In the course of a stormy meeting with the king, Gloucester amazingly advanced a theory of parliamentary sovereignty and went so far as to invent a non-existent 'ancient statute' for annual parliaments. Richard, evidently as a piece of rhetorical emphasis, said that he would rather ask help from the king of France than submit to control by parliament. Gloucester's treasonable reply was to remind the king of the fate of Edward II. That a son of Edward III, speaking to his own nephew as well as sovereign, could descend to such depths almost passes belief, but is fully confirmed by later events.

Parliament, which in fact means Gloucester and his party of magnates, insisted on a Commission of Government and forced the king to accept humiliating tutelage. Richard, however, put on record his protest that he did not accept anything that was done against his prerogative and the liberties of the Crown. Suffolk was impeached and condemned to death on the flimsiest evidence but the king was able to pardon him and send him to nominal imprisonment in Windsor Castle. There he was welcomed at Richard's splendid Christmas festivities, which enabled him to consult with Robert de Vere and his other staunch friends. The petty nature of the attack on the Court is shown, among many other acts, by the dismissal of Chaucer from his post as comptroller of customs. During the earlier part of 1387 the king went on progress in the North and through Cheshire and North Wales, accompanied by Sir Simon Burley and Burley's nephew Sir Baldwin Raddington. The opportunity was taken to raise a bodyguard of archers from Cheshire and pikemen from Wales, as the nucleus of a strictly loyal force attached to the person of the sovereign. In August Richard summoned to him at Shrewsbury five of the Chief Justices headed by Sir Robert Tresilian. They gave it as their unanimous legal opinion that the parliamentary Commission was contrary to the royal prerogative and that those who had procured it were worthy of the supreme penalty of the law; and further, that the person who had advised parliament to look up the deposition of Edward II was a traitor.

Fortified by this confidential verdict on his legal position, the king prepared to take action with such forces as he could place under De Vere's command at Chester. It was an unfortunate complication that De Vere, who had been married to a niece of Gloucester's, managed to get a divorce in order to marry one of the queen's Bohemian ladies, Agnes Launcekron. Gloucester was affronted and enraged, but at the same time was warned by Robert Wickford, archbishop of Dublin, of the questions that Richard had put to the Justices. Not to be forestalled, he and the other leaders of the illegal Commission raised private armies and met at Waltham Cross, where on 14 November they published their notorious 'appeal of treason' against the king's friends, archbishop Alexander Neville of York, De Vere, Suffolk, Chief Justice Tresilian, and Nicholas Brembre, former mayor of London and the king's best friend in the City. Gloucester, as constable of England, was able to summon the defendants to the Court of Chivalry over which he presided, and he seems at first to have intended to avoid bringing the alleged treason before Parliament. The Appellants managed to bring into their camp Henry earl of Derby, Gaunt's son, whom they put in command of their joint army; and Thomas Mowbray earl of Nottingham. There is some reason to think that Derby at least was mainly concerned to see that Richard was not deposed in favour of Gloucester rather than his father John of Gaunt, still absent in Spain.

De Vere marched towards London via the Severn and Thames valleys and Derby succeeded in ambushing his little army at Radcot Bridge near Eynsham. De Vere escaped to France, and the earl of Suffolk also reached Paris. The long proceedings in the following weeks were dreadful and it is only necessary to stress their illegality. Even the new justices, appointed by the Appellants, declared that the methods being adopted to condemn the king's friends were completely illegal. After one of the most monstrous mockeries of justice in English history, the upshot was that Chief Justice Tresilian was hanged at Tyburn; Brembre, denied counsel, denied a copy of the indictment, denied time to prepare his defence, and found guiltless by a legal committee specially appointed, was beheaded. A large group of persons attached to the royal household, from Sir Simon Burley and the steward, Sir John Beauchamp of Holt, down to clerks and chaplains, were added to those under attack, as well as the king's confessor, Thomas Rushock bishop of Chichester, and the other justices consulted by the king. The bishop and the justices were exiled to Ireland; most of the rest were condemned to death and executed.

For Burley's life the king risked his own position to the utmost, but Gloucester taunted him that he would lose the throne as well as Burley. Queen Anne actually knelt before Gloucester to beg for Burley's life, and was told she would do better to pray for herself and for her husband. At this point, too late, a rift appeared in the Appellants' ranks: both Derby and Nottingham were revolted by Gloucester's cruelty and told him so; so did his brother Edmund, the duke of York. Edmund, along with John lord Cobham, another veteran of the Black Prince's wars, actually pleaded with the Commons, but only secured a commutation of hanging to beheading. On 5 May 1388 Burley, Sir John Beauchamp, and two other knights of the household, were done to death. From the story of this appalling crime and injustice one consolatory fact emerges: King Richard did everything that any man could have done to save his friends. If ever personal loyalty and devotion have been shown to have meaning in the hard world where might is right, they were displayed in the spring of 1388 by Richard II, king of England; and by his foreign queen who, like her predecessor Philippa, sought mercy even at great cost to herself.

There is no doubt whatever about the facts of this strange story of overweening arrogance and insensate cruelty. Whence did Gloucester derive the bad blood that so defaces the royal line of Plantagenet? How is it possible that a brother of the Black Prince, of Lionel duke of Clarence, of John of Gaunt, of Edmund of Langley who, though retiring by nature found the courage to plead for Burley in public, could be a monster? Even more, how could he show himself a monster so unworthy as to persecute a mere knight whose station was far below his own and who posed no real threat to him? Burley was notoriously a close friend and companion in arms of the Black Prince; but he was also a well-liked person. Froissart, who gathered together a strangely garbled account of these events, remarked that he was 'much grieved; for in my youth I found him a gentle knight, and of great good sense'.

Enough is enough, but it remains to be noted that before dispersing, the 'Merciless Parliament' voted £20,000 – not less than the equivalent of five million pounds sterling in 1975 – to the Appellants to cover 'their great expenses'. The outspoken critics of extravagance, or what they alleged to be extravagance, in the king's household, were not too proud to dip deep into the till when they had both king and parliament by the throat. In the meantime the country had been run down to a very weak state, ironically enough by the leaders of the party determined on pursuing the war against France to the bitter end, and unmeasured in their opposition to the king's efforts for peace. Their government, mighty as it was, put up no official defence when the Scots invaded on two fronts, in Cumberland and as far as Newcastle, in the summer. It was left to the sons of the earl of Northumberland, Henry Percy ('Harry Hotspur') and his brother Ralph Percy, to lead out local recruits. At the battle of Otterburn or Chevy Chase the English were heavily defeated and both the brothers Percy carried off captive to Scotland, whence they had to be ransomed at enormous cost. The sheer hypocrisy, as well as the bullying lawlessness, of the leaders of the war party who now misgoverned the country, still causes wonder and must have driven the powerless king almost to despair.

These extraordinary events did not form a landmark in English constitutional history in the sense that used to be claimed, that they marked the supremacy of parliament. They did, however, provide the first instance of the deliberate packing of parliament by a party of great magnates, the 'Whigs' of their day, led by Gloucester. To the extent that parliament played a leading part in the government of England from 1388 until the Reform of 1832, it was as an assembly that tended to be a mirror of the preponderant landed interest. The use of parliament, by means of forms of patronage, as a convenient tool of what may be termed baronial interests, does date from Gloucester's illegal innovations. It appears all but certain that he had observed with a shrewd eye the use of popular propaganda by the revolutionaries of 1381 and, for similar reasons of envy, made himself a Philippe Égalité four centuries ahead of time. It is a strange paradox that he and the other leaders of the party determined to continue the war in France, theoretically devoted to the memory of the glorious deeds of Edward III and the Black Prince, should have all but destroyed in English public life what was left of that chivalric spirit. The prince's values, though not his methods, lived on in his son and his son's friends.

Before considering the reactions of the king to the tragedy of 1388, and the greater tragedy of 1399, it is time to look at the artistic outpouring of the last years of the fourteenth century, directly and indirectly due to Richard's personal interest, taste and stimulus. A great deal was happening in building, in painting and carving, in the minor arts, in prose and verse writing and, though little that is tangible survives, in music. All that can be said of this is that both Richard II and his cousin Henry of Derby were musical and promoted music, and that there were in England in the 1380's and '90's advanced composers who had learnt from De Machaut and could train the next generation of English musicians, represented by such famous names as those of John Dunstable, Lionel Power, John Pyamour and Thomas Damett. It is unnecessary to stress the unique importance of Chaucer as a poet. His career had begun in the household of the duchess of Clarence, wife of Prince Lionel of Antwerp, and after Clarence's death in 1368 was promoted by John of Gaunt. Soon after Richard's resumption of power in the summer of 1389, Chaucer was made clerk of the works at Westminster and for the rest of his life he received good preferments in office and pensions from the king. His greatest work, the *Canterbury Tales*, was written in the years from 1387 to his death in 1400.

Apart from Chaucer, English literature was enriched by John Gower, who wrote his *Confessio Amantis* for presentation to Richard II in the years immediately before 1390. Chaucer's disciple Thomas Hoccleve was a clerk in the royal service and probably in early manhood when Richard came to the throne; certainly his formative years as a writer coincided with Richard's reign. Another servant of the court was Hoccleve's contemporary Thomas Usk, author of the allegorical *Testament of Love* attributed for nearly five hundred years to Chaucer. Poor Usk was one of the lesser victims of 1388, barbarously executed for the treason of being the king's loyal servant. As well as writings in English, matter in French was still being produced for Richard II and members of his court, by Gower, by the private herald of Sir John Chandos who wrote the poem on the life of the Black Prince somewhere about 1385, and by Froissart.

Froissart's return to the English court after an absence of 27 years gives a wonderfully personal glimpse of the court life of Richard II as it was in July 1395, when the king had just returned from his first stay in Ireland. Froissart 'had great affection to go and see the realm of England' especially 'because in my youth I had been brought up in the court of the noble king Edward the third and of queen Philippa his wife, and among their children and other barons of England that as then were alive, in whom I found all nobleness, honour, largess and courtesy'. He landed at Dover on 12 July and two days later was at Canterbury where he visited the shrine and the tomb of the prince of Wales, 'who is there interred right richly'. The king and court were about to arrive on pilgrimage and Froissart was able to get into touch with Lord Thomas Percy (later earl of Worcester), the steward of the household, who told him to follow the court to Leeds Castle. At Leeds Froissart was remembered by the duke of York who 'made me good cheer and said: "Sir John, hold you always near to us and we shall shew you love and courtesy; we are bound thereto for the love of time past and for love of my lady the old queen my mother, in whose court ye were"'. Froissart had been at the christening of prince Richard of Bordeaux in 1367 but had never seen him since. Now he was presented to the king and delivered letters from the duke of Bavaria and duke of Brabant, which the king read. 'Then he said to me that I was welcome, as he that had been and is of the English court.' At the time the king was busy with state affairs, so Froissart had to follow on to Eltham, where he met his old friend Sir Richard Stury, whom he had not seen for 24 years. They talked together at great length, walking up and down the gallery before the king's chamber and in the garden 'where it was very pleasant and shady, for those alleys were then covered with vines'. Froissart had brought with him 'engrossed in a fair book well enlumined all the matter of amours and moralities that in four and twenty years before I had made and compiled', to present to the king. Percy and Stury arranged for the book to be laid on the king's bed; it was 'covered with crimson velvet, with ten buttons of silver and gilt, and roses of gold in the midst, with two great clasps gilt, richly wrought'. The king came, and 'demanded me whereof it treated, and I shewed him how it treated matters of love; whereof the king was glad and looked in it and read it in many places, for he could speak and read French very well'. Altogether Froissart spent more than three months following the court, and King Richard 'made me good cheer, because that in my youth I was clerk and servant to the noble king Edward the third his grandfather, and with my lady Philippa of Hainault, queen of England, his grandam; and when I departed from him, it was at Windsor, and at my departing the king sent me by a knight of his called Sir John Golofre a goblet of silver and gilt weighing two mark of silver, and within it a hundred nobles'.

Richard's love of art of every kind exceeded that of the rest of his family, but directly continued the fine taste of his father and Edward III. From 1387 onwards he gave £100 a year towards the completion of the nave of Westminster abbey, a work directed by his own architect Henry Yeveley. He contributed also to the new choir of York Minster and the west front of Canterbury cathedral; the privileges he granted to Winchester College amounted to a most substantial subsidy to Wykeham's foundation. For himself Richard refitted his father's manor-house at Kennington, improved King's Langley, and in the period around 1385 had a great deal done to modernize both Eltham and Sheen. Eltham had a new royal bathroom fitted and a dancing chamber built, and Sheen was greatly extended, while on an island in the Thames, 'La Nayght', a garden pavilion or kiosk was made, apparently as a private retreat for the king and Queen Anne. Kennington had already had important gardens in the Black Prince's time, for in 1362 timber and poles were used to support the prince's vines and to mend the alleys of his garden there. This may then have been fairly new, as Henry Yeveley in one of his first works for the prince, built a wall of hardstone along the side of the garden in 1358: the gardener from 1349, John Aleyn, and his successor Nicholas le Gardyner after 1353, had wages of 2d. a day, but also robes befitting their estate. Richard II's new garden at Eltham was being turfed by 1387 and this was presumably where Froissart walked and talked under the vines with Sir Richard Stury eight years later.

All these works have disappeared and left hardly a trace, but Richard's noble rebuilding of the great hall of Westminster Palace has survived down to our times. When it was first built, as an aisled hall with roof-trusses carried on rows of timber posts, for William Rufus in 1097–99, it was the largest room in Europe north of the Alps, and held the record for 150 years until the new hall of St Louis was built in Paris. That is divided by stone pillars, and cannot compare in splendour with the renewed concept of Richard II's hall, where the overall width of 68 feet is spanned in the clear by thirteen arched trusses of oak, designed by the chief carpenter Hugh Herland. The Norman walls and the main entrance front at the north end were transformed into Perpendicular Gothic at the same time, 1393–1400, to the design of Henry Yeveley. The new hall has strong claims to be regarded as the finest surviving work of architecture, as well as of building construction, from the European Middle Ages.

In sculpture there were the grand cast metal effigies of Edward III and the Black Prince, made early in the reign, and that of Richard himself beside Queen Anne, made after her death by two London coppersmiths, Nicholas Broker and Godfrey Prest. The statues of kings in Westminster Hall are probably those made for its Norman predecessor in 1385 by Thomas Canon of Corfe. Three taller statues of kings are probably survivors of four carved by William Chuddere in 1398–99 to stand in the pinnacle above the north gable of the Hall. At Winchester the exquisite figure of the Virgin and Child, standing in a niche on the Outer Gate of the College, has been attributed to the French sculptor André Beauneveu, who is known to have worked in England. All these statues were originally painted and gilt, like most mediaeval carvings of all kinds. Colour, in splendid harmonies such as we still see in the illuminations of the time, added an additional dimension to life.

Painting included large-scale work on walls and panels as well as the colouring of statues and the production of brilliant windows of glass, showing religious figures and scenes in churches, and in houses the heraldry of the home. According to the stage of the French War the windows of the royal palaces might display the royal arms of England, or of France and England quartered; after Richard's return from his Irish journey in 1395 he started a new fashion of impaling his arms with those imagined by the heralds for St Edward the Confessor. The king's windows, like the king's gold and silver plate, were destroyed and remade in accordance with these changing modes or campaigns of political and religious propaganda. Similarly the silver seals were made and remade by the greatest goldsmiths of London, displaying on a small scale not only the figure sculpture and heraldry, but the architectural detail and the lettering of the time. Not much of the magnificent jewellery and metalwork has come down to us: little more than the exquisite crown made in England before 1399 and now at Munich; and the engraved plate of Richard's personal quadrant, made in 1399.

A single work of art remains to personify the aims of Richard towards the end of his reign, but as in a glass darkly: the Wilton Diptych. Heraldry and costume indicate that it was painted after Queen Anne's death – the king's white hart couches in a flowery mead strewn with branches of Anne's badge, rosemary, in remembrance of her – and had some special significance in relation to Richard's feelings and policy in regard to his sovereignty over England. It is portable, so that he might have it everywhere with him; but it would serve as the altarpiece for his private oratory, such as the chapel in the Old Manor in Windsor Park which he had decorated in 1397 with harts with gilt antlers painted by Thomas Litlyngton, pupil and successor of Gilbert Prince. The king kneels before the Virgin bearing the Child; he is about to do homage for her Dowry, the kingdom of England: behind him are St John the Baptist and the two royal saints, Edward the Confessor and Edmund the Martyr. It is all but certain that St John also represents the Black Prince, and the two crowned saints the king's grandfather Edward III and great-grandfather Edward II, of whose miracles he had sent a book to the Pope in 1395. Around the Virgin stand eleven angels, wearing the king's collar of broomcods and his badge of the white hart, and on their heads chaplets of red and white roses. The rose is the flower of the Virgin and of England, and moreover, *sub rosa*, hints at a secret. The secret we shall never know, but can guess. Most probably when king Richard gazed at the painting on his private altar he dwelt upon the sacred trust handed down to him by his progenitors; his bounden duty to govern England on behalf of the Queen of Heaven with truth and justice. In the Virgin's face he saw the lineaments of Anne, loved and lost, but now in the safe keeping of the Mother of God. But the angels? Were they not eleven, the number of the faithful apostles who upheld Christ the King? Might they not also stand for living human beings, as the three saintly figures behind him could also portray three generations of his ancestry? And if so, who should they be but members of an Order closely bound to him, tighter knit than the Garter, as it was a closer and more intimate bond than the Round Table 300 strong? Such was the web of dreams in the mind of the king: his hope, his aspiration, his pledge, his prayer.

Catastrophe

For one whole year from the tragic conclusion of the great Appeal in the deaths of Burley and the king's other servants, Richard had to possess himself in patience while the unfitness of the Appellants to govern was made manifest. When, in May 1389, it was known that John of Gaunt might fairly soon return from Spain, he felt able once more to take the initiative. In a meeting of the Great Council, whose members still included many sympathetic royalists, he asked if he were not of full age, and on being told that he was – indeed he had turned 22 – insisted on freely conducting his own business, that of governing the country. The astonished lords had no answer to this and the Great Seal was meekly surrendered by bishop Thomas Arundel, to be entrusted next day to William of Wykeham, now 65 but still in full possession of his powers and lifelong experience of the king's work. Richard's success in this manoeuvre shows that he had matured an imaginative brilliance in action which, in a different field, rivalled or even surpassed that of his father. So coolly to call the bluff of the all-mighty Appellants was a stroke of genius.

What had been achieved was still precarious, and it was not possible to recall from exile the three friends who had escaped at the time of Radcot Bridge: archbishop Neville, De Vere, and Suffolk. The king had to walk warily and could but content himself with removing Gloucester and the earl of Warwick from the Council, and superseding the earl of Arundel as admiral by his half-brother John Holand, back from Spain. As keeper of the privy seal he appointed Edmund Stafford, dean of York and then bishop of Exeter, a competent and honest administrator who was later to be chancellor. It is striking that from this time onwards the city of York played a more important part in affairs and may even, as a counterpoise to London, have been marked out as an alternative capital after 1392. It was then that the king's great quarrel with the City occurred, destined as it proved to be a lethal factor in the fatal conclusion of his reign.

Three months later Richard wrote to his uncle Gaunt desiring him to come back as soon as he possibly could, and the duke landed at Plymouth on 19 November. For almost ten years, until Gaunt's death, the throne was secure and England attained prosperity in a period of truce prolonged into real peace with France. Here at last was the justification of so much blood and toil, so much nervous strain. Thanks to the chivalry of the Black Prince and to the sense and sensibility of his son, this country reached its cultural peak. Never before had it been in an economic position to spend adequately on building and art; never again would the artistic quality of its productions – taken as a whole through the whole gamut of national skill – rise to the same supreme level. The last decade of the fourteenth century, the seventh from the birth of the Black Prince in 1330, brought to fruition all the promise of his generation. In the nature of things this would almost certainly have been, even had he lived, the end of the age associated with Edward of Woodstock. If we disregard what came after and accept the year 1400 as a terminus, then the last was best.

The age was the achievement of three men in direct line, grandfather, father and son: Edward III, the Prince, and Richard II. They were ably assisted by an amazing all-star cast of companions in arms, companions in peace: knights, esquires, philosophers, scholars, statesmen, artists of every kind. At the centre of the age, not chronologically but spiritually, lay the creation of the Order of the Garter as a perpetual reminder of the highest aims of chivalry, the impossible standard of perfection laid down in Arthur's Court. It was a military order but was enshrined in the king's chapel of St George at Windsor Castle and sanctified by the association of the bishops of Winchester as prelates of the Order. Such a body at the centre of court life was in some sense a declaration of the supremacy of honour. The knights of the order, and by reflex imitation all knights and worthy esquires, might fight ruthlessly and kill without compunction, but they fought by the rules and without taking any unfair advantage. Once the heat of battle was over it was their pride to return to a cheerful equanimity and behave with courtesy to their enemies. As victors they could demand ransom from their prisoner, but not such as would deprive him or his dependents of reasonable support.

In the modern age so mistakenly devoted to the search for equality of the sexes, it is worth remembering that the society which had the Garter as its fairest flower was more rationally concerned with an equipoise between them. It was, among much else, the duty of the knight to look to the safety of all ladies and damsels; on the other hand, the savagery of male combat and the harshness of social and economic conditions were modified by the intercession of women – queens first – and the divine attribute of mercy, even if a prerogative of the king, was especially urged by women under the auspices of the Virgin Mary herself. It is reassuring that while the Black Prince married for love – unusually for his rank and period – both his father and his son had their marriages arranged; yet all three marriages were ideally happy while they lasted. The real importance of this background of domestic well-being is emphasized by the sad falling-off of Edward III's last years and Richard's increasing tension, bordering on frenzy, after Anne's death.

As we know, Richard ordered the demolition of Sheen Palace, where his wife had died, and even if this were an extreme instance of the blazing Plantagenet temper, it has to be accepted as genuine evidence of his grief. At the queen's funeral the earl of Arundel, who had been restored to the Council with Gloucester and Warwick after Gaunt's return, went out of his way to slight the king's mourning. He absented himself from the lying-in-state at St Paul's and the funeral procession; arrived late for the service at Westminster, and then insolently demanded the king's leave to quit the proceedings for urgent private business. Richard struck him and drew blood, polluting consecrated ground. In all the circumstances the king's violence is understandable on grounds of grief combined with affront alone, but there may have been a contributory cause. The references to Richard's outbursts of temper, though exaggerated by the historians and in some cases fabricated out of misunderstanding of the documents, are consistent with the agonizing pains of calculus, probably in the kidney. A prescription for the stone actually tried upon King Richard II is on record, but the date of his illness is not stated. The accounts of his wardrobe, however, in the year 1395–96 show immense payments for medicines for the king's body and fees paid to his chief physician John Middelton and second physician Geoffrey Melton, as well as to William Bradewardyn his surgeon and the apothecaries John Leche of Bury and William Waddesworth of London. The later case of Judge Jeffreys, whose attacks of the stone over a period of years gave rise to his violent outbursts on the bench, provides an analogy.

The king's doctors had careers of genuine distinction. Both were Oxford men and took holy orders. Middelton came from county Durham, studied at University College where he was a fellow in 1381–88, and became a canon of Beverley in 1391 and soon afterwards the king's clerk and physician. He ended his life, after having attended on Henry IV, as master of St Nicholas's Hospital outside York and a canon of Howden. Melton may have been rather older, as he took his M.A. by 1377, but his clerical career came later. By 1388 he was attending Henry earl of Derby and by 1395 was a king's clerk and physician. Both men received handsome grants from Richard II and were continued in their offices and pensions by Henry IV. The medical manuscript implies that the prescription was successful: it consisted of a handful each of saxifrage, fennel root, parsley, filipendula (? dropwort), root of water-flag, watercress, radish, made into a decoction with white wine and drunk, as well as being applied as poultices as hot as the patient could bear on the belly and loins. If, as seems likely, the king was an ill man in the years after Anne's death, it fully explains the appearance of premature age in some of his later portraits without recourse to the hypothesis of neurosis or acute melancholia.

Before the queen's death Richard had begun to plan his great expedition to Ireland, and after her funeral proceeded with it. If, as seems likely, he was then suffering from attacks of the stone, it was a courageous even if somewhat foolhardy act to carry on regardless. The pressure of serious work involved in leading such a major military and diplomatic campaign would, all the same, distract his mind from his recent loss, and so his physical pain and discomfort would be acceptable. There were real problems in Ireland to be solved. Primarily the king's intervention may be seen as a major part of his policy of appeasement, of bringing peace to his subjects and healing their wounds. Next there was the harsh economic fact that, whereas the English exchequer in Dublin had, in Edward III's time, lived on its own Irish revenues of some £30,000 a year, the maintenance of the much reduced English Pale was now costing England about £20,000 annually. There was also a tinge of religious orthodoxy in the king's move, for the 'Wild Irish' supported the Popes at Avignon, Clement VII (who died just at this time) and Benedict XIII, while England was faithful to the Roman obedience.

The choice of commanders makes an interesting study. John of Gaunt, now duke of Aquitaine, was going to Gascony, so that the regency of England was left to the duke of York. Gloucester was taken to Ireland where the king could keep an eye on him; and to do him justice, he had shown himself in the past a competent soldier. Sir Baldwin Raddington, Burley's nephew and one of the king's most trusted aides, had gone ahead with the vanguard. With Richard were a number of his younger supporters: the duke of York's son Edward earl of Rutland, now created earl of Cork; the earl of March, Roger Mortimer, heir presumptive to the throne; Thomas Mowbray earl of Nottingham; Thomas Holand son of the king's half-brother the earl of Kent; Sir Thomas Despenser; and Thomas Merke a monk of Westminster, who later became bishop of Carlisle and a faithful supporter of his king to the end. The great force sailed from Haverfordwest to Waterford, where it landed on 2 October 1394.

The campaign was in its way a strange and remarkable demonstration of real peace-making from strength. Richard seems himself to have worked out the grand strategy, which included a blockade of the ports used by the wild Irish. The army, though harassed on its flanks while marching from Waterford to Dublin, was overwhelming by Irish standards, and the king of Leinster, Art Oge MacMurrough, was too wily to dream of offering pitched battle. The diplomatic masterstroke was the use, on Richard's banners, of his royal arms impaled with those of Edward the Confessor. The Confessor, as the saintly king who had recovered England from the Danes, was automatically revered by the Irish, who loathed the Danes. Richard's reverence for the Confessor probably went back to that famous day in 1381 when he had taken the communion and prayed in Westminster Abbey before dealing with Wat Tyler. It was always the Abbey, close by his palace, that meant most to him among the great churches of England. The heraldic juxtaposition of the Confessor's arms and his own went back at any rate to the spring of 1393, but the impalement of the two coats on a single shield seems to have started with the expedition, and first of all with the device on the king's new signet then made. Whether the decision to couple the arms of his patron with his own was deliberate, or a happy chance, it worked like a charm on Irish tempers.

In Dublin the winter was spent in discussion with the Irish leaders, the earl of Ormond 'who could right well speak the language' and other Anglo-Irish in the forces acting as interpreters. Eighty chiefs paid homage, and the four kings of Meath, Thomond, Connor and Leinster were brought to accept knighthood from Richard after learning the usages of chivalry and spending a night in vigil in Christ Church cathedral. The whole story was told to Froissart the next year by Henry Christead, who had himself become Anglo-Irish and was one of the interpreters. Froissart was puzzled by the failure of earlier English kings to tame the Irish, contrasting with this sudden and unexpected success. Christead's explanation is revealing, in that he stressed, beyond the obvious material factors and the happy display of the Confessor's arms, the fact that the Irish kings 'repute king Richard a good man and of good conscience, and so they have done to him faith and homage'. This is an outstanding testimonial to the real base of Richard II's power over men of good will. He had the challenging sincerity which had in former years won men to his father the Black Prince.

The achievement of Richard II in Ireland was unique. He went, as a king intending to govern, but in good faith and with good will towards his Irish subjects. In all the centuries, from the twelfth to the twentieth, in which there has been the problem of a political relationship between England and Ireland, this remains the one high-water mark of genuine understanding. It is not the smallest part of the tragedy of Richard of Bordeaux that his most serious undertaking in the political field – in itself completely successful – should have remained unfulfilled and without any natural sequel. Had he remained on the throne for perhaps another 20 years or so, we cannot doubt that he would have placed England and Ireland in a permanent and positive relation to each other. The king was recalled from Ireland by the religious problem posed by the Lollard followers of Wycliffe, who had died in 1384. He did for the time being succeed in stalling off the protestantism which was to break out triumphantly

150 years later; but he was prevented from finishing in Ireland what he had so brilliantly begun.

The year 1395 was important in several ways. The king came back, dealt with Lollards in high places by his skill in making them recant their extreme doctrines, and then gave his attention to the re-burial of his exiled friend Robert de Vere, killed during a boar-hunt three years before. The body was brought back from Louvain and reburied in the family chapel of Earls Colne church with splendid ceremonial. It was made clear that the king had not forgotten the loyalty which had inspired his friend, and had led him to exile and to death abroad. We cannot say whether this symbolic act of rehabilitation portended deliberate revenge upon the king's enemies who had driven De Vere from his high position and from his country. Richard passed on to the greater project of a permanent peace with France, and it was to be secured by his own marriage to the princess Isabelle, then eight years old. Into the picture came the position of English Aquitaine, now under the diplomatic John of Gaunt, and a satisfactory settlement was made, having regard to both French and Gascon interests. Bordeaux settled, Gaunt was able to return to England and to marry his mistress, Catherine Swynford. Their children were legitimatized and became the famous Beaufort branch of the Plantagenet royal family.

From this time onwards, parallel to the foreign policy of peace with France, internal affairs took on a marked trend towards York. We saw that in 1389 Edmund Stafford, already dean of York, became keeper of the privy seal; in 1395 he was made bishop of Exeter and in the next year chancellor of England for the rest of the reign. London, whose loyalty in 1381 had been dubious, opposed the king in the crisis of 1387–88. The citizens again became troublesome in 1392 and Richard moved the courts of law and the household to York. For half the year York was the king's home; early in 1393 he gave a new and generous charter, and stayed there again for part of August and for Christmas. In 1395 Richard presented to the Minster a relic of one of the Holy Innocents, and returned for Easter 1396. At the Royal Maundy he gave 'with his own hands' a silver groat, 4d. each, to over 12,000 poor people; his father's magnificent largess poured out once more. In May he granted another, more extensive, charter and gave a state sword to be borne before the Mayor of York. He subscribed 100 marks (£66 13s. 4d.) to the Minster works in 1395 and by 1397 was shown as Emperor, bearing a sword and wearing a triple crown, on a carved bust supporting the central tower. This must date from the period when the archbishop of Cologne and three other electors became his vassals, along with other German knights. Before this, he had kept the feast of Corpus Christi on 1 June 1396 at York, when he witnessed the Mystery Plays and presided over an important meeting with the Mayor and Aldermen in the chapter house of the Minster.

Even without the need to keep the Londoners in their proper place, York would have had great advantages as a capital of Britain, roughly equidistant from London, Dublin and Edinburgh; in easy communication with the whole of northern Europe by sea, and notably with the Empire and England's economic dependencies in Scandinavia. An alternative possibility is that Richard, envisaging himself as Emperor, saw York as an Imperial Free City with unusually wide privileges, meant to be a counterbalance to London. Through this period relations with Cologne were particularly close, and this is shown by strands of artistic style and the presence of artists from Cologne such as Herebright the painter, who worked in London, for St Paul's cathedral, and for William of Wykeham. The English contribution to the International Style in these last years of the fourteenth century became more closely linked with that of the Rhineland and somewhat less with those of Paris and Prague.

It was, nevertheless, towards Paris that the king's foreign policy was now oriented. The celebrations for Richard's second marriage, with Isabelle of France, were the occasion for unprecedented demonstrations of friendship. Nearly sixty years of war, broken by temporary truces, separated the two countries, and this dynastic bridal from Philip of Valois's attacks on the England of Edward III. It seemed as though the war party, the baronial opposition led by Gloucester and the Arundels, had finally been overcome in favour of sweet reason and Richard's genuine desire to achieve and maintain peace in Europe. Within a year or two of his marriage on 1 November 1396 he might well expect to control Germany and the imperial states as well as England, Ireland and Aquitaine. With the friendly assistance of his uncle Gaunt, now not only duke of Aquitaine but father-in-law to Portugal and to Castile, he would be the arbiter of the western world. Unlike most of his predecessors in that capacity, he would owe his position to reason and tact rather than to armed force.

These hopes and expectations were not megalomania: bit by bit the pieces of the jigsaw were falling into place, and as things stood there was no substantial obstacle to success. It had been remarked that the forces in Ireland in 1395 were punctually paid, a clear sign that the chronic state of financial difficulty which had beset the Crown was now a thing of the past. The enormous burden of the French war had been shifted and real national prosperity lay ahead. In the course of a couple of years several successive accidents were, however, to bring the house down. The first of these was the quarrel deliberately picked with Richard by his murderous and uncouth uncle Gloucester, who might have been expected to keep his mouth discreetly shut. The circumstances hinged upon the refusal of the war party to see any good in the king's policy of peace. Back in 1378 England had occupied the ports of Brest and Cherbourg in return for substantial loans to the duke of Brittany and the king of Navarre respectively. In both cases there were explicit arrangements for return if the loan was paid off, which happened in the case of Cherbourg in 1393. Charles VI of France advanced the money and Richard II handed back the fortress; he was criticized at home for doing so by the war party, but in honour could have done nothing else. At Brest there was an added condition, that the English should garrison it for the duration of the war: but the treaty of marriage in 1396 provided for a definite truce of 28 years. Richard in 1397 released Brest to Brittany and the English garrison came home. In the course of a celebration banquet Gloucester deliberately taunted the king by declaring: 'Sire, you ought first to hazard your life by capturing a city before you give up one conquered by your ancestors.' Although the open breach was patched up, Gloucester must have seen that he had gone too far to be safe, and plunged into conspiracy. With the connivance of the abbot of St Albans and the prior of Westminster a fresh plot was hatched by the Appellants.

The whole of the old gang met at Arundel Castle, including the earl of Nottingham and Henry Bolingbroke, Gaunt's son. The earl of Arundel's brother had by now been made archbishop of Canterbury by the forgiving king, but he joined in an oath to imprison Richard and the dukes of Lancaster and York and to execute all of the king's councillors. Nottingham informed the king of the plot and Richard himself rode to Gloucester's home at Pleshey to find his uncle ill, probably in reality rather than diplomatically. Gloucester was arrested and sent in Nottingham's custody to imprisonment at Calais. The earls of Arundel and Warwick were also arrested and sent to the Tower. The king caused the three ringleaders to be appealed of treason in the same manner that, in 1387, they had appealed his loyal servants. The new Appellants were the informer Nottingham, with the king's nephew the young earl of Kent; his half-brother John Holand earl of Huntingdon; his nephew Edward earl of Rutland, York's son; the earl of Somerset, Gaunt's son John Beaufort; John Montague, earl of Salisbury, who had just succeeded his aged uncle William; Sir Thomas Despenser; and Sir William Scrope. The guilt of Arundel was manifest and he was condemned and executed on the same spot where Sir Simon Burley had suffered. Warwick confessed his guilt humbly and was sent to exile in the Isle of Man. It was then revealed that Gloucester had died in prison at Calais, but had left a long written confession. On the petition of Parliament, archbishop Arundel was impeached, and allowed to proceed to Rome, where he was deprived of his archbishopric by the Pope. The king expressly proclaimed that no proceedings would be taken against any other members of the improper, and probably illegal, Commission of 1386.

Even those who regard the king's proceedings as his 'revenge' have to admit that it was a very mild vengeance considering the appalling and vindictive bloodbath of 1388. But there is no doubt of the reality of the quite new plot of 1397, and of its having been precipitated by Gloucester's own boorish rudeness to the king's face. Richard had done nothing, except restore Brest to the duke of Brittany, to provoke his uncle to insult and subsequent attempted injury. The king's enemies had at last been humbled and their estates forfeited. His friends were now advanced in honour: his brother Huntingdon became duke of Exeter; his nephew Kent duke of Surrey; Rutland was promoted to duke of Albemarle or Aumale; John Beaufort, earl of Somerset, was now marquis of Dorset. Sir Thomas Despenser was given the vacant earldom of Gloucester, William Scrope was made earl of Wiltshire; Thomas Percy, earl of Worcester; and Ralph Neville earl of Westmorland. Not only did the rehabilitated Nottingham become duke of Norfolk, but Henry of Derby, as John of Gaunt's son, was made duke of Hereford. The king himself added the Arundel estates in Denbighshire and Shropshire to the county palatine of Chester and Flint, to make a new Principality of Chester. His additional title of Prince of Chester was a reward to the men of Cheshire for the steadfast loyalty they had shown him.

Parliament was adjourned after all members, lords and commons, had taken oath to maintain its acts for ever, and was to meet again at Shrewsbury in the New Year. It must have been somewhere about this time that Richard wrote his memorable letter to his cousin Albert, duke of Bavaria and count of Holland, Zealand and Hainault. From it we can sense both his exasperation at repeated treachery, and his religious beliefs:

We render humble and devout thanksgiving to the Highest Observer of human minds, in Whose hand are not only the hearts but the bodies of kings and princes, Who has until now protected beneath favouring auspices by His powerful right hand our royal throne and person since the very cradle from the hands of all enemies, and especially those of household and intimacy, whose contrivances are notoriously more destructive than any plague. For noblemen and leaders of our household, whom we have respected, whom we have brought to the highest peak of honour, to whom we have opened a generous hand and whom we have treated with real affection, have for long and since we were of tender years traitrously conspired to disinherit our crown and usurp our royal power, raising themselves with many abettors of their iniquity to rebel against our royal will, publicly condemning our faithful servants to death and doing whatsoever they pleased at their own will. Thus have they striven damnably to spend their malice even upon our person, having wrongfully usurped the royal power by going about among our privy affairs, so that they left us hardly anything beyond the royal name. And though our royal clemency indulged these traitors with time enough to change their hearts and show the fruits of repentance, so deeply rooted in evil seemed their obstinacy that by the just judgment of God our avenging severity has been meted out to the destruction and ruin of their persons. Thus through the accompanying providence of God we have brought together the right hands of our power, bruising these confessed and convicted traitors and, threshing them out even to the husks, we have adjudged them to natural or civil death, so bringing to our subjects a peace which, by the grace of God, may last for ever. . . .

It is hard to see in this any personal triumph in a long-sought vengeance at last achieved; what is there is a sense of relief – misplaced, as we can see with after knowledge – that the terrifying obstacle to a lasting peace had been removed for good and all. So long as there was a war party of the greatest magnates in the realm, England could never be sure of external peace; so long as the legitimate king was threatened by traitors there could be no real peace at home for honest citizens and countrymen. Richard here expressed in his own way that solidarity with his subjects that his father had proclaimed to his archers before Poitiers forty-one years earlier, which he himself had shouted to Wat Tyler's mob more than half his lifetime back. Within the next twelve months the links by which he felt himself bound to his father and to the men of Cheshire were to be particularly exemplified. While some of the Black Prince's knights and captains had already been enjoying pensions, others came forward and obtained annuities which they had not previously claimed. Much more recently men of the county, a few of them veterans of the old war, had served under De Vere in 1387 and been wounded or dispersed at Radcot Bridge. For these victims of the long-standing treason of the Appellants the king set up a special fund of 4,000 marks, deposited in Chester Abbey. By the end of 1398, after scrutiny of all petitions, the whole of it had been distributed. In all the documents connected with the new principality Richard used to repeat his 'immense friendship and affection' for Cheshire.

The renewed parliament at Shrewsbury set what seemed to be the stamp of final national approval on what had been achieved. The king was given a grant of the customs and other duties for life, to secure financial solvency; all the former acts which might have trespassed upon the royal sovereignty were completely traversed and annulled; the law of treason was amended to prevent any future reversal; all three estates took fresh oaths perpetually to maintain this settlement. Excommunication was promulgated against all who should contravene the present statutes and ordinances, and papal confirmation of this was sought and obtained. To maintain the settlement a Parliamentary Commission of eleven magnates was set up, consisting of the dukes of Lancaster, York, Albemarle, Surrey and Exeter, the marquis of Dorset, and the earls of March, Salisbury, Northumberland, Gloucester and Wiltshire. It might seem at first sight likely that the eleven angels of the king's private altar-piece could symbolize these eleven men, but it is not at all probable that Richard would have relied implicitly upon his kindly but ineffective uncle of York, nor is there any reason to think that John Beaufort, marquis of Dorset, was one of his closest friends. Again, the list does not include some of his most eminent and staunchest supporters: Richard Scrope archbishop of York, Thomas Merke bishop of Carlisle, William Colchester, abbot of Westminster, and Stephen Scrope.

Before the Shrewsbury Parliament sat the last act of the royal tragedy was being prepared. Henry Bolingbroke, now duke of Hereford, came to the king accusing Mowbray – the former Nottingham, now duke of Norfolk – of treason. The quarrel, immortalized by Shakespeare, was a strange case of rogues falling out amongst themselves. Both men had guilty consciences: they had attached themselves to the original Appellants, though in their favour it has to be said that they opposed Gloucester's cruelty and particularly his inexcusable murder of Burley. Nottingham, by giving away the second conspiracy of 1397, had been restored to favour and might consider himself safe. Henry, though not accused of his share in the doings either of 1387 or 1397, must have been aware of the precariousness of his position, and seized a chance to ingratiate himself at the expense of Norfolk. As everyone knows, the matter was brought to judicial combat at Coventry and at the very last moment stopped by the king, who banished Henry for ten years and Norfolk for life. Later on Richard reduced Henry's exile to six years as a concession to his father John of Gaunt.

While all this was happening in England, the king's heir Roger Mortimer, earl of March, had been killed in an ambush in Ireland. Art MacMurrough, king of Leinster, had broken his oath of fealty to his suzerain Richard and was in armed rebellion. Mortimer's son Edmund, only seven years old, was recognized by the king as his heir, but obviously the pacification of Ireland needed to be done again. Months went by in equipping another great expedition and it was during those months that the next accident of fate befell: John of Gaunt, duke of Lancaster, died on 3 February 1399 at the age of only 59, leaving the king without that elder support which he most needed. What was even worse, Gaunt's death reopened the whole question of Henry Bolingbroke and the enormous, disproportionate riches and power of the duchy of Lancaster. After six weeks of consideration, Richard decided on 18 March 1399 to confiscate the inheritance of Lancaster and unite it to the Crown of England. It has remained so united ever since, and this is the ultimate justification for the act. It was an impossible anachronism in the England of that time that there should be a realm within the realm, of enormous proportions and protected by castles of great strength, in which the king's writ did not run. Richard in principle made the right decision; but as regarded his own immediate interests it was a mistake.

There is not much doubt that, had the king remained in England, there would have been no successful invasion by Henry and his supporters, coming on the plea of recovering his own rights in land and property. Richard, however, had sworn to avenge Mortimer's death, and he never broke his pledge. Aware of the risks at sea and in Ireland on campaign, he made his will on 16 April and completed it with final alterations just before he sailed on 29 May. His chief concern was the maintenance of the statutes and ordinances of the parliament of Westminster and Shrewsbury and with the judgment at Coventry and confiscation of the Lancastrian estates. His successor, not named but by implication the boy Edmund Mortimer, was to confirm all these decisions as a condition of inheriting the king's residuary estate. Charged with holding the residue in trust to this end were four principal executors, the dukes of Surrey, Albemarle, and Exeter, and the earl of Wiltshire. The remaining executors were the bishops of Salisbury, Exeter, Worcester, Carlisle and St Davids; Richard Clifford, dean of York, keeper of the privy seal; the faithful clerks Richard Maudeleyn, William Fereby and John Ikelyngton; and two laymen, John Lufwyk and William Serle. The archbishops of Canterbury and York, the bishop of Winchester, the abbot of Westminster, the king's uncle the duke of York and the earl of Northumberland were to be overseers as a control upon the executors. Three witnesses, probably cognisant of the terms of the will, were the bishop of London, the marquis of Dorset and the earl of Worcester. Among these 24 men were probably most of the eleven members of the king's innermost circle of supporters.

There is no need to retell the well known story of Henry's landing at Ravenspur and occupation of England – ostensibly of his own, but confiscated, estates – while Richard and his army were enduring hardship and privation in the mountains between Kilkenny and Dublin. There the king showed himself a true heir to Edward I, true son to the Black Prince, as a leader of his men and sharer of their hardships. There, 'out of true and entire affection' as the French esquire Creton put it in his journal, Richard knighted the young Henry of Monmouth, his bitter rival's son and later king Henry V. Again, it is unnecessary to recapitulate the betrayals of the king in detail: by the duke of York, left as regent; by York's son the duke of Albemarle; by the earl of Northumberland who led him into a trap after swearing upon the Host at Conway that Henry had no treasonable purpose but had come only to claim his own duchy. Worse than all this, and even worse than the indignities which Richard suffered on his journey to London as a prisoner and witnessed by Creton, is the beginning of the long and shameful story of glossing over illegality, of hushing up the truth, of palming off a blatant usurpation as a popular revolt against a tyrant.

Some of the king's friends were already dead, murdered by Henry's men; others would die in their forlorn hope at the end of the year. The king was condemned as unworthy by an indictment of 33 accusations; he demanded the right to reply but it was not granted him. Parliament acclaimed Henry and made him occupy the vacant throne; but there was one dissentient voice. Thomas Merke, the bishop of Carlisle, got up and made a pungent speech which resulted in imprisonment and loss of his see: 'There is not one present who is competent and fit to judge such a sovereign as my lord the King whom we have acknowledged our lord for the space of twenty years and more . . . there never was any false traitor nor wicked murderer who is not at least brought before the judge. It appears that you are about to condemn King Richard without hearing his answer and without his even being here . . . my lord the duke has more offended against King Richard than the King against him . . . he has seated himself on the throne where none should sit but the King of England lawfully crowned; . . . you should bring King Richard to the full Parliament to hear him and . . . to see if he is willing to give up his crown to the duke or not.'

Next day a parliamentary deputation visited Richard in the Tower to tell him that he had been deposed and that allegiance to him had been renounced. He replied that he could not renounce that essential kingship which was his by virtue of the anointing at his coronation. The son of the Black Prince could be deposed, imprisoned, destroyed – in a few months he would be dead; but he could not be brought to deny the true principles in which he firmly believed, the inner spiritual kingship by which men were governed for God. He could indeed be saddened at the instability of the people: a few days earlier the chronicler Adam of Usk who, though on Henry's side, admitted that he was 'much moved at heart', had heard Richard say sadly:

My God! a wonderful land is this, and a fickle; which hath exiled, slain, destroyed or ruined so many Kings, rulers and great men, and is ever tainted and toileth with strife and variance and envy.

Appendix

THE WILL OF EDWARD THE BLACK PRINCE, 1376

(translated from the French text printed by A. P.
Stanley in *Historical Memorials of Canterbury*, 10th edition,
1883, 168–75, from the register of Archbishop Sudbury)

In the name of the Father, of the Son, and of the Holy Ghost, Amen. We, Edward, eldest son of the King of England and of France, prince of Wales, duke of Cornwall and earl of Chester, the 7th day of June in the year of grace a thousand three hundred seventy and sixth, in our chamber within the palace of our well redoubted lord and father the King at Westminster, being in good and whole memory and having consideration of the brief continuance of human frailty and how uncertain is the time of its reduction to the divine will, and ever desiring to be with the help of God prepared for His disposition, we ordain and make our testament in the manner following. Firstly we bequeath our soul to God our Creator and to the Holy Blessed Trinity, and to the glorious virgin Mary and to all the saints both men and women (*a tous lez sainz et seintez*); and our body to be buried in the cathedral church of the Trinity at Canterbury, where the body of the true martyr my lord St Thomas rests, in the midst of the chapel of Our Lady Undercroft directly before the altar, so that the end of our tomb towards the feet be ten feet distant from the altar, and that the said tomb be of marble and built in sound masonry. And we will that around the said tomb there be twelve brass scutcheons each of one foot in breadth, six of which shall be of our whole arms and the other six of ostrich feathers, and that above each scutcheon be written, that is to wit above those of our arms [? *ich diene* omitted] and above the others of ostrich feathers – *Houmout*.* And upon the tomb let there be made a table of gilt brass of the breadth and length of the same tomb, on which we will that there be set an image of work in relief of gilt brass (*un ymage d'overeigne levez de latoun suzorrez*) in memorial of us, fully armed in plate of war with our quartered arms and half the face exposed (*et le visage mie*), with our leopard helm set

---

* On the tomb the mottoes of *Houmout* are placed above the shields of arms, and those of *ich diene* above the shields bearing the badge of three ostrich feathers, each feather also carrying the motto *ich diene* on a scroll.

beneath the head of the image. And we will that upon our tomb in the place where one may be able most clearly to read it at sight there be written this following, in the way that seems best to our executors: –

Tu qe passez ove bouche close, par la ou cest corps repose
Entent ce qe te dirray, sicome te dire la say,
Tiel come tu es, Je au ciel [*autiel*] fu, Tu seras tiel come Je su,
De la mort ne pensay je mie, Tant come j'avoy la vie.
En terre avoy grand richesse, dont Je y fys grand noblesse,
Terre, mesons, et grand tresor, draps, chivalx, argent et or.
Mes ore su je povres et cheitifs, perfond en la terre gys,
Ma grand beaute est tout alee, Ma char est tout gastee,
Moult est estroite ma meson, En moy na si verite non,
Et si ore me veissez, Je ne quide pas qe vous deeisez,
Qe j'eusse onqes hom este, si su je ore de tout changee.
Pur Dieu pries au celestien Roy, qe mercy eit de l'arme de moy.
Tout cil qe pur moi prieront, ou a Dieu m'acorderont,
Dieu les mette en son parays, ou nul ne poet estre cheitifs.*

And we will that at the time when our body be brought through the town of Canterbury to the priory, two destriers be trapped with our arms, and two men armed in our arms and in our helms watch before our said body, that is to wit one for war with our whole arms quartered, and the other for peace with our badges of ostrich feathers with four banners of the same suit, and each of them who shall carry the said banners shall have upon his head a hat of our arms. And he who shall be armed for war is to have an armed man bearing by him a black pennon with ostrich feathers. And we will that the herse be made between the high altar and the choir, and within it we will that our body be placed while the vigils, masses and divine services are performed; and these services so performed, let our body be carried to the foresaid chapel of Our Lady where it shall be buried. Also we give and devise to the high altar of the said church our clothing of green velvet embroidered with gold with all that belongs to the said clothing. Also, two basins of gold, a chalice with the paten of gold and our arms engraved on the foot, and two cruets of gold, and an image of the Trinity to place on the said altar and our great cross of silver gilt and enamelled, that is to wit the best silver cross we have; all which things we give and devise to the said altar to serve there for ever without ever putting them to another use for any mishap. Also we give and devise to the altar of Our Lady in the chapel abovesaid our white clothing diapered all

---

* For translation of the poem see p. 166.

over with a blue vine, and also the frontal that the bishop of Exeter'gave us, which is of the Assumption of Our Lady in the midst bordered with gold and other imagery, and a tabernacle of the Assumption of Our Lady which the said bishop also gave us, and two great twisted candlesticks of silver, and two basins of our arms and a great chalice gilt and enamelled with the arms of Warenne, with two cruets carved like two angels to serve the same altar for ever without ever putting them to another use for any mishap. Also we give and devise our chamber-hangings of ostrich feathers of black tapestry with a red border and swans with the heads of ladies, that is to wit a dossal and eight pieces for the sides and two bankers, to the said church of Canterbury. And we will that the dossal be cut as shall seem best to our executors to serve before and round the high altar, and what shall not be needed to serve there of the remnant of the said dossal, and also the said bankers, we will should be shared out to serve before the altar where my lord Saint Thomas lies, and for the altar where the head is, and for the altar where the sword point is (*ou la poynte de l'espie est*), and about our body in the said chapel of Our Lady Undercroft, as far as it may suffice. And we will that the sides of the said chamber-hangings be for hanging in the choir along above the stalls and in this manner we ordain them to be used to serve as a memorial for us on the feast of the Trinity and on all the principal feasts of the year and on the feasts and day of my lord Saint Thomas, and on all the feasts of Our Lady, and also on the days of our anniversary for ever as long as they may last without ever putting them to another use. Also we give and devise to our chapel in this said Our Lady Undercroft, in which we have founded a chantry of two chaplains to sing for us for ever, our missal and our portifory, which we ourselves have had made and illuminated with our armorials in divers places and also with our badges of ostrich feathers; and we ordain that this missal and portifory serve for ever in the said chapel without ever putting them to another use for any mishap; and for all these things we charge the souls of the Prior and Convent as they will answer before God. Also we give and devise to the said chapel two single vestments that is to wit, alb, amice, chasuble, stole and maniple, with towels suitable to each of the said vestments; to serve also in the said chapel for ever. Also we give and devise our great retable of gold and silver, full of precious relics, and in the midst a cross of the wood of the Holy Cross, and the said table is garnished with stones and with pearls, that is to wit twenty-five balas rubies, thirty-four sapphires, fifty-eight great pearls and various other sapphires, emeralds and small pearls, to the high altar of our house of Ashridge which is of our foundation, to serve for ever at the said altar without ever putting it to another use for any mishap; and with this we charge the souls of the Rector and Convent of the said house to answer before God. Also we give and devise the remnant of all our clothing, cloths of gold, the tabernacle of the Resurrection, two shrines of silver gilt and enamelled as one set, cross, chalice, cruets, candlesticks, basins, books [or liveries? – *liveres*] and all our other ornaments belonging to holy church, to our chapel of St Nicholas within our castle of Wallingford, to serve and remain there for ever without ever putting it to another use; and with this we charge the souls of the dean and subdean of the said chapel to answer before God; always excepted the blue clothing with golden roses and ostrich feathers, the whole of which clothing with all that belongs to it we give and devise to our son Richard, together with the bed that we have of the same suit and all the apparel of the said bed, which our well redoubted lord and father the King gave us. Also we give and devise to our said son our bed striped with brocade and red camaca (*palee de baudekyn et de camaca rouge*), which is altogether new, with all belonging to the said bed. Also we give and devise to our said son our great bed embroidered with angels, with the pillows, carpets, coverlet, sheets and all other apparel belonging to the said bed. Also we give and devise to our said son the arras chamber-hangings of the passage [of arms] of Saladin (*du pas de Saladyn*), and also the worsted hangings embroidered with mermen of the sea (*mermyns de mier*) and the border of red with black stripes and embroidered with swans with the heads of ladies and with ostrich feathers, which hangings we will that our said son should have with all that belongs to them. And as for our silver vessels, since we think that with our consort the princess we received at the time of our marriage up to the value of seven hundred marks sterling of the vessels of our said consort, We will that she should have up to that said value of ours; and of the remnant of our said vessels we will that our said son should have a part suitable to his estate according to the advice of our executors. Also we give and devise to our said consort the princess the red worsted chamber-hangings embroidered with eagles and griffons, with the border of swans with ladies' heads. Also we devise to Sir Roger de Clarendon a silk bed according to the advice of our executors, with all that belongs to the said bed. Also we give and devise to sir Robert de Walsham our confessor a great bed of red camoca embroidered with our arms at each corner, and the said Camaka is diapered in the same with the arms of Hereford, with the whole canopy (*celure*), curtains, pillows, bolster, carpets of tapestry and all the other apparel. Also we give and devise to Mr Alan Cheyne (*monsieur Alayn Cheyne*) our bed of white camoca powdered with blue eagles, that is to wit quilt, dorser, whole canopy, curtains, pillows, bolster, carpets and all other apparel. And all the rest of our goods and chattels as well vessels of gold and jewels as all other goods wherever they may be, apart from those which we have given and devised above as is said, as well as all manner of debts to us due in whatever manner it may be, together with all the issues and profits which may arise and come from all our lands and lordships, for three years after God shall have worked His will upon us, the which profits our said lord and father has granted us to pay our debts, We ordain and devise as well for the funeral expenses which must necessarily be incurred for our estate, as for discharging all our debts by the hands of our executors, that they should pay firstly the said funeral expenses and afterwards chiefly discharge all the debts by us truly owed. And after these things have been performed, as is said, if anything remain of our said goods and chattels, we will that therefrom our said executors should according to the amount reward our poor servants equally according to their degrees and deserts if beforehand they may obtain information of those who have best knowledge of them, as they would answer before God at the Day of Judgment, when none will be judge save One alone. And as for the annuities which we have granted to our knights, esquires, and other our servants in reward for the services they have done us and the labours they have had about us, our whole and last will is that the said annuities should stand and that all those to whom we have granted them should be well and loyally served and paid, according to the purport of our grant and of our letters which they have of us. And we charge our son Richard upon our blessing to keep and confirm to everyone as much as we have so given them, and as far as God has given us power over our said son we give him our curse if he hinder or suffer to be hindered as much as is our said gift. And of this our testament, which we will should be kept and performed as our last will, we make and ordain executors our very dear and well beloved brother of Spain, Duke of Lancaster; the reverend fathers in God William bishop of Winchester; John bishop of Bath; William bishop of St Asaph; our very dear in God sir Robert de Walsham our confessor; Hugh de Segrave steward of our lands; Alan de Stokes; and John de Fordham; whom we pray, require and charge to execute and loyally accomplish all the things abovesaid. In witness of all and each of the things abovesaid we have caused to be set to this our testament and last will our privy and secret seals, and have also commanded our notary underwritten to put our said last will and testament into public form and by him to be subscribed and signed and marked with his accustomed sign, in witness of all and each of the things abovesaid.

Notarial attestation by John de Ormeshevede, clerk of the diocese of Carlisle and notary public by apostolic authority, in the presence of the reverend father lord John bishop of Hereford, Sir Louis de Clifford, Sir Nicholas Bonde and Sir Nicholas de Scharnesfelde knights, and sir William de Walsham clerk.

Probate of the testament before Simon archbishop of Canterbury, 4 Ides (10) June, 1376, in the chamber within the screens of the house of the convent of Friars Preachers of London.

Note that John, bishop of Durham, and Alan Stokes, executors, had rendered account and have a full acquittance, and an acquittance from the Prior and Chapter of Christ Church, Canterbury, for the legacies bequeathed to that church.

The poem on the tomb of the Black Prince

The wording given in the prince's will is not precisely followed by what is engraved on his monument, but the sense is roughly the same. Another text was set down, from the tomb inscription, by Chandos Herald at the end of his life of the prince. The verses were not an original composition but based on an anonymous French translation, of the thirteenth century, of the *Clericalis Disciplina* written in Latin by the converted Jew Petrus Alphonsi. Born in 1062–63, he was baptized in 1106 at Huesca, king Alfonso I of Aragon standing sponsor. Petrus collaborated in the translation of Euclid and other scientific writers from Arabic into Latin with the Englishman Adelard of Bath, moved to England, and became physician to Henry I. His work was profoundly inspired by the joint civilization, in Spain, of the 'three faiths of the Book' and in this poem we find a reflection of the attitude of mind of the orthodox Muslim who, on passing any cemetery of no matter what religion, prays for those who sleep in death. It is singular that the Black Prince should thus by a roundabout route return to the Mozarabic culture so dear to his friend Don Pedro.

The general sense of the poem is clear, but there are obscure points, particularly the words '*ove bouche close*' or '*de bouche close*', with shut mouth, in the first line. This apostrophizes the passer-by who remains silent that he should open his mouth to pray aloud. Apart from the omission of this detail the version in Elizabethan English by the antiquary John Weever is extremely faithful to the sense and spirit and is reprinted here as it captures far better than a more literal rendering the mediaeval quality of the French text which meant so much to Edward of Woodstock.

(J. Weever, *Ancient Funerall Monuments*, 1631, 205)

Who so thou be that passeth by,
Where these corps entombed lie:
Understand what I shall say
As at this time speak I may.

Such as thou art, some time was I,
Such as I am, such shalt thou be.
I little thought on the hour of death
So long as I enjoyed breath.

Great riches here I did possess
Whereof I made great nobleness.
I had gold, silver, wardrobes and
Great treasure, horses, houses, land.

But now a caitiff poor am I,
Deep in the ground, lo here I lie.
My beauty great is all quite gone,
My flesh is wasted to the bone.

My house is narrow now and throng,
Nothing but Truth comes from my tongue:
And if ye should see me this day,
I do not think but ye would say
That I had never been a man;
So much altered now I am.

For God's sake pray to the heavenly King
That he my soul to heaven would bring.
All they that pray and make accord
For me unto my God and Lord:
God place them in his Paradise,
Wherein no wretched caitiff lies.

Bibliography and Abbreviations

Armitage-Smith 1904   S. Armitage-Smith, *John of Gaunt* (1904)

Barnie 1974   J. Barnie, *War in Medieval Society* (1974)

C. M. Barron, 'The Tyranny of Richard II', *Bulletin of the Institute of Historical Research*, XLI (1968), 1–18

Beltz 1841   G. F. Beltz, *Memorials of the Most Noble Order of the Garter* (1841)

BPR   *The Black Prince's Register* (4 vols, 1930–33)

D. A. Bullough, 'Games People played: Drama and Ritual as Propaganda in Medieval Europe', *Transactions of the Royal Historical Society*, 5th Series, XXIV (1974), 97–122

Burne 1955   A. H. Burne, *The Crecy War: a military history of the Hundred Years War from 1337 to the peace of Bretigny, 1360* (1955)

R. V. H. Burne, 'Richard II and Cheshire', *Chester Archaeological Society's Journal*, XLVIII (1961), 27–34

J. Cammidge, *The Black Prince* (1943)

CLibR   *Calendar of Liberate Rolls*

Cobb 1883   J. W. Cobb, *History and Antiquities of Berkhamsted* (1883)

A. Collins, *Life of Edward, Prince of Wales* (1740)

M. Coryn, *The Black Prince* (1934)

Coulton 1918   G. G. Coulton, *Social Life in Britain from the Conquest to the Reformation* (1918 etc.)

CPatR   *Calendar of Patent Rolls*

Louise Creighton, *Life of Edward the Black Prince* (1876)

Curtis 1927   E. Curtis, *Richard II in Ireland* (1927)

Curtis 1938 — — *A History of Medieval Ireland* (2nd ed., enlarged, 1938)

N. Denholm-Young, *The Country Gentry in the Fourteenth Century* (1969)

Dobson 1970 — R. B. Dobson, *The Peasants' Revolt of 1381* (1970)

DuBoulay & Barron 1971 — F. R. H. DuBoulay & C. M. Barron, eds., *The Reign of Richard II* (1971)

Dunn-Pattison 1910 — R. P. Dunn-Pattison, *The Black Prince* (1910)

Emden 1957 — A. B. Emden, *A Biographical Register of the University of Oxford to A.D. 1500* (3 vols, 1957–59)

Froissart A — *The Chronicles of Froissart*, ed. G. C. Macaulay (Globe Edition, 1895 etc.)

Froissart B — *The Chronicles of England, France and Spain by Sir John Froissart*, ed. H. P. Dunster (Everyman edition)

Goodman 1971 — A. Goodman, *The Loyal Conspiracy* (1971)

V. H. H. Green, *The Later Plantagenets* (1955; corrected ed., 1966)

Harvey 1943 — J. H. Harvey, 'The Medieval Office of Works', *Journal of the British Archaeological Association*, 3rd Series, VI for 1941 (1943), 20–87

Harvey 1944 — — *Henry Yevele* (1944; 2nd rev. ed., 1946)

Harvey 1946 — — 'Side-Lights on Kenilworth Castle', *Archaeological Journal*, CI (1946), 91–107

Harvey 1947A — — *Gothic England* (1947; rev. ed., 1948)

Harvey 1947B — — 'Some London Painters of the 14th and 15th Centuries', *Burlington Magazine*, LXXXIX No. 536, November 1947, 303–5

Harvey 1948 — — *The Plantagenets* (1948)

Harvey 1950 — — *The Gothic World 1100–1600* (1950; paperback 1969)

Harvey 1952 — — 'Henry Yevele Reconsidered', *Archaeological Journal*, CVIII (1952), 100–8

Harvey 1954 — — *English Mediaeval Architects* (1954)

Harvey 1957 — — 'The Masons of Westminster Abbey', *Archaeological Journal*, CXIII (1957), 82–101

Harvey 1961A — — 'The Wilton Diptych – a Re-examination', *Archaeologia*, XCVIII (1961), 1–28

Harvey 1961B — — 'The Architects of St George's Chapel, Part I', *Annual Report of . . . the Society of the Friends of St George's Chapel . . .* (1961), 48–55

Harvey 1962 — — 'The Origin of the Perpendicular Style', in E. M. Jope ed., *Studies in Building History* ('1961'; 1962), 134–65

Harvey 1971   —— —— 'Richard II and York', in DuBoulay &
                       Barron 1971, 202–17
Harvey 1972   —— —— *The Mediaeval Architect* (1972)
Harvey 1975A   —— —— *Early Nurserymen* ('1974'; 1975)
Harvey 1975B   —— —— *Mediaeval Craftsmen* (1975)
Harvey & King 1971   —— —— & D. G. King, 'Winchester College
                       Stained Glass', *Archaeologia*, CIII (1971), 149–77
                       H. J. Hewitt, *The Black Prince's Expedition of
                       1355–57* (1958)
HKW   *History of the King's Works*, ed. H. M. Colvin, vols.
                       I, II (1963)
Hope 1913   W. H. St. J. Hope, *Windsor Castle* (2 vols, 1913)
Hughes 1918   Dorothy Hughes, *Illustrations of Chaucer's England*
                       (1918)
Hutchison 1961   H. F. Hutchison, *The Hollow Crown: a Life of
                       Richard II* (1961)
                       G. P. R. James, *Life of Edward the Black Prince* (2 vols,
                       1836; 2nd rev. ed., 1839)
JGR (1)   *John of Gaunt's Register 1372–76*, ed. S. Armitage-
                       Smith (Camden 3rd Series, XX, XXI, 1911)
JGR (2)   *John of Gaunt's Register 1379–83*, ed. E. C. Lodge &
                       R. Somerville (Camden 3rd Series, LVI, LVII,
                       1937)
                       R. H. Jones, *The Royal Policy of Richard II: Absolutism
                       in the later Middle Ages* (1968)
Leroux 1906   A. Leroux, *Le Sac de la cité de Limoges* (Limoges, 1906)
                       E. C. Lodge, *Gascony under English Rule* (1926)
Longman 1869   W. Longman, *Life and Times of Edward III* (2 vols,
                       1869)
Lydon 1963   J. F. Lydon, 'Richard II's Expeditions to Ireland',
                       Journal of the Royal Society of Antiquaries of Ireland,
                       XCIII (1963), 135–49
                       May McKisack, *The Fourteenth Century* (Oxford
                       History of England, 1959)
Mathew 1968   G. Mathew, *The Court of Richard II* (1968)
                       J. Moisant, *Le Prince Noir en Aquitaine* (1894)
                       C. Oman, *The Great Revolt of 1381* (1906)
Pauli 1861   R. Pauli, *Pictures of Old England* (1861)
                       E. Perroy ed., *The Diplomatic Correspondence of
                       Richard II* (Royal Historical Society, Camden 3rd
                       Series, XLVIII, 1933)
                       —— —— *La Guerre de cent ans* (Paris, 1945)
                       —— —— *The Hundred Years War* (English trans.
                       by W. B. Wells, 1951)

Pope & Lodge 1910   Mildred K. Pope & Eleanor C. Lodge, eds, *Life of the Black Prince by the Herald of Sir John Chandos* (1910)

RS   Rolls Series

Russell 1955   P. E. Russell, *The English Intervention in Spain and Portugal in the Time of Edward III and Richard II* (1955)

Salzman 1923   L. F. Salzman, *English Industries of the Middle Ages* (1913; new ed. rev. and enlarged, 1923)

Salzman 1968   —— —— *Edward I* (1968)

Seeley 1872   [R. B. Seeley], *The Life and Reign of Edward I* (1872)

Sharpe 1889   R. R. Sharpe, *Calendar of Wills in the London Court of Husting* (2 vols, 1889)

Stanley 1883   A. P. Stanley, *Historical Memorials of Canterbury* (10th ed., 1883)

    A. Steel, *Richard II* (1941)

Strickland 1840   Agnes Strickland, *Lives of the Queens of England* (rev. ed., 1864–73, 6 vols), I, 377–410

    W. Stubbs, *The Constitutional History of England*, vol. II (1875)

Terry 1914   S. B. Terry, *The Financing of the Hundred Years War 1337–1360* (1914)

Thomas 1888   E. C. Thomas, ed., *The Philobiblon of Richard de Bury* (ed. 1903)

    E. M. Thompson, *Chronicon Galfridi le Baker de Swynebroke* (1889)

Tuck 1973   A. Tuck, *Richard II and the English Nobility* (1973)

    H. Wallon, *Richard II* (Paris, 2 vols, 1864)

Worcestre 1969   *William Worcestre: Itineraries*, ed. J. H. Harvey (Oxford Medieval Texts, 1969)

Notes to the Text

References are in general not given for material from the chronicles of Froissart, Chandos Herald, and Le Baker (see Bibliography above: Froissart, Pope & Lodge 1910, E. M. Thompson).

Page   PREFACE
- 11   Quotation – *The Plantagenets* (1st ed., 1948), vi
- 12   Numbers – see René Guenon, *La Règne de la Quantité et les Signes des Temps* (Paris, 1946); English translation by Lord Northbourne, *The Reign of Quantity and the Signs of the Times* (1953)
- 14   Edward I – see Salzman 1968 for a detailed modern biography, and Seeley 1872 for the best of the older studies
- 15   Black Armour – F. C. Louandre, *Histoire d'Abbeville et du Comté de Ponthieu* (Paris, 2 vols, 1844–45), 230

INTRODUCTION

- 25   War – see J. Barnie, *War in Medieval Society* (1974)
- 26   Limoges – Leroux 1906
       Bensington – BPR, IV, 7–8; cf. JGR (2), i, pp. xxi–ii, no. 125 (p. 48)
- 27   Edward I – Seeley 1872, chap. xi, esp. 250–7
- 28   Guild Codes – see Harvey 1972, 139, 149, 199–207; Harvey 1975B, 81–3, 184
       Ars Nova – Harvey 1947A, 53
- 30   Calveley – Barnie 1974, 85–6
       Chivalry – for a much more recent instance of chivalric attitudes transcending the war mentality, see *The Memoirs of James II (1652–60)*, ed. A. Lytton Sells (1962)
- 31   Technology – Harvey 1975B, 12–16, 96–100
- 32   Edward III and Germany – Pauli, 1861, 151

CHAPTER I

36 Linen – Salzman 1923, 226, 239; CLibR 1226–40, 34, 36

Gardens – Harvey 1972, 66; Harvey 1975A, 16, 33

37 Philippa – G. G. Coulton, *Medieval Panorama* (1940), 644; Strickland 1840

38 Burley – Emden 1957, I, 312–14

Bury – Emden 1957, I, 323–6; Thomas 1888, chap. ix; v

39 Bacon – Emden 1957, I, 87–8

41 Rusticiano – T. F. Tout, *Edward the First* (1893 etc.), 71

Chambers – in *History*, III (1918–19), 225

CHAPTER II

47 Woodstock – William of Malmesbury, *Gesta Regum Anglorum* (RS, 90), ii (1889), 485; HKW, II, 1009–17

48 Coutances – Harvey 1972, 59

Kenilworth – Harvey 1946, 93

49 Dominicans – HKW, I, 257–63; Harvey 1961A, 18 n.1; Harvey 1971, 210 and n. 32

51 Stratford, Shordich – Emden 1957, III, 1796, 1695

52 Damsel of Dijon – Worcestre 1969, 5; cf. Longman 1869, 104–5

57 English Sea – Longman 1869, 74

Rationing – Act 10 Edw. III, Stat. 3

CHAPTER III

59 Prince William – the year, 1336, of his birth and early death, is given by Walsingham, *Ypodigma Neustriae* (ed. H. T. Riley, RS, 28, vii), 274; I am indebted to Mr Christopher Hohler for this reference

60 Philippa – CPatR 1327–30, 257; the girl was Agnes, daughter of Alice de Penrith

St Omer family – CPatR 1334–8, 247, 559

61 Rosemary – J. H. Harvey in *Garden History*, I, No. 1 (1972), 14–21; Harvey 1975A, 135–7

62 Alice Causton – H. T. Riley, *Memorials of London* (1868), 319

Salad – Harvey 1947A, 179

63 Equatory – D. J. Price ed., *The Equatorie of the Planetis* (1955)

Constitutions of Masonry – full text in Harvey 1972, 191–207

Arab Botany – see J. H. Harvey in *Garden History*, III No. 2, Spring 1975, 10–21

64 Kempe – Strickland 1840, I, 382

Spanish Gardeners – Salzman 1968, 99

65 Yellow Stain – Harvey 1975B, 14–15

Llull – C. A. Burland, *The Arts of the Alchemists* (1967), 45

65 Bradwardine – Emden 1957, I, 244–6
66 Gaddesden – Ibid, II, 739
    Tingewick – Ibid, III, 1877
67 Guns – T. F. Tout, *Firearms in England in the Fourteenth Century*, ed. C. Blair (1968); J. Lavin in *Journal of the Arms & Armour Society*, IV (1962–4), 163–9
68 Edward III – Longman 1869, 14; translation of challenge in Harvey 1948, App. V (2nd ed. 1959, etc., App. II)
70 Cologne – Pauli 1861, 151

CHAPTER IV

72 Florentine Bankruptcy – Terry 1914, 107–8
73 Windsor – Hope 1913, I, 11–12
74 Coinage – Terry 1914, 88, 103
    Standards – CPatR 1330–34, 417; Public Record Office, DL 29/728/11977
75 St Stephen's Chapel – Harvey 1962, 144–50; cf. HKW, I, 514–22
76 Kennington – HKW, II, 967–8; Harvey 1954, 17, 163, 243, 269, 313. Important excavations on the site of Kennington Palace have been carried out since 1965 by Mr G. J. Dawson
    Yeveley – Harvey 1944
77 Avignon – Harvey 1950, 102–3
    Fonoll – Harvey 1954, 107; Fonoll's career has been worked out in meticulous detail by the late Josep Vives i Miret, *Reinard des Fonoll* (Barcelona, 1969)
78 Perpendicular – Harvey 1962
79 Bardi etc. – Terry 1914, 106
80 Expedition – Dunn-Pattison 1910, 53–9
82 Poix – Froissart A, 99
    Crecy – Burne 1955

CHAPTER V

84 Ostrevant – *Archaeologia*, XXXII (1847), 69–71
85 Song – Henry Bett, Nursery Rhymes and Tales (1924), 83
    Manny – Froissart A, 108–9
87 Christmas – Dunn-Pattison 1910, 109
88 Garters – Beltz 1841, 385
    French Colours – A. R. Wagner, 'The Order of the Garter, 1348–1948', *Annual Report of . . . the Society of the Friends of St George's Chapel . . .* (1946), 13
    College – Hope 1913, I, 129; CPatR 1348–50, 144, 147
89 Windsor Works – Harvey 1961B, 52–5
    Plague – Hughes 1918, 145–54, especially 151–2

91 Joanna's Death – Harvey 1948, 91–2 (2nd ed., 145; paperback, 144–5)
Calais – Froissart A, 117–18; Froissart B, 51–3; Worcestre 1969, 347–9

92 D'Enne – this is the knight whose name is generally given as 'Eam'.
Enne or Esnes is a village 6 miles south-east of Cambrai (see G. E. C.,
Complete Peerage, new ed., II, 1912, App. B, 535)
Spaniards-on-the-Sea – Hughes 1918, 123–9, from Froissart's chronicle
and other sources

95 Poitiers – Burne 1955

96 Prince's Letter – Hughes 1918, 77–80

CHAPTER VI

100 Rewards – BPR, IV, 193, 206–7, 291
Linch – Ibid, II, 98

101 Chartres Vow – Froissart B, 72

102 Prince's son – Beltz 1841, 384
Chantry – Stanley 1883, 163–8; Harvey 1944, 27

103 Berkhamsted – Cobb 1883, 21; Froissart A, 473
Vauxhall – Stanley 1883, 143; cf. BPR, IV, 508
Minstrel etc. – BPR, IV, 304; I, 16
Gifts – Beltz 1841, 383

105 Spain – Russell 1955

106 Battle of Thirty – Coulton 1918, 294–300
Calveley – see C. Blair, *The Effigy and Tomb of Sir Hugh Calveley* (The
Bunbury Papers, 4, 1951)

108 Richard's Baptism – Froissart A, 472

CHAPTER VII

111 Ibn Khaldun – C. Issawi, *An Arab Philosophy of History* (1950 etc.), 2–3
Prince's Counsel – Pope & Lodge 1910, 165

112 Prince's Reputation – Froissart A, 181; Froissart B, 109
Burgos – Russell 1955, 108 ff.

113 Return to Bordeaux – Dunn-Pattison 1910, 250

114 Chaucer – Monkes Tale, lines 3565–72
Blanche – Coulton 1918, 148

115 Manny – For the rediscovery of Manny's tomb in 1947, and his foundation of the London Charterhouse, see D. Knowles & W. F. Grimes,
Charterhouse (1954)

117 Chandos Herald – Pope & Lodge 1910, 130, lines 4184–6

119 Arthurian Oath – *Le Morte Darthur*, ed. Sir E. Strachey (Globe Edition,
1868/1901), 74–5

120 Gifts – see particularly the extracts from accounts, now lost, in Beltz
1841, 383 ff.

120 Engineers – Froissart A, 201; Froissart B, 132–3

Yeveley – Harvey 1952, 101; Harvey 1954, 313; cf. J. G. O. Whitehead, 'Henry Yeveley, Military Engineer', *The Royal Engineers Journal*, 1974, 102–10

Funeral – Stanley 1883, 150–3

CHAPTER VIII

122 Gaunt – Armitage-Smith 1904; cf. Russell 1955

123 Painters – Harvey 1947B; Harvey 1961

Bullok – will in Sharpe 1889, II, 179

Horewode – Harvey 1943, 76

Geddyng – dead by 18 Feb 1378 when his successor, John of Brampton, was appointed (CPatR 1377–81, 120)

Arderne – D'Arcy Power, ed., *Treatises of Fistula* (Early English Text Society, OS 139, 1910), x–xiii; Harvey 1948, 92 (Westminster Abbey Muniments 19356)

Bray – CPatR 1374–77, 354, 355, 368, 382; Ibid 1377–81, 136, 320, 340; Ibid 1381–85, 37; his vocabulary is British Museum, Sloane MS. 282, ff. 167v–173v; JGR (1), 547, 1706; JGR (2), 48 n. 1

124 Edward III – see R. P. Howgrave-Graham, 'The Earlier Royal Effigies: New Light on Portraiture in Westminster Abbey', *Archaeologia*, XCVIII (1961), 160–2

125 Gloucester – Goodman 1971, x, quoting Froissart in Berners' translation (Pynson 1525), f. cclxxxvii

126 Challenge – see above, note to p. 68

Peasants' Revolt – Dobson 1970

127 Will of Richard II – translated from sealed original in Harvey 1948, 2nd ed. 1959, 222–7; paperback 1967/72, 219–24

128 Ireland – Curtis 1927; Curtis 1938

130 Marcus Aurelius – *Thoughts*, transl. by G. Long, I.14

131 Letter – Hughes 1918, 233–4

Confession – Dobson 1970, 365–6

132 Appleton – JGR (1), 72, 557, 836

CHAPTER IX

136 Wykeham's Plan – A. F. Leach, *A History of Winchester College* (1899), 68–70; for Richard's charter of privileges see T. F. Kirby, *Annals of Winchester College* (1892), 25, 452–5

138 Stafford's Death – Mathew 1968, 169, 196 n. 4; A. Emery, *Dartington Hall* (1970), 31

Aljubarrota – Russell 1955, 381–99

143 Music – B. Trowell in *Acta Musicologica*, II–III (1957), 65–75; cf. M. F. Bukofzer, *Studies in Medieval and Renaissance Music* (New York, 1950)

144 Westminster – Harvey 1957, 87–8
York – J. H. Harvey in DuBoulay & Barron 1971, 207, 209
Canterbury – Harvey 1961A, 18; Harvey 1962, 156 n. 51
Royal Houses – see HKW as indexed
Kennington – BPR, IV, 247, 441
Gardeners – Ibid, 36, 91, 237, 363, 433

145 Sculpture – A. Gardner, *English Medieval Sculpture* (1951), 229–30;
L. Stone, *Sculpture in Britain: the Middle Ages* (1955), 193–4; Helen J.
Dow, 'André Beauneveu and the sculpture of Fourteenth-century
England', *Peregrinatio*, I (1971), 19–38
Painting – E. W. Tristram, *English Wall Painting of the Fourteenth
Century* (1955); cf. Margaret Rickert, *Painting in Britain: the Middle Ages*
(1954)

146 Wilton Diptych – G. Scharf, *Description of the Wilton House Diptych*
(Arundel Society, 1882); Joan Evans, 'Le diptyque de Wilton', *L'Oeil*,
No. 24 (Noël 1956), 18–23; Harvey 1961A

CATASTROPHE

147 York – J. H. Harvey, 'Richard II and York', in DuBoulay & Barron
1971, 202–17

149 Richard's Illness – Harvey 1961A, 13 and nn. 2, 3
Doctors – Emden 1957, 1257, 1276–7
Prescription – BM, Royal MS. 12 E.xxii, f. 132

153 Herebright – Harvey & King 1971, 150–1

154 Gloucester's Confession – Tuck 1973, from *Rotuli Parliamentorum*, III
(1783), 379

155 Chester – R. R. Davies, 'Richard II and the Principality of Chester', in
DuBoulay & Barron 1971, 256–79
Richard's Letter – translated from BM, Cotton MS. Galba B.i, f. 22

158 Richard's Will – see above, note to p. 127.

159 Merke's Speech – Hutchison 1961, 230–1
Richard's Remarks – Ibid, 226

Index

Numerals in *italics* are principal references; those in **heavy** type refer to the figure numbers on the plates. The following abbreviations are used: abp, archbishop; bp, bishop; emp, emperor.

Abbeville, Ponthieu, 23
Abingdon abbey, Berks., 66
Absentee landlords, 128
Abulwalid Ismail, sultan of Granada, 67
'Acacia', 124
Adelard – see Bath
Adrianople (Edirne), Turkey, 32
Agace, Gobin, 82
Agen, bp of, 108
Ages, critical, 30–1, 59–60
Agitators, 131–2
Aiguillon, 85
Ailyngton, Nicholas de, mason, 76
Airaines, 82
Aire, Jean d', 86
Álava, Spain, 107
Albert, duke of Bavaria, 33, 155
Alery, William, 110
Alexander the Great, 15, 30, 118, 127
III, king of Scots, 50
Aleyn, John, gardener, 144
Alfaro, Spain, 107
Alfelin *facetus* (Curteys), 44
Alfonso VI, king of Castile, 111
VII, 111
X, 23, 24, 63, 65
XI, 106
Alfred, king of England, 34, 58
Algeciras, Spain, 67, 105, 123
Aljubarrota, battle of, 138
Alps, 35, 120, 145
Amiens, France, 81, 82, 119
André, Andrieu d', 86
Angevin Empire, 101
Angoulême, 104, 113
Angoumois, 106
Anjou, 100, 101
Anne of Bohemia, queen of England, 135, 138, 141, 144, 146, 149, 150
Antwerp, Brabant, 55, 59, 61, 62, 69, 70
Appellants, the, 27, 125, 136, *140–2*, 147, 154, 156, 157
Appleton, William de, O.F.M., 132

Aquitaine, 22–3, 50–2, 55, 76, 79, 81, 93, 95, 100–2, 104, 106, 113, 115, 118, 131, 150, 152–3
Arabic language, 39, 63, 111, 166
Arabs, 39, 48, 65, 66
Aragon, Spain, 64
Architecture, 28, 35, 43–5, 75–7, 89, 123, 135, 144–5, 148
Arderne, John, surgeon, 123
Aristotle, 28, 38, 65
Armagnac, count of, 113
'Ars Nova' music, 28
Art, 36, *43–6*, 87, 103, 108, 120, *122–3*, 135, *142–6*, 148
Art Oge MacMurrough, king of Leinster, 150–1, 157
Arthur, king of Britain, 41, 58, 72–3, 88, 118–19, 120, 148
prince (d. 1203), 53
Arundel Castle, Sussex, 154
Arundel, earl of – see Fitzalan Thomas – see Fitzalan
Ashmole, Elias, antiquary, 88
Ashridge, Herts, college, 162
Astrology, 30, 103
Athens, Greece, 34
Auberoche, battle of, 79
Audley, Sir James the younger, 92, 98, 100, 114
Aungerville – see Bury, Richard de
Auray, battle of, 105
Avignon, France, 77, 122, 150

Babur, emp of India, 30
Babylonia, 39
Bacon, Roger, O.F.M., 28, 39, 65, 67, 77
Baliol, John de (1249–1315) – see John, king of Scots
Ball, John, rebel, 131, 134
Bangor, bp of – see Gilbert, John
Bardi and Peruzzi, bankers, 72, 78–9
Barnie, Mr John, 30
Basque provinces, 107, 112

Bath abbey, 45
Bath, Adelard of, 35, 166
Bathrooms, 144
Bavaria, dukes of, 33, 143
Bayonne, 106, 116
Baza, Spain, 67
Beauchamp of Holt, Sir John, 141
Thomas de, 11th earl of Warwick, 73, 83, 92, 137; **12**
Thomas de, 12th earl of Warwick, 137, 147, 149, 154
Beaufort family, 152
John, marquis of Dorset, 154, 155, 156–7, 158
Beaumont, Richard de, standard-bearer, 83
Beauneveu, André, sculptor, 145
Beauty, 13
Beauvais, France, 81, 82, 131
Becket, Thomas (d. 1170), 20, 71, 87, 100
Beddington, Surrey, 123
Bede, the Venerable, 23, 40
Beeston, Cheshire, 48
Belgium, 24, 104
Belinus, king of Britain, 41
Bells, ringing of, 11
Benedict XIII, Pope, 150
Bensington (Benson), Oxon., 26
Bergerac, 79
Berkhamsted Castle, Herts., 22, 87, 103, 115
Bermeo, Spain, 107
Berwick-upon-Tweed, 37, 100
Beverley, Yorks., 138, 149
Bilbao, Spain, 107
Bindweed, 123
Binomial nomenclature, 124
Biscay (Vizcaya), Spain, 107
Bishopthorpe, Yorks., 60
Black Death, plagues, 11, 45, 59, 65, 66, 75, 76, 78, *89–91*, 115, 124, 130, 136
Blackheath, Kent, 131, 132
Blair, Mr Claude, 18

Blanche of the Tower, princess, 59
  countess of Champagne, 43
  of Lancaster (d. 1369), 101, 114,
  139
Blenheim Palace, Oxon., 47
Boccaccio, writer, 122
Bohemia, 135
Bologna, Italy, 39
Bonde, Sir Nicolas, 164
Books, 39, 143, 144
Bordeaux, 15, 23, 52–3, 58, 64, 76,
  79, 91, 93–4, 99, 100, 102, 104,
  106, 107, 108, 113, 115, 116, 118,
  152
Botany, 123–4
Boulogne, France, 105
Bourbon, duchess of, 114
Bourges, France, 94
Bourne, Lincs., 40
Box, John, mason, 103
Boycott, Charles C., 128
Brabant, duchy of, 55, 57, 69, 70,
  71, 143
Bradewardyn, William, surgeon,
  149
Bradwardine, Thomas, abp of
  Canterbury, 65
Bramble, 124
Brampton, John of, glazier, 176
Bray, John, physician, 123
Brembre, Nicholas, mayor of
  London, 140
Brest, Brittany, 153–5
Bretigny, Peace of, 18, 30, 100, 102,
  104, 105, 113, 124
Brie, France, 106
British Empire, 40, 98
Brittany, 72, 93–4, 100, 101, 106,
  153–5
Brock, Thomas, sculptor, 20
Broker, Nicholas, coppersmith, 145
Bruce, Robert (1210–1295), 50
  Robert (1274–1329) – see Robert
  I, king of Scots
Bruges, Flanders, 55, 67, 116
Brusa, Turkey, 32
Brussels, Brabant, 55, 69, 71
Brutus the Trojan, 40–1
Buildings, 12, 35, 43 – see also
  Architecture
Building trades, 35
Bullok, John, tapestry-maker, 123
Burghersh, Sir Bartholomew, 92,
  103, 114
Burgos, Spain, 112
Burgundy, count of, 104
Burley, Sir John, 38
  Sir Simon, 38, 114, 125, 140–1,
  147, 150, 154, 157
  Walter, 38, 49, 65, 118
Bury St Edmunds, Suffolk, 149
Bury, Richard de (Aungerville),
  bp of Durham, 38–40, 49, 65
Butler, James, 3rd earl of Ormond,
  151
Byzantium – see Constantinople

Cadzand, Holland, 57–8, 59, 61, 69
Caen, Normandy, 80–1, 119
Caerphilly Castle, Wales, 45
Caesar – see Julius Caesar
Cairo, Egypt, 35, 78
Calahorra, Spain, 107
Calais, 23, 58, 60, 68, 81, 85–7,
  91–2, 100, 116, 154
Calveley, Sir Hugh, 30, 106, 112

Cambrai, 67, 92, 175
Cambridge, King's College, 14
Canon, Thomas, sculptor, 145
Canterbury, Kent, 121, 123, 143, 161
  cathedral, 20–1, 44, 49, 66, 87,
  100, 102, 103, 143, 144, 160–2,
  165; 1, 5, 6, 16
Canterbury Tales, 143
Canterbury, Michael of, mason, 44
  Thomas of, mason, 44, 75
  Walter of, mason, 44
Capet, House of, 22, 50, 53
  Hugh, 50
Captal de Buch – see Grailly, Jean de
Carlisle cathedral, 44
Carrillo, Gómez, traitor, 26, 112
Carrión, Spain, 112
Castles, works on, 137
Castro Urdiales, Spain, 107
Catalonia, 77
Catherine of Lancaster, queen of
  Castile, 139
Causton, Alice, alewife, 62
Caxton, William, 118
Ceuta, 23, 139
Chambers, R. W., 41
Champagne, France, 43
Chandos, Sir John, 69, 82, 83, 92–3,
  98, 99, 100, 103, 105, 108,
  109–10, 112, 114, 119, 120
  Herald of, 117, 143, 166, 172
Channel Islands, 57
Chargny, Sir Geoffrey de, 91–2
Charlemagne, emp, 31, 69
Charles I, king of Great Britain, 49,
  128
  II, 20
  IV, emp, 122, 135
  IV, king of France, 50, 52, 54, 77
  V, 17, 105, 106, 109, 113, 114,
  120, 122
  VI, 154
  II 'the Bad', king of Navarre,
  105–6, 107, 108
  of Blois, claimant of Brittany, 87,
  105
Chartres, France, 94, 101
Chatellerault, 94
Chaucer, Geoffrey, poet, 13, 16, 20,
  63, 66, 113–14, 140, 142–3
Cherbourg, Normandy, 80, 106,
  153–4
Cheshire, 87, 93, 106, 140, 155, 156
Chester, 48, 76, 80, 156
  principality of, 155
Chevy Chase – see Otterburn
Cheyne, Alan, 163
China, 13, 31, 34, 36, 89
Chivalry, 24–5, 30, 79, 85, 111–12,
  114, 118–20, 129, 141–2, 148
Christead, Henry, 151
Chuddere, William, sculptor, 145
Civil service, 136
Clarendon, Sir Roger, 102, 163
Clement IV, Pope, 39
  V, Pope, 39
  VII, Pope, 150
Clifford, Sir Louis de, 164
  Richard, dean of York, 158
Cloth trade, 55
Coal-mining, 60
Cobham, John, 3rd baron, 141
  Sir Reginald, 83
Coinage, 12, 74–5, 93
Cokard, John, minstrel, 103
Colchester, Essex, 131

Colchester, William, abbot of
  Westminster, 157, 158
Collins, Arthur, 16
Cologne, Germany, 70, 152–3
Cologne, Herebright of, painter, 153
Common Market, European, 75
Companies, Free, 104, 105
Compostela, Spain, 79, 109
Confucius, 31
Connor, king of, 151
Constance of Castile, duchess of
  Lancaster, 115, 138
Constantine the Great, Roman
  emp, 73
Constantinople (Byzantium), 32,
  35, 135
Conway Castle, Wales, 76
Corbie, France, 82, 119
Cordova, Spain, 35
Corfe, Dorset, 145
Cornwall, 48, 87
Corruption, political, 115–16, 141–2
Corunna, Spain, 106, 108
Coucy, Enguerrand de, earl of
  Bedford, 59
Courtrai, battle of, 51, 55
Coutances, Normandy, 48
Coventry, Warwicks., 157, 158
Craftsmen, 27–8, 33, 36, 60
Crecy, battle of, 15, 18, 20, 21, 41,
  59, 65, 68, 82–3, 84, 85, 95, 98,
  109, 112, 118, 129, 134, 135
Crete, 34
Creton, chronicler, 158
Croydon, Surrey, 123
Crusades, 22, 25, 28, 41, 55, 56, 77
Curvilinear style, 44
Customary law, 52
Cuthbert, St, 60

Damett, Thomas, musician, 142
Danes, 58, 151
Dante, poet, 32, 63
Danyel, Henry, O.P., 62
Darcy, Sir John, 71–2
Dark Ages, 29
David, king of Israel, 49
  II, king of Scots, 41, 55, 72, 87,
  100, 101, 123
  of Huntingdon, 50
Dawson, Mr G. J., 174
Dax, 108
Dean, Forest of, 80
Death-mask, 124
Demarcation disputes, 90
Derby, earl of – see Henry, 1st duke
  of Lancaster; Henry IV
Despenser, Thomas, earl of
  Gloucester, 154, 155, 156
Diamond Necklace, 52
Dijon, Damsel of, 52
Dissolution of monasteries, 40
Dock, plant, 124
Domesday Book, 29, 35, 36
Dominican Order, 49
Dordogne, 94
Dordrecht, Holland, 57
Dorking, Surrey, 123
Douglas, Sir William, 94–5
Dover, Kent, 76, 143
Duarte (Edward), king of Portugal,
  139
Dublin, Ireland, 150, 151, 153, 158
Du Guesclin, Bertrand, 17, 25, 30,
  91, 105, 106, 109, 112, 113
Dunn-Pattison, R. P., 16

Dunstable, John, musician, 13, 142
Dupplin Moor, battle of, 55
Duras, Sir Robert de, 99
Durham, 60, 149

Earls Colne, Essex, 152
Eastry, Henry, prior, 66
Ebenbürtigkeit, 28
Edinburgh, Scotland, 37, 123, 138, 153
Edington, William, bp of Winchester, 103
Edirne – see Adrianople
Edith Matilda, queen of England, 22
Edmund, St, king and martyr, 146 of Lancaster, 43
of Langley, duke of York, 59, 101, 122, 128, 137, 141, 143, 150, 154, 156–7, 158
of Woodstock, earl of Kent, 102
Education, 27, 49, 136
Edward the Confessor, St, king of England, 145, 146, 151
I, 14, 22, 23, 27, 31, 34, 36, 37, 40, 41, 42, 48, 51, 60, 61, 65, 66, 72–3, 75, 77, 82, 93, 102, 119, 126, 158
II of Caernarvon, 14, 28, 31, 34, 37, 48, 49, 51, 60, 65, 77, 102, 118, 120, 136, 139, 140, 146
III, 11, 15, 17, 20, 27, 28, 31, 32, 33, 37, 38, 41, 46, and passim: at siege of Calais, 86; founds Order of the Garter, 87–92; at rescue of Calais, 91–2; leads expedition of 1359–60, 101; tourneys, 101; leads expedition of 1372, 115; death, 124; 3
VIII, 49
Baliol, king of Scots, 55, 72 of Angoulême, prince, 104, 108, 114, 129
of Woodstock, the Black Prince, passim: cognomen, 15; portraits 19; statue, 20; armour, 20; mottoes, 21; magnanimity, 25; birth, 47; earl of Chester, 48; duke of Cornwall, 57; prince of Wales, 72; on Crecy campaign, 80–2; knighted, 80; a founder of the Garter, 88; at rescue of Calais, 91–2; in sea battle, 93; duke of Aquitaine, 93; leads expedition to Narbonne, 93; wins battle of Poitiers, 94–7; letter to London, 96–7; his prayer, 97; on expedition of 1359–60, 101; tourneys, 101; prince of Aquitaine, 102; keeps court at Bordeaux, 104; leads expedition to Spain, 108; wins battle of Nájera, 109–10; counsels Don Pedro, 111; his illness, 112–13; 115–17; leaves Bordeaux, 115; surrenders Aquitaine, 115; his will, 116, 160–7; death, 116–17; character, 117–20; funeral, 120–1; tomb, 143, 160–1, 166–7; 1, 2, 4, 6
duke of Albemarle, 150, 154, 156, 158
illegitimate son of the Black Prince, 102
Effigies, 124, 145
Eglesfield, Robert de, chaplain, 38
Egypt, ancient, 13, 39

Eketon, Peter de, messenger, 47
Eleanor of Aquitaine, queen of England, 22
of Castile, 23, 64, 102
of Provence, 35
countess of Gelderland, 70
Élite, 13
Elizabeth I, queen of England, 31 of Lancaster, 139
Eltham, Kent, 139, 143–4
Ely cathedral, Cambs., 14, 45, 74
Embroidery, 46
Enghien, duc d', 25
Engineers, 120
English language, 14, 40, 43, 62, 63, 96, 123, 143
Enne, Sir Henry d', 92
Enrique II, king of Castile – see Henry
Eu, count of, 80
Eversley, Geoffrey of, clerk, 65
Everswell, Oxon., 47
Evreux, Normandy, 106
Exeter, bp of, 37, 162 cathedral, 44
Exeter, duke of – see Holand, John
Eynsham, Oxon., 140

Falkirk, Scotland, 73
Famine, 33
Farleigh, Richard of, mason, 45
Felton, Sir Thomas, 104
Fereby, William, clerk, 158
Fernando, the Constant Prince, 139
Ferrant, Martin, 110
Fiennes, Jean de, 86
Fitzalan, Richard, 3rd earl of Arundel, 73
Richard, 4th earl of Arundel, 137, 139, 147, 149, 153, 154
Thomas, abp of Canterbury, 137, 139, 147, 153, 154
Fitzgerald, Edward, poet, 63
Flagellants, 89
Flamboyant style, 28, 44, 78
Flanders, Flemings, 32, 55, 56, 58, 60, 61, 64, 67, 69, 71, 72, 75, 78, 84, 92, 100, 104, 112, 116, 128, 132
Flint, North Wales, 48
Folk-song, 85
Fonoll, Reinard, mason, 77, 174
Fordham, John de, (bishop of Durham), 164, 165
Forests, 27
Fortune, Wheel of, 118
France, passim
Francis I, king of France, 95
French language, 24, 40, 41, 43, 62, 63, 96, 117, 123, 143, 144
French, Mr T. W., 19
Froissart, Jean, chronicler, 18, 26, 32, 56, 58, 72, 79, 85, 86, 92, 96, 103, 108, 112, 114, 120, 125, 141, 143–4, 151, 172
Fulk II, the Good, count of Anjou, 126

Gaddesden, Dr John, physician, 66
Galicia, Spain, 108, 139
Gardens, 36, 48, 61–2, 63, 64, 144
Gardyner, Nicholas le, gardener, 144
Garter, Order of the, 74, 87–8, 92, 124, 148
Geddyng, John, glazier, 123
Gelderland, county of, 69

Genoese, 83, 91
Geoffrey Plantagenet, count of Anjou, 22
George, St., 45, 58, 88, 99
III, king of Great Britain, 31
German language, 62, 63, 84
Germany, Germans, 24, 32, 35, 84, 112, 153
Ghent, Flanders, 32, 56, 59, 61, 70
Gibraltar, Spain, 23
Gibson, Mr Robin, 19
Gilbert the Englishman, physician, 66
Gilbert, John, bp of Hereford, 117, 164
Glanville, Bartholomew de, encyclopaedist, 62
Glass-painting, 46, 65, 145
Glazing, 36
Gold coinage, 12, 74, 93
Goldsmiths, 46, 145
Golofre, Sir John, 144
'Good Parliament', 116, 137
Gordon, Bernard, physician, 66
Gothic architecture, 14 – see also Architecture
Gower, John, poet, 143
Grail, Temple of the, 74
Grailly, Jean de, Captal de Buch, 17, 92, 96, 98, 121
Granada, Spain, 24, 48, 67, 80, 111
Grandvilliers, France, 82
Gravesend, Kent, 57
Greece, Greeks, 13, 39
Greek language, 39
Greenfield, John, 132
Gregory XI, pope, 115
Grimes, Professor W. F., 175
Guildford, Surrey, manor, 87
Guilds, 27–8, 35
Guipúzcoa, Spain, 107
Gunpowder, 67
Guns, 67–8, 120, 138

Hainault, county of, 32–3, 37, 38, 57, 60, 69, 70
countess of, 61, 103
Hales, Sir Robert, 132
Halidon Hill, battle of, 37, 55
Hannibal, 120
Harcourt, Sir Geoffrey de, 81
Harewell, John, bp of Bath and Wells, 164
Haro, Spain, 107
Hastings, John, 2nd earl of Pembroke, 59
Laurence, 1st earl of Pembroke, 73
Hatfield, Yorks., 59
Haverfordwest, Wales, 150
Hawking, 87, 100, 101
Hebrew language, 39
Helpeston, William, mason, 93
Henry I Beauclerk, king of England, 22, 34, 35, 36, 41, 48, 166
II, 13, 22, 34, 47, 52, 91, 119, 126, 128
III, 34, 35, 48, 60, 88, 89
IV of Derby, 53, 127, 137, 140, 141, 142, 149, 154, 155, 157, 158–9; 16
V of Monmouth, 158
VI, 14
VII, 14
VIII, 13
(Enrique) II of Trastamara, king of Castile, 30, 91, 105, 106–13,

116, 119, 138
III, king of Castile, 139
earl of Lancaster (d. 1345), 47
1st duke of Lancaster (d. 1361),
57–8, 71, 73, 79, 92–3, 94, 101,
123; **10**
earl of Derby and of Lancaster –
see Henry IV
the Navigator, prince of
Portugal, 139
Heraldry, 37, 70, 145, 146, 150–1,
160, 162, 163
Herbs, medicinal, 123–4
Hereford, arms of, 163
bp of – see Gilbert, John
Heretics, 127
Herland, Hugh, carpenter, 145
William, carpenter, 123
sHertogenbosch, Brabant, 69
Higden, Ralph, chronicler, 62–3
Hippocratic Oath, 119
Hocart, A. M., anthropologist, 18
Hoccleve, Thomas, poet, 143
Hohler, Mr Christopher, 173
Holand, John, duke of Exeter, 138,
139, 147, 154, 155, 156, 158
Sir Thomas, 80, 83, 92, 102, 119
Thomas, duke of Surrey, 150,
154, 155, 156, 158
Holland, county of, 34, 57, 69, 104
Honour, 17–18, 23, 30, 148
Horewode, Robert, plumber, 123
Hospitallers, Order of, 132
Howden, Yorks., 149
Huesca, Spain, 166
Hundred Years War, 11, 25, 32, 50,
54, 58, 68, 78, 126
Hunting, 87, 100, 101
Huntingdon, Hugh de, mason, 76
Hurley, William, carpenter, 45,
73–4, 123

Ibn Bassal, agriculturist, 63
Ibn Khaldun, philosopher, 111
Ibn Wafid, agriculturist, 63
Ich dien, motto, 84
Ikelyngton, John, clerk, 158
Illuminators, 46
Imworth, Richard, 132, 133
India, 34
Industrial Revolution, 28
Inequality, 34
Inflation, 11, 12, 130
Inheritance, rules of, 50
Innocent VI, Pope, 99
International Style, 78, 153
Invasion, French, 79, 81, 137, 139
Inventions, 31, 124
Ireland, Irish, 126, 128, 141, 143,
145, 150, 151, 153, 157, 158
Irish language, 151
Isabel, princess (1332–1379), 48, 59
of Castile, duchess of York, 122
Isabella of France (d. 1358), queen
of England, 38, 39, 47, 54
Isabelle of Valois, queen of
England, 152, 153
Islam, Muslims, 24, 25, 29, 30, 32,
68, 77, 111, 127, 166
Italy, Italians, 28, 32, 34, 45, 48, 63,
72, 74, 76–7, 78, 122, 135

Jacquerie, revolt, 131
James III, king of Majorca, 108, 112
James, George P. R., historian, 16
Japan, 36

Jeanne, princess (1333–1348), 59,
66, 91
Jeffreys, George, 1st baron, judge,
149
Jerusalem, Palestine, 43
Jesus, 30
Jewellery, 145
Jews, 89, 111, 127
Joan, 'The Fair Maid of Kent', 19,
80, 101–2, 113, 119, 125, 127,
133, 134, 135, 136; **5, 8**
of Arc, 29
John the Baptist, St, 146
Lackland, king of England, 23,
34, 53, 128
Baliol (1249–1315), king of
Scots, 29, 50, 55
king of Bohemia, 84, 135
(Juan) I, king of Castile, 138, 139
II, king of France, 25, 94–6,
99–101, 105, 106
I, king of Portugal, 50, 138
XXII, Pope, 55
of Gaunt, duke of Lancaster, 26,
32, 53, 59, 61, 75, 101, 107, 108,
114, 115, 116, 122, 123, 125–6,
137, 138, 139, 140, 141, 143, 147,
148–9, 150, 153, 154, 156, 157,
164; **9**
IV, duke of Brittany, 59
'Anglicus', 43
Johnson, Samuel, 29
Julian, Roman emp, 30
Julius Caesar, 15, 127
Juniper tree, 123
Justinian, Byzantine emp, 31

Kempe, John, weaver, 64
Kenilworth Castle, Warwicks., 48
Kennington, Surrey, 21, 75–6, 144,
174
Kilkenny, Ireland, 158
King's Lynn Cup, 46
Kingship, theory of, 49, 54, 125–6,
127–8, 130, 136, 139–40, 146, 159
Knollys, Sir Robert, 133–4
Knowles, David, 175
Kublai Khan, emp of China, 31

Lambeth, Surrey, 75, 102, 132
Lancaster, duchy of, 53, 75, 157–8
earls and dukes of – see Henry,
John
Landscape gardening, 48
Langley, King's, Herts., 48–9, 59,
62, 64, 144
Langtoft, Peter de, chronicler, 41
Language, 24
Languages, oriental, 39
Lao-tzu, sage, 31
La Réole, 79
La Rochelle, 103, 115
Latimer, William lord, K.G., **11**
Latin language, 24, 29, 39, 40, 41, 49,
62, 63, 64, 96, 123, 166
Launcekron, Agnes, 140
Law, rule of, 128, 130, 133
systems of, 52
Le Baker, Geoffrey, chronicler, 172
Leche, John, apothecary, 149
Le Crotoy, 82
Leeds Castle, Kent, 143
Leeds, Yorks., 20
Leonora de Guzmán, 106
Le Puy, France, 64
Leroux, Alfred, historian, 26

Lettuce, Wild, 124
Libourne, Treaty of, 107, 112
Lichfield cathedral, Staffs., 45
Limburg, duchy of, 70
Limoges, capture of, 25–6, 81, 114,
120, 129
Linch, William, 100
Lincoln cathedral, 14
Lincoln, Philip of, carpenter, 123
Linnaeus, Carl, scientist, 124
Lionel of Antwerp, duke of
Clarence, 32, 59, 61, 101, 122,
141, 143
Lisieux, Normandy, 81
Lithuania, 127
Llull – see Lully
Logroño, Spain, 107
Lollards, 127, 151–2
London, 35, 52, 53, 56, 57, 64, 68,
73, 74, 87, 91, 101, 104, 116, 131,
132–3, 140, 147, 149, 152–3
Black Friars (Preachers), 164
Bridge, 100, 121
Charterhouse, 175
Cheapside, 60, 133
Clerkenwell, 132, 134
Fish Street Hill, 76
Guildhall, 45
Merchant Tailors' Hall, 76
Mile End, 132–3
St Bartholomew's Hospital, 35
St Martin Vintry, 132
St Paul's cathedral, 44, 66, 149,
153
Savoy Palace, 100, 105, 132
Smithfield, 133
Strand, 121
Temple, 132
Tower of, 45, 59, 71, 74–5, 132,
154, 159
Wardrobe, 133–4
– see also Westminster
Longevity, 31, 59–60
Lorraine, duke of, 84
Loryng, Sir Nele, 92, 100, 125
Louis IV the Bavarian, emp, 32, 70,
72, 75
VII, king of France, 22
IX, Saint, king of France, 145
XIV, 24, 31, 95
prince of France, 105
de Nevers, count of Flanders, 55–6
Louvain, Brabant, 55, 71, 152
Louviers, Normandy, 81
Low Countries, 35, 55, 61, 69 – see
also Flanders, Holland
Loyalty, 18, 30, 127, 136, 141, 150,
152
Lufwyk, John, 158
Lully, Raymond (Ramon Llull),
39, 65
Lusignan, 114
Lyons, Richard, merchant, 116, 132

Machaut, Guillaume de, musician,
123, 142
Machinery, 31, 33
Madagascar, 34
Magna Carta, 49
Maine, France, 100, 101
Malines, Brabant, 55
Malory, Sir Thomas, 118–19
Man, Isle of, 154
Manny, Sir Walter, 18, 32, 57–8,
60–1, 68, 69, 72, 79, 85, 86, 91,
115, 118, 175

Mannyng, Robert, writer, 40, 41, 62
Mantes, France, 81
Marco Polo, 31
Marcus Aurelius, Roman emp, 130
Margaret of France, queen of
    England, 102
'The Maid of Norway', 50, 51
    princess (1346–1361), 59, 87
Margate, Kent, 57
Maria of Portugal, queen of
    Castile, 106
Marlborough, 1st duke of, 15
Mary, princess (1344–1361), 59
Masonry, Constitutions of, 63
Masons, 28, 64
Maudeleyn, Richard, clerk, 158
Maupertuis, 94, 96
Meath, king of, 151
Meaux, France, 131
Medicine, 35, 66–7, 123–4, 149–50
Melilla, 23
Melton, Geoffrey, physician, 149
    William, abp of York, 44
Merchants, 60, 98, 116, 130
'Merciless Parliament', 141
Merke, Thomas, bp of Carlisle,
    150, 157, 158, 159
Merlin, prophet, 107
Mes'ud III, sultan of Rum, 32
Middleton, John, physician, 149
Military engineers, 35
Miners, 60, 64
Minot, Laurence, poet, 41–2
Mongol empire, 31–2, 34
Monmouth, Geoffrey of, writer,
    40–1
Montague, John, earl of Salisbury,
    154, 156
    William, de, earl of Salisbury, 73,
    80, 92, 102, 123, 125, 134, 135;
    13
Montbray, Geoffrey de, bp of
    Coutances, 48
Montfort, John de, duke of
    Brittany, 72
Montiel, battle of, 113
Montserrat, Spain, 74
Morocco, Moors, 23, 67, 111
Mortimer, Edmund, 5th earl of
    March, 157, 158
    Roger, 1st earl of March (d.
    1330), 16, 39, 125
    Roger, 2nd earl of March, 80
    Roger, 4th earl of March, 150,
    156, 157, 158
Mowbray, Thomas, duke of
    Norfolk, 137, 140, 141, 150,
    154, 157
Munich, Germany, 145
Murder, political, 132, 140–1
Murimuth, Adam, chronicler, 73
Music, 13, 123, 142

Nájera, battle of, 15, 20, 25, 109–10,
    111, 118, 119, 128
Napoleon I, emp of the French,
    25, 30, 95, 127
    III, 95
Nationalism, 28–9, 40–1, 54
National consciousness, 42, 54
Nationality, 23–4
Navarre, 105, 112, 154
Neville, Alexander, abp of York,
    140, 147
    Ralph, earl of Westmorland, 155
Neville's Cross, battle of, 42

Nevin, Wales, 72
Newark-upon-Trent, Notts., 123
Newcastle-upon-Tyne, 60, 138, 142
New Guinea, 34
Newton, Sir John, 133
Niort, 103
Norfolk, earls of – see Thomas of
    Brotherton; Mowbray
Norman Conquest, 22, 35, 40, 48
Normandy, Normans, 23, 48, 50,
    79, 85, 100, 101
Norwich, 45, 46, 60, 64, 69
Norwich, Sir Thomas, 83

Ockham, William of, philosopher,
    28, 65, 77
Official Secrets Act, 30
Opium, 124
Oppression, 130
Orhan, Turkish sultan, 32
Orleans, France, 85
Ormeshevede, John de, notary, 164
Ormond, earl of – see Butler, James
Osman, Turkish chief, 32
Ostrevant, 84
Ostrich feathers, badge, 84
Otterburn (Chevy Chase), battle
    of, 142
Ottoman Empire, 13, 32, 34
Ottonian Empire, 13
Ouistreham, Normandy, 80
Oxford, 39, 149
    Merton College, 66
    New College, 14, 136
    The Queen's College, 38
    University College, 149
Oxford, Joan of, nurse, 47

Pacifism, 127, 128
Painters, 45–6, 145–6
Palestine, 25
Pamplona, Navarre, 108
Paris, France, 24, 38, 39, 43, 51, 52,
    53, 81, 85, 100, 101, 104, 113,
    140, 145, 153
    Cluny Museum, 46
    Palace Hall (Salle des Pas Perdus),
    145
    Sainte Chapelle, 120
    Temple, 121
Parks, 36, 47–8
Parliament, supremacy of, 142
Party politics, 130, 136, 142
Patrington, William, sculptor, 123
Pavia, Americ of, 91
Peace, policy of, 126, 142, 148, 150,
    152, 153–4, 156
Peasants' Revolt, 115, 125, 126,
    129–34, 137
Pedro (Peter) 'the Cruel', king of
    Castile, 23, 25, 30, 91, 105,
    106–10, 111–14, 115, 118, 119,
    122, 128, 138, 166
Peking, China, 31
Pembroke, earl of – see Hastings
Penrith, Agnes de, 173
Percy, Henry, 1st earl of
    Northumberland, 142, 156, 158
    Sir Henry 'Hotspur', 142
    Sir Ralph, 142
    Thomas, earl of Worcester, 133,
    143–4, 155, 158
Périgord, Cardinal de, 94, 99
Perpendicular style, 44, 76, 78, 135,
    145
Perrers, Alice, 116

Persia, 32, 34, 36, 48, 78
Perth, Scotland, 37
Peruzzi – see Bardi
Peter de Lusignan, king of Cyprus,
    104
Peterborough, Northants., 46
Petrarch, poet, 28, 122
Petrus Alphonsi, physician, 35, 166
Pevensey, Sussex, 75
Philip III, king of France, 50
    IV, 77
    V, 52
    VI of Valois, 41, 50–1, 54, 56, 68,
    69, 72, 79, 80–2, 84, 85, 86, 94,
    103, 126, 153
    prince of France, 96
Philippa of Hainault, queen of
    England, 18, 28, 32, 33, 37–8,
    47, 48, 60, 62, 86, 87, 92, 100,
    102, 103, 114, 115, 124, 136, 141,
    143, 144
    of Lancaster, queen of Portugal,
    138, 139
Philippe Égalité, duke of Orleans,
    142
Picquigny, France, 82
Pipe Rolls, 36
Pisa, Rusticiano of, writer, 41
Plague – see Black Death
Plantagenet family, 11, 22, 23, 34,
    53, 60, 105, 126, 149, 152
Plants, 123–4
Plate, gold and silver, 46
Plays, 87
Pleshey, Essex, 154
Plumpton, Matilda, cradle-rocker,
    47, 117
Plymouth, Devon, 93, 148
Poetry, 33, 40
Poissy, France, 81
Poitiers, 103, 115
    battle of, 15, 20, 42, 94–7, 98–101,
    109, 112, 156
Poix, France, 82, 119
Pole, Michael de la, earl of Suffolk,
    136, 139, 140, 147
Poll-tax of 1381, 131
Pontchardon, Sir Richard, 108
Pont de l'Arche, Normandy, 81
Ponthieu, county of, 23, 82, 100
Poor, relief of the, 27
Poppy, white, 124
Population, transfers of, 86–7
Portraiture, 18–19, 146
Portsmouth, Hants., 81
Portugal, Portuguese, 24, 29, 34, 50,
    78, 105, 116, 138, 153
Powell, George F. (d. 1962), 18
Power, Lionel, musician, 142
Prague, Bohemia, 153
Prescription, medical, 149–50
Prest, Godfrey, coppersmith, 145
Prince, Gilbert, painter, 46, 123, 146
Prior, Edward S., architect, 78
    Thomas, messenger, 47
Prophecies, 103, 107
Provençal language, 24
Prussia, 80
Pyamour, John, musician, 142
Pyrenees, 21, 23, 51, 108, 113, 120

Quadrant, 145–6; 17
Quantity, 12

Radcot Bridge, Oxon., 140, 147,
    156

Raddington, Sir Baldwin, 140, 150
Radish, 124
Raghton, Ivo de, mason, 44
Rahere, minstrel, 35
Ramsey, abbot of, 44
Ramsey, William, mason, 44–5, 73–5
Rationing, 11, 57
Raughton, Cumberland, 44
Ravenspur, Yorks., 158
Reading abbey, Berks., 45
Reading, Richard of, sculptor, 45
Records, 36
Reform of 1832, 142
Reformation, 13
Reinald II, count of Gelderland, 69
Rents, money, 42
Revolution, French, 37
Revolutionaries, 131–4, 142
Rheims, France, 43, 101
Rhineland, 70, 153
Rhuddlan, Flintshire, 48
Ribemont, Sir Eustace de, 92, 94, 95
Richard I Coeur-de-Lion, king of England, 23, 25
    II of Bordeaux, 11, 14, 15, 16, 17, 27, 30, 31, 33, 49, 53, 54, 62, 75, 78, 108, 116, 119, 120, 125–59 *passim*, 163, 164; birth, 108; coronation, 124; meets rebels, 133–4; stand against Appellants, 141; as art patron, 144–6; takes charge, 147; illness, 149; in Ireland, 150–2; aims at the Empire, 152–3; triumphant, 156–7; deposition, 159; **17** portraits of, 19, 150; **7, 15**
    III, 30
Rickman, Thomas, architect, 44
Robert I Bruce (1274–1329), king of Scots, 22, 29, 50, 55
    king of Sicily, 103
    II, count of Artois, 51
    of Artois, count of Beaumont, 51–2
Robin Hood, 58
Rochester Castle, Kent, 133
Rodez, 104
Roman Empire, Romans, 29, 34, 39
    Law, 52
Rome, 39, 64, 74, 122, 150, 154
Romorantin, France, 94
Roncevalles, 105
Roofs, 45
Rosamund, 'The Fair', 47
Rosemary, 61–2, 63, 146
Round Table, 72–4, 76, 87, 88, 108, 119, 146
Roxburgh, Scotland, 37
Rushock, Thomas, bp of Chichester, 141
Ruskin, John, writer, 31
Russia, 34
Rusticiano – see Pisa
Rye, Sussex, 93

St Albans, Herts., 45
    abbey, 66
    abbot of, 154
St Albans, Hugh of, painter, 45, 76, 123
St-Lo, Normandy, 80
St-Omer, France, 91
St-Omer, Bertram, 60
    Elizabeth, 60
    William, 60

Saint-Pierre, Eustache de, 86
St-Vaast-la-Hougue, Normandy, 80
St-Valery, Ponthieu, 82
Saintes, 115
Salad, 62
Saladin, sultan, 25
Salamanca, Spain, 39
Salerno, Italy, 61
'Salic Law', 50–1, 54
Salisbury cathedral, 45, 66
Salisbury, Oath at, 55
Salisbury, countess of, 88
    earl of – see Montague
Saltash ferry, Cornwall, 100
Sancho of Castile, Don, 112
Sandwich, Kent, 100
Sanitation, 36, 144
San Juan del Pie del Puerto, Navarre, 108
San Sebastián, Spain, 106, 107
Scharnesfelde, Sir Nicholas de, 164
Scherfgin, Heinrich, 70
Schism, the great, 122
Scholasticism, 28, 77
Schwarz, Berthold, 67
Science, 28, 63–8, 123–4
Scone, Scotland, 55
Scotland, Scots, 14, 22, 24, 29, 37, 41, 50, 52, 55, 56, 68, 72, 77, 78, 89, 100, 105, 126, 138, 142
Scrope, Richard, abp of York, 157
    Stephen, 157
    William, earl of Wiltshire, 154, 155, 156, 158
Sculptors, 45, 145
Seals, 145, 147
Segrave, Hugh de, 164
    Margaret lady, 61
Seljuk kingdom, 32
Senna tree, 124
Sens, abp of, 99
Serle, William, 158
Seville, Spain, 111, 112
Sex equality, 148
Shakespeare, William, 157
Sheen Palace, Surrey, 136, 144, 149
Ship Money, 128
Shooter's Hill, Kent, 123
Shordich, John de, lawyer, 51
Shrewsbury, 140, 155, 156–7, 158
Sicilian Vespers (1282), 24
Sicily, 25, 29, 48
Silver stain on glass, 65
Sloes (wild plums), 124
Sluys, Flanders, 69, 70
Smithfield, rebels at, 27, 133
Snelleston, Henry de, mason, 76
Socrates, 31
Solon, 31
Sondergotik, 28, 78
Soria, Spain, 108, 112
Sounder, Sir John, 102
Southampton, 70, 81, 115
Spain, Spaniards, 20, 21, 23, 24, 25, 32, 33, 35, 48, 51, 64, 78, 91, 93, 105–13, 116, 128, 137, 139, 140, 147, 153, 166
Spaniards on the Sea, battle, 92–3
Spanish language, 62, 63
Speeches to troops, 95–6
Spridlington, William, bp of St Asaph, 164
Stafford, Edmund, bp of Exeter, 147, 152
    Sir Ralph, 138

Standish, Sir Ralph, 133
Statistics, 12
Statues, 45, 145
Stephen, king of England, 22, 41
Stirling, Scotland, 37
Stokes, Alan de, 164, 165
Stone (calculus), 149
Strassburg cathedral, Germany, 28, 77
Stratford, John, abp of Canterbury, 51, 71
    Robert, bp of Chichester, 71
Straw, John (Jack), 131–2
Strickland, Agnes, historian, 68
Stubbs, William, bp of Oxford, 71
Stury, Sir Richard, 117, 144
Sudbury, Simon, abp of Canterbury, 132, 137, 164
Suffolk, earl of – see Pole; Ufford
Swynford, Catherine, 152

Tancarville, count of, 80
Taste, 13, 33, 43
Taxation, 53, 113, 128, 131
Terry, Schuyler B., economist, 12
Thirty, Battle of, 106
Thomas of Brotherton, earl of Norfolk, 61
    of Woodstock, duke of Gloucester, 59, 75, 125–6, 137, 139–42, 147, 149, 150, 153, 154, 157
Thomond, king of, 151
Thopisfield, John de, goldsmith, 103
Thouars, 115
Three Kings, 108
Timur (Tamerlane), 31
Tingewick, Nicholas de, physician, 66
Toledo, Spain, 63
Tonbridge Castle, Kent, 45
Touraine, France, 101
Tours, France, 94
Trades Unionism, 90
Travel, 65–6
Treason, 26, 107, 109, 119, 120, 133, 143, 156
Tresilian, Sir Robert, C. J., 140
Trevisa, John, translator, 62–3
Troyes, France, 43
Trust funds, 127
Tudor dynasty, 13
Turkestan, 32
Turkey, 13
Tyler, Wat, rebel, 133–4, 151, 156

Ufford, Robert de, 1st earl of Suffolk, 73
United States of America, 34
Upwell, Norfolk, 44
Usk, Adam of, chronicler, 159
    Thomas, poet, 143

Valenciennes, Hainault, 32, 57, 79, 85
Vale Royal abbey, Cheshire, 93
Valladolid, Spain, 112
Van Artevelde, Jakob, 32, 55, 61, 70, 72, 78
Vauxhall manor, Surrey, 103
Venice, Italy, 31, 78
Vere, Sir Aubrey de, 133
    Robert de, duke of Ireland, 133, 136, 139, 140, 147, 152, 156
Vernon, Normandy, 81
Versailles, abbot of, 52

Vestments, 161–3
Victoria, queen of Great Britain, 31
Vienne, Council of, 39
Vienne, Sir Jean de, 86
Vierzon, France, 94
Villein tenants, 26–7
Vitri, Philippe de, musician, 28
Vives i Miret, Josep, 174
Volunteer soldiers, 27

Waddesworth, William,
    apothecary, 149
Wagner, Sir Anthony, 88
Wales, 14, 21, 22, 42, 48, 72, 76, 77,
    83, 87, 128, 140
Waleys, Henry le, merchant, 64
Wallingford, Berks., 26, 163
Walsham, Robert de, chaplain, 163
    William de, clerk, 164
Waltham Cross, 140
Walworth, Sir William, mayor of
    London, 133–4
Waqfs, 127
War, 11, 25, 29, 53–4, 57, 126, 128,
    130, 142, 153, 156
Warenne, arms of, 162
Warwick, earl of – see Beauchamp
Waterford, Ireland, 150
Waterloo, battle of, 30, 37
Weavers, 35, 55, 56, 60, 64
Wedmore, treaty of, 58
Weever, John, antiquary, 166
Weights and Measures, 74–5
Wellington, 1st duke of, 15

Wells cathedral, Somerset, 14, 44
Westminster abbey, 21, 48, 61, 114,
    123, 132, 133, 144, 149, 151;
    2, 15
    Henry VII's Chapel, 14
    prior of, 154
    Hall, 14, 21, 145
    Palace, 21, 44–5, 48, 87, 102, 116,
        120, 143, 145
    Retable, 14
    St Stephen's Chapel, 21, 44, 45,
        75, 76, 88
Whipsnade, Beds., 48
Whitehead, Col. J. G. O., 18
Wickford, Robert, abp of Dublin,
    140
Wight, Isle of, 57
Wilde, Oscar, 31
William I the Conqueror, king of
    England, 22, 29, 35, 50, 79
    II Rufus, 145
    IV, 16
    II, count of Hainault, 69
    of Hatfield (d. 1336), 38, 59, 173
    of Windsor (d. 1348), 59, 91
Wilton Diptych, 14, 146; **7**
Wiltshire, 123
Winchester, bishops of, 148
    cathedral, 44
    College, 14, 19, 136, 144, 145; **14**
Windsor, Berks., 22, 59, 73, 87, 88,
    100, 101, 102, 104, 115, 144
    Castle, 45, 59, 73–4, 76, 87, 102,
        139
        Great Hall, 123

St George's Chapel, 88–9, 148
    Park, Old Manor, 146
    Treaty of, 116
Wissant, Jacques de, 86
    Pierre de, 86
Witney, Thomas of, mason, 44
'Wonderful Parliament', 139
Woodland, Sir Walter, 99
Woodstock, Oxon., 36, 38, 47–8, 59
Worcester, earl of – see Percy,
    Thomas
World War, 91
Wren, Sir Christopher, 44
Wycliffe, John, 137, 151
Wykeham, William of, bp of
    Winchester, 14, 116, 122, 136,
    144, 147, 153, 158, 164; **14**
    portrait of, 19; **14**
Wynford, William, mason, 19

Yeveley, Henry, mason, 16, 18, 76,
    103, 120, 144–5
York, 60, 74–5, 131, 138, 147, 152–3
    mayor of, 152
    Minster, 19, 38, 43, 44, 59, 65,
        123, 144, 152; **3, 4, 10, 11, 12,
        13**
        chapter house, 14, 45, 152
    Mystery Plays, 152
    St Nicholas's Hospital, 149

Zeeland, 69
Zouche, William, abp of York, 42
Zuider Zee, Holland, 69